Cointegration Analysis in a German Monetary System

Contributions to Economics

Giuseppe Gaburro (Ed.)
Ethics and Economics
1997. ISBN 3-7908-0986-1

Frank Hoster/Heinz Welsch/
Christoph Böhringer
CO_2 Abatement and Economic Structural Change in the European Internal Market
1997. ISBN 3-7908-1020-7

Christian M. Hafner
Nonlinear Time Series Analysis with Applications to Foreign Exchange Rate Volatility
1997. ISBN 3-7908-1041-X

Sardar M. N. Islam
Mathematical Economics of Multi-Level Optimisation
1998. ISBN 3-7908-1050-9

Sven-Morten Mentzel
Real Exchange Rate Movements
1998. ISBN 3-7908-1081-9

Lei Delsen/Eelke de Jong (Eds.)
The German and Dutch Economies
1998. ISBN 3-7908-1064-9

Mark Weder
Business Cycle Models with Indeterminacy
1998. ISBN 3-7908-1078-9

Tor Rødseth (Ed.)
Models for Multispecies Management
1998. ISBN 3-7908-1001-0

Michael Carlberg
Intertemporal Macroeconomics
1998. ISBN 3-7908-1096-7

Sabine Spangenberg
The Institutionalised Transformation of the East German Economy
1998. ISBN 3-7908-1103-3

Hagen Bobzin
Indivisibilities
1998. ISBN 3-7908-1123-8

Helmut Wagner (Ed.)
Current Issues in Monetary Economics
1998. ISBN 3-7908-1127-0

Peter Michaelis/Frank Stähler
(Eds.)
Recent Policy Issues in Environmental and Resource Economics
1998. ISBN 3-7908-1137-8

Jessica de Wolff
The Political Economy of Fiscal Decisions
1998. ISBN 3-7908-1130-0

Georg Bol/Gholamreza Nakhaeizadeh/Karl-Heinz Vollmer (Eds.)
Risk Measurements, Econometrics and Neural Networks
1998. ISBN 3-7908-1152-1

Joachim Winter
Investment and Exit Decisions at the Plant Level
1998. ISBN 3-7908-1154-8

Bernd Meyer
Intertemporal Asset Pricing
1999. ISBN 3-7908-1159-9

Uwe Walz
Dynamics of Regional Integration
1999. ISBN 3-7908-1185-8

Michael Carlberg
European Monetary Union
1999. ISBN 3-7908-1191-2

Giovanni Galizzi/
Luciano Venturini (Eds.)
Vertical Relationships and Coordination in the Food System
1999. ISBN 3-7908-1192-0

Gustav A. Horn/
Wolfgang Scheremet/
Rudolf Zwiener
Wages and the Euro
1999. ISBN 3-7908-1199-8

Dirk Willer
The Development of Equity Capital Markets in Transition Economies
1999. ISBN 3-7908-1198-X

Karl Matthias Weber
Innovation Diffusion and Political Control of Energy Technologies
1999. ISBN 3-7908-1205-6

Heike Link et al.
The Costs of Road Infrastructure and Congestion in Europe
1999. ISBN 3-7908-1201-3

continued on page 177

Kirstin Hubrich

Cointegration Analysis in a German Monetary System

With 19 Figures and 30 Tables

Physica-Verlag
A Springer-Verlag Company

Series Editors
Werner A. Müller
Martina Bihn

Author
Dr. Kirstin Hubrich
De Nederlandsche Bank
Econometric Research
and Special Studies Department
P.O. Box 98
1000 AB Amsterdam
The Netherlands

Dissertation, Humboldt-Universität zu Berlin, June 1999

ISSN 1431-1933

Cataloging-in-Publication Data applied for
Die Deutsche Bibliothek – CIP-Einheitsaufnahme

Hubrich, Kirstin: Cointegration analysis in a German monetary system: with 30 tables/Kirstin Hubrich. – Heidelberg; New York: Physica-Verl., 2001
(Contributions to economics)
Zugl.: Berlin, Humboldt-Univ., Diss., 1999
ISBN 978-3-7908-1352-4 ISBN 978-3-642-99815-7 (eBook)
DOI 10.1007/978-3-642-99815-7

Physica-Verlag Heidelberg New York
a member of BertelsmannSpringer Science+Business Media GmbH

Softcover Design: Erich Kirchner, Heidelberg

SPIN 10784648 88/2202-5 4 3 2 1 0 – Printed on acid-free paper

Acknowledgements

While working on the research projects that resulted in this thesis I received advise and encouragement from my supervisors, collaegues and friends.

In particular, I would like to thank my principal supervisor, Helmut Lütkepohl, for his invaluable advice and encouragement for my research. I am also very grateful to my second supervisor, Jürgen Wolters, for his beneficial support and constructive suggestions. Especially, I would like to thank both my supervisors that they were always available for discussions as well as for their detailed comments on an earlier version of this thesis.

Furthermore, this thesis has benefitted from stimulating debates with Jörg Breitung and from valuable discussions with Pentti Saikkonen. I am also indebted to Dieter Nautz, Jörg Breitung, Sascha Djumena and Christian Müller for reading parts of the manuscript of my thesis, and I thank all of them for their critical comments.

This thesis also profited from the favourable academic atmosphere at the Institute of Statistics and Econometrics and the *Sonderforschungsbereich 373* at the *Humboldt-Universität zu Berlin* and from helpful comments in seminars and workshops in Berlin as well as at national and international conferences.

For his computational assistance with the simulations for the data-based DGP I thank Carsten Trenkler and I am grateful to Ralf Brüggemann for his assistance with the graphical presentation of the simulation results.

I would also like to thank all my colleagues in Berlin, especially Siegbert Klinke, Antje Mertens, Martin Moryson, Marlene Müller and Rolf Tschernig for various kinds of support.

Finally, my special thanks go to Sascha Djumena and my family for their support during my work on this thesis.

Amsterdam, July 2000 Kirstin Hubrich

Contents

Chapter 1

Introduction

1.1 Motivation

A lively and controversial discussion has accompanied the establishment of the European Central Bank (ECB) and its decision regarding its monetary policy strategy. With the start of the European Monetary Union (EMU) in January 1999 and the decision of the ECB to assign a publicly announced monetary reference value a prominent role within its monetary strategy, it is essential to further understand the German Bundesbank's (*Bundesbank*) policy of monetary targeting and the conditions under which it worked.

The ECB is confronted with a situation which is in many respects different and more complex than that of the Bundesbank since it will be responsible for the monetary policy of a large number of sovereign countries. Many uncertainties still remain in the project of EMU, despite a convergence of the initially participating countries of EMU with respect to economic conditions, especially interest rates, inflation rates, borrowing and debt, which has not been expected a few years ago.

As Germany is the largest economy in the EMU area, it will play a major role in the transmission process of the ECB's monetary policy. Thus, one aim of this thesis is to contribute to a further understanding of German monetary policy in the larger context of EMU.

With respect to the monetary policy of the Bundesbank, the appropriateness of a strategy of monetary targeting is a central topic. In this context, questions regarding the stability of the demand for money, the controllability of the monetary aggregate by the central bank's monetary policy actions and the question whether a causal link between the monetary aggregate M3 and inflation exists, i.e. between the intermediate target and the final target, are highly relevant.

Especially after German reunification, the question has been raised whether German money demand continues to be stable. This discussion was the original starting point and motivation for this thesis. The answer to the stability issue is crucial for the monetary policy strategy of the central bank as a stable money demand is a precondition for a policy of monetary targeting by the central bank. Since a monetary aggregate is the intermediate target of monetary policy with the final target being the inflation rate, the relationship between money and the variables influencing money demand should be stable in order to make the demand for money in the economy predictable to some extent. The literature on German money demand has - with few exceptions - found that German money demand is still stable. Recently, the analysis of the stability of money demand has also been of increasing interest with respect to the discussion of whether monetary targeting is a viable strategy for the European Central Bank.

The focus of this thesis is therefore on long-run monetary relationships in a system of macro-economic variables that influence the monetary transmission mechanism. Natural candidates for the long-run relationships besides the long-run money demand are an interest rate relation derived from the expectations theory of the term structure as well as the Fisher relation.

With respect to identification and testing of long-run relationships between economic variables, the question of the methodological approach arises. The analysis presented is set in the framework of cointegration, aiming to analyse whether and how variables are moving together over time. Cointegration analysis focuses on long-run relationships between variables, i.e. it analyses whether persistent comovements between economic time series exist.

Since the seminal work of Granger (1981) and Engle & Granger (1987) econometric modelling is not confined to stationary processes, but is expanded to include nonstationary processes. A large number of estimation and testing procedures accounting for cointegration relationships between variables have been suggested in a single equation as well as a systems context.

Engle & Granger (1987) propose a two-step procedure. They suggest to estimate the parameters by ordinary least squares (OLS) in a static regression, first, and estimate an error correction model in a second step. Despite the advantage that the parameters of the static regression can be estimated superconsistently in case of cointegration, however, the LS estimator is not efficient if autocorrelation in the residuals is present due to insufficient dynamic specification. Moreover, the estimator is biased in small samples and, additionally, the t-statistic of the estimated parameters has no standard distribution. Alternatively, a one-step procedure to estimate an error correction model can be employed, originally suggested by Stock (1987). A further contribution to the cointegration literature is the fully modified procedure suggested by Phillips (1988) and Phillips & Hansen (1990). During the last decade, a wide range of further single equation cointegration procedures have been suggested.[1]

For the analysis of monetary policy, however, it is reasonable to choose a systems approach, since the interdependences between the variables are of importance for the transmission process of monetary policy and should also be taken into account in an analysis of long-run relationships. Further, a systems approach allows testing the number of cointegration relationships between a set of economic variables. In contrast to single-equation procedures, cointegration rank tests allow testing for more than one long-run relationship.

Early tests for the number of cointegration relations have been derived by Johansen (1988) and Stock & Watson (1988). Since these early proposals, there has been a substantial growth in the literature on systems cointegration tests suggesting numerous improvements of existing tests and alternative procedures.

Since every empirical study in the context of cointegration analysis is based on the result of testing the number of cointegration relations, it is especially important to know the properties of the systems cointegration tests used. Therefore, a broad range of procedures are reviewed in the methodological part of this thesis and their small sample performances are compared in a uniform setting. The relative performance of these tests in samples relevant in economic analysis is evaluated to provide a guideline for applied research. An important property of many of these tests is their dependence on deterministic terms in the data generation process. Therefore, special emphasis is given to the sensitivity of the test performance with respect to the trending properties of the data generating process (DGP).

The Johansen approach has become widely used in empirical applications since this procedure does not only allow to test for the number of cointegration relationships, but also facilitates testing restrictions on the cointegration space. The following particular features of Johansen's systems cointegration approach should be noted. First, this framework allows testing stationarity of the variables where, in contrast to most

[1] An exposition and overview of single equation cointegration methodologies can be found in Banerjee, Dolado, Galbraith & Hendry (1993), Hamilton (1994), Lütkepohl (1995) and Wolters (1995a), among others.

univariate unit root tests, the null hypothesis is stationarity and the interdepencies between the variables are taken into account. Further, weak exogeneity of the variables can be tested within a systems approach.[2] The application of single equation procedures to estimate and test cointegration relationships will lead to a loss in efficiency if weak exogeneity is rejected (Johansen, 1992; Ericsson, Hendry & Mizon, 1998). Only the fully modified approach (Phillips, 1988; Phillips & Hansen, 1990) introduces a correction term to account for possible endogeneity of the regressors. Moreover, if there is more than one cointegration relationship further analysis should be carried out within a systems approach. Additionally, Johansen's approach facilitates testing simultaneously for long-run relationships.

Thus, the empirical analysis in the second part of the thesis will be carried out in a systems context. Rank tests will be applied to test for the number of cointegration relationships in the German monetary system that have been found to perform best in the first part of the thesis. Further, the Johansen procedure will be applied to identify long-run relationships because of the advantages of this approach discussed above. Conclusions for monetary policy can be drawn from identified long-run relationships that influence the conduct and transmission process of German monetary policy and from the analysis of their stability.

The remainder of the introduction provides an overview of this thesis, motivating the structure and presenting an outline of Chapters 2 and 3.

1.2 Outline

This thesis is divided into two main parts. Chapter 2 contains methodological issues with respect to systems cointegration tests whereas Chapter 3 presents the empirical analysis of long-run monetary relationships in Germany.

In Chapter 2, a broad range of systems cointegration tests are compared. Section 2.2 presents the framework for discussing the cointegration rank tests. Sections 2.3 and 2.4 review the alternative systems cointegration tests and the assumptions regarding the deterministic terms under which these testing procedures are supposed to work as well as a comparison of the tests in a general unifying framework.

These tests can broadly be divided into two groups: One group of rank tests is based on a well-established testing principle, i.e. the likelihood

[2] A collection of articles on exogeneity can be found in Ericsson & Irons (1994); see also Hendry (1995).

ratio tests within a parametric framework. These are reviewed in Section 2.3. The other group of tests displays more heterogeneous characteristics. These tests are based on canonical correlations of levels, principal components as well as nonparametric procedures and are presented in Section 2.4.

Since one central aim of this thesis is to gain further insights in the performance of systems cointegration tests in empirical applications, the small sample properties of the tests are especially of interest (see Sections 2.5 to 2.7). Therefore, previous small sample simulation studies are discussed in the context of the respective test (see Sections 2.3 and 2.4) and are summarized in Section 2.5.1. The details on the simulation design underlying the new simulations presented here are provided in Sections 2.5.2 and 2.5.3. Since most earlier simulation studies focus on one test only or on a small range of tests, often presenting favourable results for the author's own test, new simulations are presented in Sections 2.5.4 to 2.5.6, to compare a broad range of tests under uniform conditions. Thereby, a special focus is on the test performance with respect to the deterministic terms of the DGP.

The recommendations drawn from this comparison as well as first simulation results with respect to the impact of dummy variables on the performance of rank tests provide a guideline for testing the cointegration rank in the empirical analysis in Chapter 3.

Chapter 3 presents an empirical analysis of long-run relationships influencing the transmission process of German monetary policy within a systems cointegration analysis. It is organised as follows: Section 3.2 reviews the main aspects of the discussion of monetary policy strategies with respect to the ECB's policy framework. The relevance of the German monetary policy experience in that context is highlighted and the main features of the monetary policy of the Bundesbank are discussed emphasizing the stability of the demand for money. This section also provides the policy framework for the empirical analysis presented later.

Section 3.3 presents an overview of propositions from economic theory with respect to money demand, the term structure of interest rates and the Fisher relation that can be tested on the cointegration space of the system of variables considered here. Further, recent empirical studies on money demand, the term structure of interest rates and the Fisher equation are reviewed.

In Section 3.4 the empirical analysis is presented. Section 3.4.1 introduces the initial vector autoregressive model (VAR). The variables employed in the analysis are described and a preliminary data analysis is carried out. Especially, Perron's unit root test is applied that allows for a structural break in the series. The model specification strategy to estimate a vector autoregressive model is described and misspecification as well as stability tests are carried out.

The comparison of the small sample performance of the tests for the cointegration rank in Chapter 2 shows that tests based on the likelihood ratio principle perform best in small samples. Therefore, Johansen's likelihood ratio (LR) test as well as the trend adjusted LR test suggested by Saikkonen & Lütkepohl (2000c, 1998b) are applied.

In Section 3.4.3 restrictions on the cointegration space are tested within Johansen's maximum likelihood procedure. Stationarity tests of the variables are carried out in this framework as well as tests for weak exogeneity of the variables. Further, economically plausible long-run restrictions motivated by the theoretical considerations in Section 3.3 are tested on single cointegration vectors as well as simultaneously on all cointegration vectors. Also, the economic interpretation of the resulting vectors is discussed and their stability is examined. Section 3.4.4 contains concluding remarks for the empirical results.

Chapter 4 summarizes the main results of the thesis. Additionally, it provides an outlook on further research and on the lessons the German monetary policy experience can provide for the ECB.

Chapter 2

Systems Cointegration Analysis: Tests for the Cointegration Rank

2.1 Introduction

The literature on cointegration has developed into many different directions since the seminal papers by Granger (1981) and Engle & Granger (1987). One area of interest has been concerned with finding the number of cointegrating relations in a system of time series variables.[1]

A cointegration rank test is of major importance in empirical work because any further analysis within a cointegration framework depends on the result of the number of cointegration relations, i.e. it is one determinant of the choice between single equation and systems analysis, as well as being the basis for the identification of cointegration vectors or for analysing the effects of shocks within a cointegrated system. The number of cointegration relations found might depend on the deterministic terms included in the system. It will determine any further analysis and thereby also the policy conclusions drawn. Thus, the role of deterministic terms will be the focus of this chapter together with a broad comparison of cointegration rank tests.

In the following chapter, a broad range of systems cointegration tests is reviewed and compared within a general unifying framework. The chapter is based on the review paper by Hubrich, Lütkepohl & Saikkonen (2000) and the notation used is the same as in that review. However, in

[1]Broad expositions on cointegration methodologies with a specific focus on systems cointegration approaches can be found e.g. in Lütkepohl (1991), Hendry (1995) and Johansen (1995).

contrast to Hubrich et al. (2000) the main focus is on the small sample properties of the tests. Previous small sample simulation results are discussed more extensively and the test statistics for the new simulation study are chosen in the light of these results.[2] The small sample simulation evidence for a wide range of systems cointegration tests in Hubrich et al. (2000) is extended to further DGPs, but excluding some alternative variants of a number of tests. An additional focus is on the differences between tests based on trend-adjusted data and tests that are derived from a model including deterministic terms using unadjusted time series.

Many of the tests considered have first been derived for a DGP without deterministic terms. These test statistics are not included in this thesis since they are not relevant for applied research, but are only of theoretical interest.[3] A comparison of the asymptotic properties and local power results for some of the tests is provided in Saikkonen & Lütkepohl (1999).

The Wald counterparts of the LR statistics have been presented in Saikkonen & Luukkonen (1997). These authors find that the Wald tests are outperformed by the LR tests in small samples in terms of size as well as power. Therefore, Wald tests are not considered here.

Saikkonen & Luukkonen (1997) and Saikkonen & Lütkepohl (2000c, 1998a,1999) have proposed Lagrange Multiplier (LM) type tests that base the estimation of the trend parameters as well as the test statistics on the cointegration rank assumed under the null hypothesis. These tests are shown to be asymptotically equivalent to the trend-adjusted LR tests proposed by the same authors. However, in small samples the LM type tests are in most situations outperformed by the trend-adjusted LR tests (see Hubrich et al., 2000). Therefore, the following presentation focuses on LR tests. LM type tests are mentioned in the relevant context, but are not discussed any further.

The lag augmentation test proposed by Lütkepohl & Saikkonen (1999a), the fully modified test suggested by Quintos (1998a, b), choosing the cointegration rank by model selection criteria (e.g. Gonzalo & Pitarakis, 1998; Lütkepohl & Poskitt, 1998) as well as some further proposals are discussed in Hubrich et al. (2000) and are therefore not presented here.

This chapter has the following structure. Section 2.2 describes the general framework in which the various cointegration rank tests can be analyzed and compared. Likelihood ratio testing procedures are reviewed

[2] An exposition on Monte Carlo experimentation can be found e.g. in Hendry (1984).

[3] These versions of the tests are, however, considered in Hubrich et al. (2000).

in Section 2.3. The different assumptions for the asymptotic validity of these tests, e.g. the underlying DGP, are discussed. An important property of many of these tests is their dependence on deterministic terms in the data generation process. Therefore, the presentation is structured according to the properties of deterministic terms. In applied research the specification of the deterministic terms, e.g. whether a linear trend in the data should be allowed or whether a deterministic trend term should be included in the cointegration relation, is of great importance. The respective section provides a discussion of the alternative tests for the cointegration rank, the appropriate references as well as the small sample evidence for the respective test. In Section 2.4 some other tests are considered. These include tests based on canonical correlations as well as the Stock & Watson and Bierens' nonparametric tests.

Section 2.5 presents the new small sample results. In Section 2.5.1 previous simulation results are summarized which explore and compare the size and power properties of some of the tests in small samples. In Section 2.5.2, details for the setup of the new simulations are provided. Section 2.5.3 presents the DGP proposed by Toda (1994, 1995) on which a large part of the simulation is based. In Sections 2.5.4 to 2.5.6 own simulations are presented to compare the full range of tests under uniform conditions employing different DGPs.

Section 2.5.7 provides conclusions from the new simulations as well as a discussion extending the LR framework to allow for dummy variables modelling structural breaks. This section also includes some first simulation results for original and trend-adjusted LR tests allowing for dummy variables on the basis of a data-based DGP derived in a bootstrap procedure. Finally, recommendations for applied research are brought forward.

2.2 Cointegration Rank Tests: The Framework

2.2.1 Data Generating Process

The representation of the DGP considered in this thesis, is the same as in a series of papers by Lütkepohl and Saikkonen (e.g. Lütkepohl & Saikkonen, 1999c; Saikkonen & Lütkepohl, 2000c).

The tests for the cointegrating rank considered in the following are presented in the general framework in which an observable n-dimensional time series $y_t = (y_{1t}, \dots, y_{nt})'$, $t = 1, \dots, T$, is assumed to be generated as

$$y_t = \mu_0 + \mu_1 t + x_t, \qquad t = 1, 2, \ldots, \tag{2.2.1}$$

where μ_0 $(n \times 1)$ and μ_1 $(n \times 1)$ are parameters which may be zero. The first of these parameter vectors will be referred to as the mean term or mean parameter and μ_1 will be called trend term or trend parameter. The quantity x_t is an unobservable process with zero mean. The different tests make different assumptions regarding μ_0, μ_1, and x_t.

The components of x_t are assumed to be at most $I(1)$, that is, x_t is nonstationary and the first difference of x_t is stationary. This implies that y_t is also at most $I(1)$. Cointegration among the variables of x_t, i.e. stationary linear combinations of the elements of x_t, is allowed. The cointegration rank r might equal the dimension n of the system, i.e. x_t may be $I(0)$ altogether. If x_t is cointegrated, y_t is also cointegrated where some linear combinations of y_t might be trend stationary.

Some of the tests assume that x_t has a finite order error correction (EC) representation, e.g. Johansen's LR tests as well as the LR type tests suggested by Lütkepohl and Saikkonen, whereas others allow a more general DGP, e.g. an infinite order VAR, like Bierens' nonparametric test or the mean-adjusted LR test suggested by Saikkonen & Luukkonen (1997). However, the simulations presented in Section 2.5 are carried out for DGPs that follow a finite order VAR to receive comparable results for all tests. To present all tests in a uniform setting, the following exposition of the tests assumes a finite order VAR(p) process for x_t of the following form

$$x_t = A_1 x_{t-1} + \cdots + A_p x_{t-p} + \varepsilon_t, \tag{2.2.2}$$

where the A_j are $(n \times n)$ coefficient matrices and ε_t is Gaussian white noise, that is, $\varepsilon_t \sim iid\ N(0, \Omega)$. By subtracting x_{t-1} on both sides of (2.2.2) and rearranging terms, the process can be rewritten in EC form

$$\Delta x_t = \Pi x_{t-1} + \sum_{j=1}^{p-1} \Gamma_j \Delta x_{t-j} + \varepsilon_t, \qquad t = 1, 2, \ldots, \tag{2.2.3}$$

where Π and the Γ_j are $(n \times n)$ matrices of unknown parameters, $\varepsilon_t \sim (0, \Omega)$ is white noise and the initial values x_t, $t \leq 0$, are assumed to be zero for convenience.[4] Furthermore, $\Pi = -(I_n - A_1 - \cdots - A_p)$ and $\Gamma_j = -(A_{j+1} + \cdots + A_p)$ for $j = 1, \ldots, p-1$.

[4] Alternatively, it may be assumed that the initial values are fixed constants or that they are stochastic with some fixed distribution (see e.g. Hubrich et al., 2000). It is important, however, that the initial conditions do not depend on the sample size.

This framework allows at most a deterministic linear trend in the data and the cointegration relation, but not a quadratic deterministic trend as this is not considered to be realistic for economic time series.[5]

The decomposition of y_t (see (2.2.1)) in the deterministic and stochastic components helps to clarify the following presentation where the performance of the tests with respect to the deterministic terms is emphasized. Furthermore, this presentation facilitated the derivation of some of the tests (e.g. the tests proposed by Lütkepohl & Saikkonen, 1999c). A similar presentation can be found in Schmidt & Phillips (1992) for the univariate case. Additionally, one strategy to obtain similarity of tests with respect to deterministic terms is to adjust the data for mean and trend parameters before constructing the test statistic. Consequences of trend-adjustment will be analysed on the basis of the small sample simulations presented below.

2.2.2 Hypotheses and Testing Procedure

The number of linearly independent cointegration vectors of y_t is called the cointegrating rank of y_t and will be denoted by r in the following. In this thesis the focus is on testing the hypotheses

$$H_0(r_0) : r = r_0 \qquad \text{vs.} \qquad H_1(r_0) : r > r_0, \tag{2.2.4}$$

with r_0 denoting the cointegration rank under the null hypothesis. Alternatively, tests for the hypotheses

$$H_0(r_0) : r = r_0 \qquad \text{vs.} \qquad \bar{H}_1(r_0) : r = r_0 + 1 \tag{2.2.5}$$

can be constructed. If $H_0(r_0)$ in (2.2.4) is true and x_t has the representation (2.2.3), the matrix Π in the EC form is zero if $r_0 = 0$. The matrix Π can be written as a product $\Pi = \alpha\beta'$, where α and β are $(n \times r_0)$ matrices of rank r_0. The matrix β is the cointegration matrix whereas α is often referred to as loading matrix or matrix of adjustment coefficients.

The test statistics of the systems cointegration tests discussed below are based on the generalized ordered eigenvalues of the system.

For example, when applying the LR tests a sequential procedure is carried out to test whether the eigenvalues are significantly different from zero, starting with the largest eigenvalue. More specifically, sequential testing $r_0 = 0, 1, 2, ..., n$ (or $n-1$)[6] continues until the null hypothesis is not rejected any more.

[5]For more about the difference between Johansen's representation and the representation considered here, see Section 2.3.1.1.

[6]This is the end of the testing sequence when a linear trend is in the data, but not in the cointegration relation; see Section 2.3.1.2

2.3 Likelihood Ratio Tests

Likelihood ratio (LR) tests for the cointegration rank have been suggested in a series of papers by Johansen (1988, 1991a, 1992, 1994). In contrast to those tests, Saikkonen & Luukkonen (1997), Saikkonen & Lütkepohl (2000c, 1998a,1999) suggest to adjust the data for estimated mean (and trend) terms, first, and base the test statistics on the trend-adjusted time series.

To derive LR tests, x_t is assumed to be a Gaussian VAR(p) process of the form 2.2.3.[7]

For this DGP, tests under different assumptions for the mean and trend parameters μ_0 and μ_1 in representation (2.2.1) will be considered in the following.

Three possible specifications of deterministic terms, relevant in applied work are considered. These include tests based on a model that allows a linear trend in the data as well as in the cointegration relation, second, tests that allow for a linear trend in the data but not in the cointegration relation and, third, tests based on a model that excludes a linear trend in the data. A DGP with zero mean and zero trend term, i.e. $\mu_0 = \mu_1 = 0$ so that $y_t = x_t$, is not considered in the following since this case is not relevant for applied work.[8]

In this section, the trace statistics of the LR tests will be presented. The maximum eigenvalue versions are not considered explicitly in the following. The reason for concentrating on the trace tests is that the trace and the maximum eigenvalue statistic have been found to perform similarly in small samples (see, for example, Cheung & Lai, 1993; Toda, 1994, 1995). Toda (1994) even finds that the trace test performs better in some cases where the power of both statistics is quite low.

Modifications of some of the test statistics discussed in this section, proposed by Reinsel & Ahn (1992) and Yap & Reinsel (1995) to account for small sample distortions of the test size, are not considered in this thesis. Although these modifications were found to improve the size or power performance of some tests in specific situations, Cheung & Lai (1993) showed that these modifications are inadequate in parts of the parameter space. Therefore, the focus will be on the original versions of the statistics in the following.

---

[7]It should be noted, however, that the asymptotic distribution remains valid if the ε_t are not Gaussian, but have other suitable distributions (see e.g. Lütkepohl, 1991, p.359).

[8]This case is presented in Hubrich et al. (2000), Section 2.3.1., for comparison purposes.

2.3.1 DGPs and Test Statistics

2.3.1.1 Arbitrary Mean and Trend Term (μ_0, μ_1 arbitrary)

The most general model in the framework considered here will allow both μ_0 and μ_1 to be nonzero. In that case the DGP has the following EC representation

$$\Delta y_t = \nu_0 + \nu_1 t + \Pi y_{t-1} + \sum_{j=1}^{p-1} \Gamma_j \Delta y_{t-j} + \varepsilon_t, \qquad t = p+1, p+2, \ldots \quad (2.3.1)$$

where $\nu_0 = -\Pi\mu_0 + \left(\sum_{j=1}^{p} jA_j\right)\mu_1$ and $\nu_1 = -\Pi\mu_1$. Johansen (1995) starts with this model, but does not constrain ν_0 and ν_1 and thereby allows y_t to have a quadratic trend. In contrast, the DGP (2.2.1) underlying the presentation in this thesis can have linear deterministic trends at most. Since higher order deterministic trends are not relevant in the context of economic time series the presentation of the tests in the following will use (2.2.1) as the basic model and thereby rule out quadratic trends.

Therefore, using $\Pi = \alpha\beta'$, (2.3.1) can alternatively be written as

$$\begin{aligned} \Delta y_t &= \nu + \alpha(\beta' y_{t-1} - \tau(t-1)) + \sum_{j=1}^{p-1} \Gamma_j \Delta y_{t-j} + \varepsilon_t \\ &= \nu + \Pi^+ y_{t-1}^+ + \sum_{j=1}^{p-1} \Gamma_j \Delta y_{t-j} + \varepsilon_t, \qquad t = p+1, p+2, \ldots, \end{aligned} \quad (2.3.2)$$

where $\nu = -\Pi\mu_0 + (I_n - \Gamma_1 - \cdots - \Gamma_{p-1})\mu_1$, $\tau = \beta'\mu_1$, $\Pi^+ = \alpha[\beta' : -\tau] = \Pi[I_n : \mu_1]$ and $y_{t-1}^+ = [y_{t-1}' : t-1]$. The Maximum Likelihood (ML) estimators and the LR statistics based on these estimators can be obtained from these representations using reduced rank (RR) regression.

This model allows a linear trend in some or all of the variables, but can also be applied if there is no trend in the data.[9]

The consequences of such an overparameterization in small samples will be analysed in the simulations of Section 2.5.

Tests Based on Original Data Johansen (1994) proposed a test using (2.3.2) as a basis for estimation. The model underlying the DGP restricts the linear trend to lie in the cointegration space.

[9] In this context, see Perron & Campbell (1993) for the terminological difference between stochastic and deterministic cointegration.

An LR test version for a sample $y_1, \cdots, y_T$ including an unrestricted intercept, thereby allowing a trend in the data as well as a trend restricted to the cointegration relation, is obtained calculating

$$M_T^+ = (T-p)^{-1} \left[\sum_{t=p+1}^{T} y_{t-1}^+ y_{t-1}^{+\prime} - \sum_{t=p+1}^{T} y_{t-1}^+ z_t' \left(\sum_{t=p+1}^{T} z_t z_t' \right)^{-1} \sum_{t=p+1}^{T} z_t y_{t-1}^{+\prime} . \right] \tag{2.3.3}$$

with $z_t' = (1, \Delta y_{t-1}', \ldots, \Delta y_{t-p+1}')$ and $y_{t-1}^+ = [y_{t-1}' : t-1]'$.

The LS estimators $\hat{\Pi}$ and $\hat{\Omega}$ can be obtained from (2.3.2). Moreover, denote the corresponding LS residuals by $\hat{\varepsilon}_t$ and define

$$\hat{\Omega} = (T-p)^{-1} \sum_{t=p+1}^{T} \hat{\varepsilon}_t \hat{\varepsilon}_t' . \tag{2.3.4}$$

The resulting estimators and the weighting matrix M_T^+ are then substituted in the determinantal equation

$$\det(\hat{\Pi} M_T^+ \hat{\Pi}' - \lambda \hat{\Omega}) = 0 \tag{2.3.5}$$

and, denoting the resulting generalized eigenvalues obtained by $\hat{\lambda}_1^+ \geq \cdots \geq \hat{\lambda}_n^+$, leads to the trace statistic

$$LR^+(r_0) = (T-p) \sum_{j=r_0+1}^{n} \log(1 + \hat{\lambda}_j^+). \tag{2.3.6}$$

The limiting null distributions are nonstandard and depend on the dimension of the process and the cointegration rank r_0. They are derived in Johansen (1994, 1995). Critical values for these distributions are given in Johansen (1994, Table V; 1995, Table 15.4).

It should be noted that this statistic, although presented in a slightly different way, is identical to the one given by Johansen (1995).

Another possibility is to base an LR type test on the representation (2.3.1) by estimating ν_0 and ν_1 unrestrictedly as proposed by Perron & Campbell (1993). They suggest to calculate M_T^{PC} as in (2.3.3) using $z_t' = (1, t, \Delta y_{t-1}', \ldots, \Delta y_{t-p+1}')$ and $y_{t-1}^{PC} = [y_{t-1}']$.

The test statistic, denoted LR^{PC} in the following, is then computed as in (2.3.6), but is based on the ordered generalized eigenvalues derived within the framework considered in Perron & Campbell (1993). The limiting null distributions are again nonstandard and differ from those of the previous tests. Critical values for these tests are given in Perron & Campbell (1993, Table 1) as well as in Rahbek (1994, Table 1). It should be noted that the null distribution is unchanged if in fact there is no intercept and trend term in the true DGP ($\nu_0 = \nu_1 = 0$).

Tests Based on Trend-Adjusted Data A further approach to setting up LR tests in the present framework is to adjust the data for the mean and trend term, first, and then to compute LR tests on the basis of the trend adjusted data. For VAR processes with a deterministic linear trend Lütkepohl & Saikkonen (1999c) use ideas associated with the Lagrange multiplier (LM) principle to construct tests for the cointegrating rank. In the following, two alternative methods of estimating the trend parameters are reviewed first, before the construction of the test statistics is discussed.

Some alternative methods for trend estimation have been proposed by Lütkepohl & Saikkonen (1999c) and Saikkonen & Lütkepohl (2000c), based on parameter estimators computed under the null hypothesis tested for the cointegration rank.

This additional restriction is introduced to derive more powerful tests (see e.g. the small sample properties of the univariate LM tests suggested by Schmidt & Phillips, 1992).

One method of estimating μ_0 and μ_1, suggested by Lütkepohl & Saikkonen (1999c), involves a two-step estimation procedure based on partitioning the cointegration matrix according to the cointegration rank assumed under the null hypothesis. The GLS procedure presented below, it has not been used in the simulations in Section 2.5 and is, therefore, not described any further here.[10]

Another estimator of the mean and trend parameters proposed by Saikkonen & Lütkepohl (2000c) is based on a GLS approach applied to the model $y_t = \mu_0 + \mu_1 t + x_t$. Using the RR estimators $\tilde{\nu}, \tilde{\alpha}, \tilde{\beta}, \tilde{\tau}, \tilde{\Gamma}_j$ from (2.3.2) results in the estimators of the levels VAR coefficients

$$\begin{aligned} \tilde{A}_1 &= I_n + \tilde{\alpha}\tilde{\beta}' + \tilde{\Gamma}_1, \\ \tilde{A}_j &= \tilde{\Gamma}_j - \tilde{\Gamma}_{j-1}, \quad j = 2, \ldots, p-1, \\ \tilde{A}_p &= -\tilde{\Gamma}_{p-1} \end{aligned}$$

given the definition $\tilde{A}(L) = I_n - \tilde{A}_1 L - \cdots - \tilde{A}_p L^p$. Moreover, $\tilde{G}_t = \tilde{A}(L)a_t$ and $\tilde{H}_t = \tilde{A}(L)b_t$ with

$$a_t = \begin{cases} 1 & \text{for} \quad t \geq 1 \\ 0 & \text{for} \quad t \leq 0 \end{cases}, \qquad b_t = \begin{cases} t & \text{for} \quad t \geq 1 \\ 0 & \text{for} \quad t \leq 0 \end{cases}$$

[10]See Lütkepohl & Saikkonen (1999c) for details on this estimation procedure and small sample results.

are used to estimate μ_0 and μ_1 by multivariate LS from the regression model

$$\tilde{Q}\tilde{A}(L)y_t = \tilde{Q}\tilde{G}_t\mu_0 + \tilde{Q}\tilde{H}_t\mu_1 + \eta_t^*, \quad t = p+1, \ldots, T, \tag{2.3.7}$$

where

$$\tilde{Q} = \begin{bmatrix} (\tilde{\alpha}'\tilde{\Omega}^{-1}\tilde{\alpha})^{-1/2}\tilde{\alpha}'\tilde{\Omega}^{-1} \\ (\tilde{\alpha}_\perp'\tilde{\Omega}\tilde{\alpha}_\perp)^{-1/2}\tilde{\alpha}_\perp' \end{bmatrix}$$

is a weight matrix which ensures that the error term roughly has a unit covariance matrix. Since $\tilde{Q}'\tilde{Q} = \tilde{\Omega}^{-1}$, estimating the transformed model (2.3.7) amounts to GLS estimation of the untransformed model $y_t = \mu_0 + \mu_1 t + x_t$. The resulting estimators of μ_0 and μ_1 are denoted $\tilde{\mu}_0^{GLS}$ and $\tilde{\mu}_1^{GLS}$, respectively. These estimators can also be motivated as approximate Gaussian ML estimators under the assumption of zero initial values.

The resulting test statistics are based on trend adjusted data $\tilde{x}_t = y_t - \tilde{\mu}_0^{GLS} - \tilde{\mu}_1^{GLS}t$. Lütkepohl & Saikkonen (1999c) have suggested three different test statistics, i.e. an LR statistic and two LM statistics, that will be denoted by $LR_{ta}^{GLS}(r_0)$, $LM_{ta(1)}^{GLS}(r_0)$ and $LM_{ta(2)}^{GLS}(r_0)$. The LM type statistics are based on a decomposition of the eigenvectors of the system of variables according to the cointegration rank under the null hypothesis, r_0, in β ($n \times r_0$) and $\beta_\perp$ ($n \times (n-r_0)$). These test statistics are presented in Lütkepohl & Saikkonen (1999c). The LR_{ta}^{GLS} test suggested by Lütkepohl & Saikkonen (1999c) is derived analogously to Johansen's LR test, but based on trend-adjusted data.

It is well-known that LR and LM tests are asymptotically equivalent. Lütkepohl & Saikkonen (1999c) show that $LM_{ta(2)}^{GLS}(r_0)$ has the same limiting null distribution as $LR_{ta}^{GLS}(r_0)$. The distribution of the test statistics is free of unknown nuisance parameters and does not depend on the actual trending properties of the process. Critical values are given in Lütkepohl & Saikkonen (1999c, Table 1) and Saikkonen & Lütkepohl (2000c, Table 1). Furthermore, the test statistics LR_{ta}^{GLS} as well as $LM_{ta(1)}^{GLS}$ and $LM_{ta(2)}^{GLS}$ have the same limiting distributions under H_0 as the corresponding statistics based on trend-adjusted data using the above mentioned alternative estimation method for the mean and trend parameters.

The LM type tests are not discussed any further in the following, as Lütkepohl & Saikkonen (1999c), Saikkonen & Lütkepohl (2000c) and Hubrich et al. (2000) found that these are outperformed by the original and trend-adjusted LR tests in small samples.

In the next section a model is considered that has received some attention in the theoretical literature and is often applied in empirical work. It assumes that a trend appears in the variables and not in the cointegrating relations.

2.3.1.2 Trending Variables and No Trend in the Cointegration Relations (μ_0 arbitrary, $\mu_1 \neq 0$, $\beta'\mu_1 = 0$)

Another possibility is that a linear trend is present in the data so that $\mu_1 \neq 0$, but that the trend is confined to the variables and does not appear in the cointegrating relations, that is $\beta'\mu_1 = 0$. Tests for the cointegrating rank may be constructed for such a situation, taking the additional restriction into account. The tests considered in this section are perhaps the most frequently used for determining the cointegrating rank in applied work. In empirical work, there is no prior knowledge available about the presence of a linear trend in the cointegration relation. Therefore, the starting point of any analysis should be the model presented in the previous section (Sect. 2.3.1.1).

The presence of an unrestricted trend term in the underlying DGP can be tested using an LR test, as suggested by Johansen (1994, 1995, p.162), or can be evaluated using model selection criteria (Pesaran & Smith, 1998). However, the presence of a linear trend in the cointegration relation should also be evaluated on the basis of economic considerations. This will be discussed further with respect to the empirical application in Chapter 3.

If a linear trend is to be excluded from the cointegrating relation, the following model should be considered:

$$\Delta y_t = \nu_0 + \Pi y_{t-1} + \sum_{j=0}^{p-1} \Gamma_j y_{t-j} + \varepsilon_t, \quad t = p+1, p+2, \cdots \tag{2.3.8}$$

with $\nu_0 = -\Pi\mu_0 + \left(\sum_{j=1}^{p} jA_j\right)\mu_1$.

One special feature of the model considered in this section (allowing for a trend in the variables and no trend in the cointegration relations) that has been emphasized by Saikkonen & Lütkepohl (2000a), is that the assumptions $\beta'\mu_1 = 0$ and $\mu_1 \neq 0$ imply for the $(n \times r)$ cointegration matrix β that the cointegration rank must be smaller than the number of variables $(r < n)$. This is because a stationary system $(r = n)$ is excluded by the assumption that at least one of the time series has a linear trend $(\mu_1 \neq 0)$. Consequently, the highest null hypothesis to be tested in an n-dimensional system is $H_0 : r_0 = n - 2$. For example, it would be unreasonable to test $H_0 : r = 1$ vs. $H_1 : r > 1$ in a bivariate process in the context of this model. This will be taken into account in the empirical analysis in Section 3.4.2.

Tests Based on Original Data If there is some indication for a deterministic trend ($\mu_1 \neq 0$), but μ_1 is orthogonal to β ($\beta'\mu_1 = 0$) and, therefore, $\nu_1 = 0$ in the model (2.3.1), the LS estimators $\hat{\Pi}$ and $\hat{\Omega}$ may be obtained from

$$\Delta y_t = \nu_0 + \Pi y_{t-1} + \sum_{j=1}^{p-1} \Gamma_j \Delta y_{t-j} + \varepsilon_t, \qquad t = p+1, p+2, \ldots \quad (2.3.9)$$

The corresponding test statistics are obtained calculating M_T^i as in (2.3.3), but with $z_t' = (1, \Delta y_{t-1}', \ldots, \Delta y_{t-p+1}')$ and y_{t-1}^+ is substituted by y_{t-1}, using the resulting M_T^i matrix in (2.3.5) to derive the corresponding generalized eigenvalues. The resulting LR statistics will be determined as

$$LR^i(r_0) = (T-p) \sum_{j=r_0+1}^{n} \log(1 + \hat{\lambda}_j^i), \quad (2.3.10)$$

where the i stands for 'intercept'.[11]

Critical values for these test statistics may be found in Johansen & Juselius (1990, Table A.1), Johansen (1995, Table 15.3) and Osterwald-Lenum (1992, Table 1), among others. Unfortunately, as has been pointed out in Saikkonen & Lütkepohl (2000a), the null distributions change if the true μ_1 turns out to be zero. In that case, the tests correspond to those that are constructed for data without a linear trend in the data, but that take into account that in practice it is not known whether the data actually have a linear trend (see the test statistic $LR^{i0}(r_0)$ in Section 2.3.1.3). These tests have limiting distributions quite different from those of $LR^i(r_0)$ although the test statistics are identical.

Tests Based on Trend-Adjusted Data Within the framework of the same model, i.e. a process with a deterministic linear trend in the variables but not in the cointegration relations ($\mu_1 \neq 0$ and $\beta'\mu_1 = 0$), Saikkonen & Lütkepohl (2000a) propose to write the EC form as

$$\Delta y_t - \mu_1 = \Pi(y_{t-1} - \mu_0) + \sum_{j=1}^{p-1} \Gamma_j(\Delta y_{t-j} - \mu_1) + \varepsilon_t, \qquad t = p+1, p+2, \ldots \quad (2.3.11)$$

and to base LR and LM type tests for the cointegrating rank on this model form. Again, the estimated mean and trend parameters $\hat{\mu}_0$ and $\hat{\mu}_1$ substitute μ_0 and μ_1 in (2.3.11) and the test statistics are derived in a second step as before.

[11] See Johansen (1995) for the asymptotic distribution.

It is shown in Saikkonen & Lütkepohl (2000a) that the two LM type tests and the LR test $LR^i_{ta}(r_0)$ have identical asymptotic properties. However, Saikkonen & Lütkepohl (2000a) and Hubrich et al. (2000) compare the small sample properties of these LR and LM type tests in small sample simulations and find that the trend-adjusted LR test outperforms the LM type tests in most cases. Therefore, only the LR tests are considered further in the following. They will be denoted by $LR^i_{ta}(r_0)$, representing the trace version of the LR statistic.

The application of a test that does not allow for a linear trend in the data nor in the cointegration relation will be discussed in the next section.

2.3.1.3 Arbitrary Mean and no Trend Term in the DGP (μ_0 arbitrary, $\mu_1 = 0$)

Sometimes, a system of time series that do not exhibit linear trends is analysed. In this case, Lütkepohl & Saikkonen (1999c) have shown that tests based on a model where μ_0 takes on an arbitrary value, possibly nonzero, and no linear trend enters the DGP, i.e. $\mu_1 = 0$ in (2.2.1), have higher local power than tests based on more general models. Whether the small sample power of these tests is higher than of tests based on more general models is analysed in Section 2.5.

In the framework considered in this section, y_t is a VAR(p) process with EC representation

$$\Delta y_t = \nu_0 + \Pi y_{t-1} + \sum_{j=1}^{p-1} \Gamma_j \Delta y_{t-j} + \varepsilon_t, \qquad t = p+1, p+2, \dots, \tag{2.3.12}$$

where $\nu_0 = -\Pi\mu_0$. Alternatively, the model can be written in the form

$$\Delta y_t = \Pi^* y^*_{t-1} + \sum_{j=1}^{p-1} \Gamma_j \Delta y_{t-j} + \varepsilon_t, \qquad t = p+1, p+2, \dots, \tag{2.3.13}$$

where $\Pi^* = \Pi[I_n : \mu_0]$ and $y^*_{t-1} = [y'_{t-1} : 1]'$. The LR statistics may be obtained from these representations using RR regression techniques (see below).

Tests Based on Original Data An LR test including an unrestricted intercept, thereby allowing a trend in the data, is obtained calculating the matrix M^{i0}_T as in (2.3.3) with $z'_t = (1, \Delta y'_{t-1}, \dots, \Delta y'_{t-p+1})$ and y^+_{t-1} is substituted by y_{t-1}. M^{i0}_T is introduced into (2.3.5) with $\hat\lambda^{i0}_1 \geq \dots \geq \hat\lambda^{i0}_n$

denoting the corresponding ordered generalized eigenvalues obtained as solutions of

$$\det(\hat{\Pi} M_T^{i0} \hat{\Pi}' - \lambda \hat{\Omega}) = 0. \tag{2.3.14}$$

Johansen's LR trace statistic for testing the pair of hypotheses in (2.2.4) can be derived as

$$LR^{i0}(r_0) = (T-p) \sum_{j=r_0+1}^{n} \log(1 + \hat{\lambda}_j^{i0}), \tag{2.3.15}$$

where the superscript i stands for the intercept term and 0 indicates that the trend parameters are zero.[12] The corresponding critical values are, for example, given in Johansen & Juselius (1990, Table A.2).

The intercept term in (2.3.12) is estimated unrestrictedly. This formulation of the model takes into account that it is often not known whether a linear trend in the data exists. Therefore, a linear trend in the variables is not ruled out in estimating the parameters.

In contrast, LS estimators $\hat{\Pi}^*$ and $\hat{\Omega}^*$ from (2.3.13) may be computed, where the constant is restricted to the long-run. The ordered generalized eigenvalues $\hat{\lambda}_1^* \geq \cdots \geq \hat{\lambda}_n^*$ can be obtained from $\det(\hat{\Pi}^* M_T^* \hat{\Pi}^{*\prime} - \lambda \hat{\Omega}^*) = 0$, where M_T^* is defined as in (2.3.3) with y_{t-1} replaced by $y_{t-1}^* = [y_{t-1}' : 1]'$ and $z_t' = (\Delta y_{t-1}', \ldots, \Delta y_{t-p+1}')$. Now the trace statistic similar to (2.3.15) may be defined as

$$LR^*(r_0) = (T-p) \sum_{j=r_0+1}^{n} \log(1 + \hat{\lambda}_j^*).$$

Critical values are, for instance, given in Johansen & Juselius (1990, Table A.3), Johansen (1995, Table 15.2) and Osterwald-Lenum (1992, Table 1*).[13]

Since it might be unknown in many empirical analyses whether a deterministic trend in the data exists, it should be tested whether the restriction $\mu_1 = 0$ holds. Johansen (1992) suggests to test null hypotheses for increasing ranks $r_0 = 0, 1, \ldots$, with both types of tests, the test allowing for a linear trend in the data ($LR^i(r_0)$) and the test assuming that the data do not exhibit a linear trend ($LR^*(r_0)$), using the critical values obtained under the assumption $\mu_1 \neq 0$ for the latter. If both tests reject for a given r_0 the procedure is continued to test $H_0(r_0+1)$ etc.. If at some stage $H_0(r_0)$ is rejected by $LR^*(r_0)$ and not by $LR^i(r_0)$,

[12] For the asymptotic distribution, see Johansen (1991) or, consistent with the notation presented here, in Hubrich et al. (2000).

[13] The asymptotic distribution can be found in Johansen (1995) or, in a notation consistent with the present framework, in Hubrich et al. (2000).

then r_0 is chosen as cointegrating rank and the process is assumed to have $\mu_1 \neq 0$. If $H_0(r_0)$ is not rejected by $LR^*(r_0)$ but by $LR^i(r_0)$ for some r_0, the conclusion is that $r = r_0$ and the process does not have a linear trend. The same holds, of course, if both $LR^*(r_0)$ and $LR^i(r_0)$ do not reject. However, in some cases in applied work the restriction that no linear trend is in the data might be imposed, e.g. in the analysis of interest rates.

Tests Based on Mean-Adjusted Data Another possibility to proceed in the case without a linear trend in the DGP, i.e. neither in the cointegration relation nor in the data, has been proposed by Saikkonen & Luukkonen (1997). They suggest to estimate the mean parameter μ_0 on the basis of the EC representation

$$\Delta y_t = \Pi(y_{t-1} - \mu_0) + \sum_{j=1}^{p-1} \Gamma_j \Delta y_{t-j} + \varepsilon_t, \qquad t = p+1, p+2, \ldots, \quad (2.3.16)$$

in a first step, include the estimator $\hat{\mu}_0$ in (2.3.16) and then proceed by computing LR^{SL} as in (2.3.17) below.

To obtain an appropriate estimator for μ_0 the VAR form $y_t = \nu_0 + A_1 y_{t-1} + \cdots + A_p y_{t-p} + \varepsilon_t$ is initially estimated by LS, where the estimators of ν_0 and the A_j will be denoted by $\hat{\nu}_0$ and $\hat{A}_j$, respectively. Further, the following quantities are computed:

$$\hat{d}_t = y_t - \sum_{j=1}^{p} \hat{A}_j y_{t-j} \quad \text{and} \quad \hat{C}_t = I_n - \sum_{j=1}^{t-1} \hat{A}_j, \quad t = 1, \ldots, T,$$

with $y_t = 0$ for $t \leq 0$, $\hat{C}_1 = I_n$ and $\hat{A}_j = 0$ for $j > p$. Then, the estimator of μ_0 is obtained as

$$\hat{\mu}_0 = \left(\sum_{t=1}^{T} \hat{C}_t' \hat{\Omega}^{-1} \hat{C}_t \right)^{-1} \sum_{t=1}^{T} \hat{C}_t' \hat{\Omega}^{-1} \hat{d}_t.$$

Here, $\hat{\Omega}$ is the estimator for the residual covariance matrix based on the LS estimator of the VAR(p) process in levels. As stated in Hubrich et al. (2000), the estimator $\hat{\mu}_0$ may be regarded as a GLS estimator for μ_0 and it can be motivated as an approximate Gaussian ML estimator if $x_t = 0$, $t \leq 0$ (Hubrich et al., 2000).

The test statistics are determined on the basis of model (2.3.16). Generalized eigenvalues $\hat{\lambda}_1^{SL} \geq \cdots \geq \hat{\lambda}_n^{SL}$ are again derived from $\det(\tilde{\Pi} M_T^{SL} \tilde{\Pi}' - \lambda \tilde{\Omega}) = 0$, where $\tilde{\Pi}$ and $\tilde{\Omega}$ are obtained from LS estimation of (2.3.16) and M_T^{SL} is defined as in (2.3.3) with y_{t-1} replaced by

$y_{t-1} - \hat{\mu}_0$ and $z_t' = (\Delta y_{t-1}', \ldots, \Delta y_{t-p+1}')$, as before. The trace statistic for testing the pair of hypotheses (2.2.4) then becomes

$$LR^{SL}(r_0) = (T-p) \sum_{j=r_0+1}^{n} \log(1 + \hat{\lambda}_j^{SL}). \qquad (2.3.17)$$

These test statistics have the same asymptotic null distributions as Johansen's LR tests without mean and trend term. Critical values can, therefore, be taken from Johansen (1988, Table 1; 1995, Table 15.1) and Osterwald-Lenum (1992, Table 0).

2.3.2 Summary of Models and Test Statistics

Table 2.1 provides a summary of the model types in a VAR(1) setting and the corresponding LR type test statistics with the respective references. As discussed in the previous section small sample analyses have only been carried out for a few of the original LR tests by Toda (1994, 1995) and Gonzalo & Pitarakis (1999). Also, some simulations have been carried out for the trend-adjusted LR tests (e.g. Saikkonen & Luukkonen, 1997; Saikkonen & Lütkepohl, 2000a; Lütkepohl & Saikkonen, 1999c).

In contrast, a systematic comparison of local power results of LR tests is presented in Saikkonen & Lütkepohl (1999). They conclude that it is advantageous in applied work to pay attention to the specification of the deterministic terms. If a linear trend term in the variables and the cointegration relations cannot be excluded a priori the LR^{+}, LR^{PC} or LR_{ta}^{GLS} tests have to be used. Substantial power gains are possible, if a deterministic trend can be excluded from the cointegration relations or even from the variables. Based on the local power comparison presented in Saikkonen & Lütkepohl (1999), LR^{SL} tests should be used if $\mu_1 = 0$ whereas LR_{ta}^{i} type tests might be applied if $\mu_1 \neq 0$ and $\beta'\mu_1 = 0$.

In Hubrich et al. (2000) it has been analysed whether these results from the local power analysis of the tests can also be found when analysing the power of the tests in small samples. Section 2.5 will extend the results of that paper.

2.3.3 Previous Simulation Studies

A number of simulation studies, mainly concentrating on LR tests, have been presented in the literature. Tables 2.3 and 2.4 provide an overview of a large number of small sample simulation studies that have included LR tests. These tables present information on the dimension and lag order of the DGPs as well as the sample sizes on which the simulations have

Table 2.1: Models for Lag order 1 and LR Type Tests

Assumption for deterministic terms	Model	Notation for LR statistic	References
μ_0, μ_1 arbitrary	$\Delta y_t = \nu + [\Pi : \delta] \begin{bmatrix} y_{t-1} \\ t-1 \end{bmatrix} + \varepsilon_t$	LR^{+}	Johansen (1992, 1994, 1995)
	$\Delta y_t = \nu_0 + \nu_1 t + \Pi y_{t-1} + \varepsilon_t$	LR^{PC}	Perron & Campbell (1993)
	$\Delta y_t - \hat{\mu}_1 = \Pi(y_{t-1} - \hat{\mu}_0 - \hat{\mu}_1(t-1)) + \hat{\varepsilon}_t$	LR^{GLS}_{ta}	Saikkonen & Lütkepohl (2000c)
μ_0 arbitrary, $\mu_1 \neq 0$, $\beta'\mu_1 = 0$	$\Delta y_t = \nu_0 + \Pi y_{t-1} + \varepsilon_t$	LR^{i}	Johansen (1991)
	$\Delta y_t - \hat{\mu}_1 = \Pi(y_{t-1} - \hat{\mu}_0) + \hat{\varepsilon}_t$	LR^{i}_{ta}	Saikkonen & Lütkepohl (2000a)
μ_0 arbitrary,	$\Delta y_t = \nu_0 + \Pi y_{t-1} + \varepsilon_t$	LR^{i0}	Johansen (1991)
$\mu_1 = 0$	$\Delta y_t = [\Pi : \eta] \begin{bmatrix} y_{t-1} \\ 1 \end{bmatrix} + \varepsilon_t$	LR^{*}	Johansen (1991)
	$\Delta y_t = \Pi(y_{t-1} - \tilde{\mu}_0) + \tilde{\varepsilon}_t$	LR^{SL}	Saikkonen & Luukkonen (1997)

been based. Furthermore, the tables include the information whether sequential testing procedures have been carried out as well as the main topics analysed in these simulation studies.

In the following, model selection, non-normality, the dependence of the test performance on assumptions regarding deterministic terms, the dimension of the system as well as the sample size are discussed with respect to the small sample performance of LR tests.

Model Selection In the theoretical discussion of systems cointegration tests above it has been assumed that the DGP is a finite order VAR(p) process and that the order p is known. However, the true order of the process is not known in practice. There seems to be broad agreement that lag order selection criteria should be applied to set up the model before testing for cointegration to avoid lag order misspecification, that would lead to a bias in the test decision for the cointegration rank in the system.

Lütkepohl & Saikkonen (1999b) recommend applying model selection criteria to choose the lag order in a first step before testing for the cointegration rank.[14] They show that the asymptotic properties of the LR tests remain unchanged if model selection criteria are used for order selection prior to testing for the cointegrating rank.

Hubrich et al. (2000), Section 4.5, summarize simulation evidence with respect to order selection in the context of systems cointegration tests. They find that most studies recommend using an order selection criterion to choose the lag order, but that different studies provide different recommendations regarding the choice of a specific order selection criterion.

In general, however, choosing the lag length with order selection criteria, which tend to find a balance between a good approximation of the DGP and an efficient use of the sample information, appears to be a good strategy for applied work. However, a universally optimal criterion for this purpose does not seem to exist.[15]

Non-Normality The test performance of Johansen's LR test (LR^{i0}) in small samples seems to be sensitive to non-normal processes (see e.g. Cheung & Lai, 1993).[16] Thus, the researcher has to be aware that de-

[14]For a discussion of model selection criteria, see also Lütkepohl (1991, Chapter 4).

[15]It should be noted that the small sample analysis of order selection concentrates on LR tests for data with as well as without trend.

[16]Theoretical considerations of the consequences of nonnormal processes have been reviewed in Hubrich et al. (2000).

viations of the DGP from the normal distribution might influence the result of systems cointegration tests.

Specification of Deterministic Terms Generally, simulation studies have mainly concentrated on the LR test that considers an error correction model with intercept, allowing for a trend in the data, but not in the cointegration relation (LR^i), e.g. Haug (1996). Yap & Reinsel (1995), Reimers (1992) and Saikkonen & Luukkonen (1997) consider the model where the constant is estimated unrestrictedly, whereas the DGP is assumed not to have a linear trend (LR^{i0}). Saikkonen & Luukkonen (1997) show that, if it is known that there is no deterministic trend, LR^{SL} tests can be considerably more powerful than Johansen's LR versions. However, these studies do not provide recommendations for applied work with respect to the choice of deterministic terms.

Toda (1994, 1995) analyses the dependence of the LR test statistics on deterministic terms in small samples. Further, a paper by Gonzalo & Lee (1998) considers the relevance of deterministic components with respect to testing the null of no cointegration using LR tests. Recently, in a series of papers Lütkepohl & Saikkonen (e.g. Lütkepohl & Saikkonen, 1999c; Lütkepohl & Saikkonen, 1999b) have presented comparisons of cointegration rank tests which work under alternative assumptions regarding the deterministic term in the DGP.

Toda concentrates his simulation comparison on the class of LR tests. He compares Johansen's original LR tests LR^i, LR^* and LR^0 (Toda, 1995) as well as LR^+ and LR^{PC} (Toda, 1994) using sequential test procedures.

Additionally, Toda (1995) analyses the mixed procedure LR^* & LR^i described in Section 2.3.1.2 above, as suggested by Johansen (1992), and finds that this procedure often fails to detect the presence of a linear trend, even though the cointegrating rank may be correctly determined.

Toda (1994) concludes that LR^{PC} generally outperforms LR^+ for the DGP considered, despite the fact that the latter imposes an additional (correct) constraint by excluding quadratic trends in the data. In contrast, LR^{PC} and LR^+ perform similar in the simulations presented in Hubrich et al. (2000). Therefore, the LR^+ test is presented in the simulations below, since this test is more commonly applied in empirical work.

However, Toda (1994, 1995) does not provide a comparison of the performance of tests that do allow for a linear trend in the cointegration relation relative to tests that do not allow for a linear trend in the cointegration relation. This is one extension that will be provided in the new simulation results presented in this thesis.

Toda (1994, 1995) also concludes that at least 300 observations are needed to ensure the good performance of the test procedures, in the sense that they detect the true cointegration rank even if a stationary root of the process is close to one (e.g. 0.8 or greater).

The studies considered above show that it is important which deterministic terms are considered when testing for cointegration relationships, and whether the deterministic components enter the cointegration relation.

Dimension and Sample Size Regarding the dependence of the test results to dimensionality, Cheung & Lai (1993) find that the finite-sample bias towards overrejection of the null hypothesis of no cointegration magnifies with increasing dimension of the estimated system. Gonzalo & Pitarakis (1999) base their simulations on DGPs of higher dimensions ($n = 2, 5$ and 10) and study various methods for detecting the cointegrating rank as the number of variables is increased. For Johansen's standard LR statistic without deterministic terms they find that inferences in systems of high dimensions are highly distorted. This result might be transferred to the application of tests with deterministic terms.

Ho & Sørensen (1996) employ 4- to 9-dimensional data based DGPs in their simulation study and come to the conclusion that in a high-dimensional system based on few data the LR^i test tends to find too much cointegration if the lag order is misspecified. This is in line with other findings, e.g. Reimers (1992). Ho & Sørensen (1996) also conclude that the performance of the testing procedure deteriorates as the ratio of parameters to data points increases to more than about 0.5.

Regarding the sample size, Toda (1994) states that a sample size as large as $T = 400$ is needed for the trace tests (LR^+ and LR^{PC}) to distinguish between eigenvalues of unity and near unity. For LR tests without a trend in the cointegration relation Toda (1995) concludes that at least $T = 300$ observations are needed to ensure a good test performance over all values of the cointegration rank and the nuisance parameters of the DGP. However, in macroeconomic applications time series are normally shorter, i.e. around 100 to 200 observations.

From the combined analysis of the influence of dimensionality and sample size on the test performance, Ho & Sørensen (1996) and Gonzalo & Pitarakis (1999) conclude that the ratio of the number of parameters to observations crucially influences the performance of the LR tests. Gonzalo & Lee (1998) show that different possibilities of misspecification, e.g. dynamic misspecification or an order of integration of the variables in the system different from one.

2.4 Other Tests

Whereas the previous section has reviewed tests based on the likelihood ratio principle, this section presents tests that are based on other ideas. Again, tests can be grouped according to whether they are based on original or trend-adjusted data. The first group includes the tests based on canonical correlations of levels suggested by Bewley & Yang (1995) and Yang & Bewley (1996) that will be described in Section 2.4.1.[17] The tests based on trend-adjusted data presented below include the test suggested by Stock & Watson (1988) as well as Bierens' nonparametric test.

Each of the tests includes different variants. However, in the small sample simulations only one variant of each test is presented. The choice will be motivated in the respective section. An overview of the tests discussed in this section is provided in Table 2.2.

In contrast to LR tests, all the tests mentioned above have only been presented in limited simulation studies so far. Some of them have been compared with LR tests. Only SW tests have been included in several simulation studies. A summary of the main available small sample simulation results is given following the respective presentation of the tests. The presentation of the underlying DGPs and the test statistics in this section is based on Hubrich et al. (2000).

2.4.1 Tests Based on Canonical Correlations of Levels

2.4.1.1 DGPs and Test Statistics

Bewley & Yang (1995) and Yang & Bewley (1996) propose tests for cointegration which may be thought of as being based on the canonical correlations of the levels y_t and y_{t-1} if the DGP is a VAR(1) process. Thereby they differ from Johansen's LR tests which, in the special VAR(1) case, may be regarded as a canonical correlation analysis for the levels and

[17]Other tests in that group are the lag augmentation test suggested by Lütkepohl & Saikkonen (1999c), who propose to add an additional lag to the VAR(p) model, and the fully modified test suggested by Quintos (1998a, b). The advantage of these tests is that the test statistics have a standard χ^2 distribution. However, these tests are not considered in the following because of some deficiencies (see Hubrich et al., 2000).

Table 2.2: Other Tests

Assumptions for the deterministic terms	Test statistic	References
μ_0, μ_1 arbitrary	SW_{ta} BI	Stock & Watson (1988) Bierens (1997b)
μ_0 arbitrary, $\mu_1 \neq 0, \beta'\mu_1 = 0$	BY^i	Yang & Bewley (1996)
μ_0 arbitrary, $\mu_1 = 0$	BY SW_{ma}	Bewley & Yang (1995) Stock & Watson (1988)

first differences. Bewley & Yang consider a VAR(p) model in EC form,[18]

$$\Delta y_t = \nu_0 + \alpha\beta' y_{t-1} + \sum_{j=1}^{p-1} \Gamma_j \Delta y_{t-j} + \varepsilon_t, \qquad t = p+1, p+2, \ldots \quad (2.4.1)$$

and construct their test statistics based on original data, similar as in the framework of Johansens's LR tests. Bewley & Yang propose to compute residuals g_t and h_t from regressions of y_t and y_{t-1} on $[1, \Delta y_{t-1}, \ldots, \Delta y_{t-p+1}]$, define $G = [g_{p+1}, \ldots, g_T]$, $H = [h_{p+1}, \ldots, h_T]$ and solve the eigenvalue problem

$$\det[GH'(HH')^{-1}HG' - \gamma GG'] = 0.$$

Let $\gamma_1 \leq \cdots \leq \gamma_n$ be the ordered eigenvalues and $q_1, \ldots, q_n$ the corresponding eigenvectors satisfying

$$GH'(HH')^{-1}HG'q_j = \gamma_j GG'q_j, \quad j = 1, \ldots, n.$$

Note that for $p = 1$ the γ_j are the canonical correlations of y_t and y_{t-1}. The first r_0 of the q_j are used to estimate the cointegration relations, i.e., $\hat{\beta} = [q_1, \ldots, q_{r_0}]$. Estimators of the other parameters in (2.4.1) are obtained by replacing β with $\hat{\beta}$ and applying multivariate LS to (2.4.1). The resulting estimators will be denoted by $\hat{\nu}_0, \hat{\alpha}, \hat{\Gamma}_j$ and the residuals are $\hat{\varepsilon}_t$. From these quantities estimators $\hat{\alpha}_\perp$ and $\hat{\beta}_\perp$ are derived in the usual way. Based on these estimators the following definitions are made:

$$\hat{C} = \hat{\beta}_\perp[\hat{\alpha}'_\perp(I_n - \sum_{j=1}^{p-1} \hat{\Gamma}_j)\hat{\beta}_\perp]^{-1}\hat{\alpha}'_\perp,$$

[18]Please note, that this model underlies the test statistics not allowing for a linear trend in the data as well as the statistics that allow for a linear trend in the data. Bewley & Yang do not consider a test with arbitrary mean and trend term.

$$h_t^{r0} = \hat{\alpha}'_\perp h_t \quad \text{and} \quad H_{r0} = [h_{p+1}^{r0}, \dots, h_T^{r0}],$$

$$g_t^{r0} = \hat{\alpha}'_\perp (h_t + \hat{C}\hat{\varepsilon}_t) \quad \text{and} \quad G_{r0} = [g_{p+1}^{r0}, \dots, g_T^{r0}].$$

Denoting the ordered eigenvalues obtained as solutions of

$$\det[G_{r0}H'_{r0}(H_{r0}H'_{r0})^{-1}H_{r0}G'_{r0} - \gamma G_{r0}G'_{r0}] = 0 \tag{2.4.2}$$

by $\hat{\gamma}_1 \leq \cdots \leq \hat{\gamma}_{n-r_0}$, the following statistic is calculated:

$$BY_{min}(r_0) = (T-p)(1-\hat{\gamma}_1). \tag{2.4.3}$$

When $\hat{\gamma}_1$ in BY_{min} is small and, thus, the statistics are large, fewer than $n - r_0$ common trends are indicated. Thus, $H_0(r_0)$ is rejected when the statistics assume large values. Alternatively, Bewley & Yang (1995) suggest the calculation of the trace statistic $BY_{trace}(r_0) = (T-p)\sum_{j=1}^{n-r_0}(1-\hat{\gamma}_j)$. The asymptotic null distributions of these statistics depend on $n - r_0$ and the trending properties of the process. BY_{min} and BY_{trace} denote the test statistics for the case without deterministic trend ($\mu_1 = 0$). Critical values for BY_{min} and BY_{trace} are provided in Table 1 of Bewley & Yang (1995).[19] The test statistics BY_{trace}^i and BY_{min}^i are calculated in the same way as BY_{trace} and BY_{min}, but different critical values for BY_{trace}^i and BY_{min}^i in the case $\mu_1 \neq 0$, $\beta'\mu_1 = 0$, may be found in Table 1 of Yang & Bewley (1996).[20]

In Bewley & Yang (1995) the authors also note that for a given cointegrating rank r_0, the hypotheses $H_0 : \mu_1 = 0$ may be tested with the statistic $BY_{max}(r_0) = (T-p)(1-\hat{\gamma}_{n-r_0})$, where H_0 is rejected if $BY_{max}(r_0)$ is small.

As argued in Hubrich et al. (2000), Section 4.2, the tests suggested by Bewley & Yang (1995) and Yang & Bewley (1996) are derived under similar conditions as the LR tests in Section 2.3, but might be more restrictive for higher order processes as the tests derived in an LR framework above.

However, Bewley & Yang (1995) and Yang & Bewley (1996) state that their tests are consistent. Small sample simulations are only presented for the BY tests in Bewley & Yang (1995). The results are discussed in the following section.

[19]The table has to be used cautiously because the legend is not fully clear and the user is expected to add minus signs to some of the entries.

[20]Further test statistics for the case of $\mu_1 = 0$ are proposed in Bewley & Yang (1995), but are not considered here since according to Bewley & Yang (1995) they either perform similarly to their minimum test statistic or are less robust to variations in the innovation correlation.

2.4.1.2 Previous Simulation Results

Bewley & Yang (1995) compare their test with Johansen's LR^{i0} test based on a two- and five-dimensional VAR(1) process. They find that the small sample power of the BY_{trace} test is not satisfactory. Therefore, its use is not recommended. On the other hand, $BY_{min}(r_0)$ may has better power than Johansen's LR tests in case of low innovation correlation. The BY tests also seem to be more robust against variation of the innovation correlation than LR tests. However, these results are exclusively based on processes without deterministic terms. For the tests allowing for a drift in the data, Bewley & Yang (1996) do not carry out any small sample simulations. Also, simulations are restricted to testing the null of no cointegration (cointegration rank of zero). The results for the five-dimensional DGP are broadly the same as for the two-dimensional process, except that the power is lower as would have been expected.

According to Bewley & Yang (1995), their trace statistic is outperformed by the minimum statistic. Therefore, only results for BY^i_{min} will be reported in the small sample simulations in Section 2.5. It should be noted that small sample simulations for BY^i_{min} have not been available yet, except for the review paper by Hubrich et al. (2000).

2.4.2 Stock–Watson Tests

2.4.2.1 DGPs and Test Statistics

For ease of exposition, the tests proposed by Stock & Watson (1988) are discussed for the case of $\mu_0 = \mu_1 = 0$, first.

The modifications for more realistic processes with deterministic terms are discussed subsequently. The Stock–Watson tests are suitable for the pair of hypotheses given in (2.2.4), that is, $H_0(r_0) : r = r_0$ is tested against the alternative $H_1(r_0) : r > r_0$. The idea underlying the tests is as follows. If r_0 cointegrating relationships exist for x_t, then $n - r_0$ common trends exist. Stock & Watson (1988) suggest performing a principal components analysis and order the principal components from smallest to largest. Denoting by Q the orthogonal matrix whose rows correspond to the principal components, $z_t = Qy_t$ where the y_t are the original data. The common trends τ_t are then chosen to be the last $n - r_0$ components of z_t. Under $H_0(r_0)$ this process has $n - r_0$ unit roots (i.e., $\Delta\tau_t$ is stationary with possibly infinite order VAR representation). Thus, computing the multivariate LS estimator of Φ in $\tau_t = \Phi\tau_{t-1} + u_t$

results in a matrix

$$\tilde{\Phi} = \left(\sum_{t=2}^{T} \tau_t \tau_{t-1}'\right) \left(\sum_{t=2}^{T} \tau_{t-1} \tau_{t-1}'\right)^{-1} \tag{2.4.4}$$

whose eigenvalues approach one in large samples. Therefore, the test rejects $H_0(r_0)$ if the eigenvalue of $\tilde{\Phi}$ with smallest modulus is much smaller than one.

In order to receive a test statistic which does not depend on unknown nuisance parameters, adjustments for the short-term dynamics are made. Two types of adjustments were suggested by Stock & Watson (1988). The first one assumes that τ_t has a VAR(p) representation. In that case $\Delta\tau_t$ has a VAR($p-1$) representation, say

$$\Delta\tau_t = \Xi_1 \Delta\tau_{t-1} + \cdots + \Xi_{p-1} \Delta\tau_{t-p+1} + v_t.$$

Denoting the LS estimators of the Ξ_i by $\hat{\Xi}_i$ residuals may be computed as

$$\hat{\xi}_t = \tau_t - \hat{\Xi}_1 \tau_{t-1} - \cdots - \hat{\Xi}_{p-1} \tau_{t-p+1}$$

and used to compute the estimator

$$\hat{\Phi} = \left(\sum_{t=p+1}^{T} \hat{\xi}_t \hat{\xi}_{t-1}'\right) \left(\sum_{t=p+1}^{T} \hat{\xi}_{t-1} \hat{\xi}_{t-1}'\right)^{-1}.$$

The test statistic proposed by Stock & Watson is then

$$SW^{VAR}(r_0) = (T-p)(\text{real}(\hat{\lambda}_{min}) - 1),$$

where real$(\hat{\lambda}_{min})$ denotes the real part of the eigenvalue of $\hat{\Phi}$ with smallest modulus. $H_0(r_0)$ is rejected if $SW^{VAR}(r_0)$ is small. The asymptotic null distribution of this test statistic is nonstandard. Its critical values are tabulated in Table 1 of Stock & Watson (1988).

This test may be regarded as nonparametric because the VAR(p) may just be an approximation to a more general DGP of the common trends τ_t. Note that, if y_t is a VAR(p) process, τ_t will in general not have a finite order VAR representation. Therefore, Stock & Watson (1988) also propose another nonparametric procedure to account for the short-term dynamics and thereby eliminate nuisance parameters in the limiting distribution of their test statistics. They suggest to compute residuals $\hat{u}_t = \tau_t - \tilde{\Phi}\tau_{t-1}$, where $\tilde{\Phi}$ is defined in (2.4.4). Then an estimator of the covariance matrix of u_t is determined as

$$\hat{\Omega}_u = \sum_{s=1}^{T} K\left(\frac{s}{h_T}\right) \sum_{t=s+1}^{T} \hat{u}_t \hat{u}_{t-s}',$$

where h_T is the bandwidth and $K(\cdot)$ is a kernel function. The nonparametric estimator of Φ is then

$$\hat{\Phi}_{NP} = \left(T^{-2}\sum_{t=1}^{T}\tau_t\tau_{t-1}' - T^{-1}\hat{\Omega}_u\right)\left(T^{-2}\sum_{t=1}^{T}\tau_{t-1}\tau_{t-1}'\right)^{-1}.$$

Denoting the real part of the eigenvalue with smallest modulus of this matrix by real$(\hat{\lambda}_{min}^{NP})$ the test statistic becomes

$$SW^{NP}(r_0) = (T-p)(\text{real}(\hat{\lambda}_{min}^{NP}) - 1).$$

Under H_0 it has the same asymptotic distribution as $SW^{VAR}(r_0)$. The two statistics will differ in small samples.

For the realistic cases that μ_0 and/or μ_1 are nonzero, the components z_t are mean- and/or trend-adjusted. If μ_0 can take on arbitrary values and $\mu_1 = 0$, then z_t is replaced by $z_t - \bar{z}$, where z_t is transformed such that the last $n - r_0$ components are noncointegrated $I(1)$ processes, i.e. the common trends. The transformation is obtained by a principal components analysis as above. If both μ_0 and μ_1 are allowed to be nonzero, then z_t is replaced by $z_t - \hat{\mu}_0 - \hat{\mu}_1 t$, where $\hat{\mu}_0$ and $\hat{\mu}_1$ are obtained by regressing z_t on a constant and a linear trend. These tests can therefore, analogously to the LR test suggested e.g. by Lütkepohl & Saikkonen (1999c), be considered as tests based on trend-adjusted data. The resulting test statistics will be denoted by $SW_{ma}^{VAR}(r_0)$, $SW_{ma}^{NP}(r_0)$ and $SW_{ta}^{VAR}(r_0)$ and $SW_{ta}^{NP}(r_0)$, respectively. The limiting distributions of these test statistics differ from those of $SW^{VAR}(r_0)$ and $SW^{NP}(r_0)$. The critical values are listed in Tables 2 and 3 of Stock & Watson (1988).

2.4.2.2 Previous Simulation Results

In the paper proposing their tests, Stock & Watson (1988) present a small simulation study based on a three-dimensional VAR(2) and VARMA(1,1). Testing the null hypothesis of $r_0 = 1$ (two common trends) against the alternative of $r_A = r_0 + 1 = 2$ (one common trend) they find that the empirical size is similar to the nominal size in all cases. SW_{ta} performs better than SW_{ma} in terms of size and power in case of the VAR(2) process, whereas the reverse is true for a VARMA process. In contrast, Yap & Reinsel (1995) and Reimers (1992), who base their simulations on different two- and three-dimensional VAR and VARMA processes, find that SW_{ma} tests display severe size distortions in some cases. This is not dependent on whether the DGP is a VAR or a VARMA process. Therefore, Yap & Reinsel (1995) conclude that these tests cannot be recommended for applied work.

In preliminary simulations for the study presented in Section 2.5 the nonparametric SW^{NP} test has been found to perform similar to SW^{VAR}. In contrast to Haug (1996), it was found that neither the SW^{VAR} test nor his variant of SW^{NP} outperforms the other. Therefore, only results for SW^{VAR} are reported in Section 2.5.

2.4.3 Bierens' Nonparametric Tests

2.4.3.1 DGPs and Test Statistics

Bierens (1997a, b) develops nonparametric tests for the cointegrating rank. In his approach y_t may have a quite general DGP which does not have to be a finite order VAR process. It is assumed that y_t is of the form (2.2.1) and x_t is such that Δx_t is stationary and ergodic. Bierens considers weighted means of y_t and Δy_t and exploits the difference in their asymptotic behaviour to construct a test for the cointegrating rank. He defines matrices

$$D_m = \frac{8\pi^2}{T}\sum_{k=1}^{m} k^2 \left(\frac{1}{T}\sum_{t=1}^{T} F_{k,T} y_t\right)\left(\frac{1}{T}\sum_{t=1}^{T} F_{k,T} y_t\right)'$$

and

$$G_m = 2T\sum_{k=1}^{m} \left(\frac{1}{T}\sum_{t=1}^{T} F_{k,T} \Delta y_t\right)\left(\frac{1}{T}\sum_{t=1}^{T} F_{k,T} \Delta y_t\right)'$$

with

$$F_{k,T} = \cos(2k\pi(t-0.5)/T).$$

Other weights than $\cos(2k\pi(t-0.5)/T)$ may be chosen here. However, to ensure invariance of the test statistics to drift terms, the present choice is recommended.

Denoting by $\hat{\lambda}_1^B \geq \cdots \geq \hat{\lambda}_n^B$ the generalized eigenvalues obtained from

$$\det[D_m - \lambda(G_m + T^{-2}D_m^{-1})^{-1}] = 0,$$

Bierens proposes to use $BI(r_0) = \hat{\lambda}_{n-r_0}^B$ as a test statistic for testing the hypotheses in 2.2.5. The null hypothesis $H_0(r_0)$ is rejected if $BI(r_0)$ becomes too small, that is, the test is left-sided. Again the asymptotic null distribution is nonstandard and critical values may be found in Bierens (1997b).

The power of the test will depend on the number of terms m. For a test with 5% significance level Bierens (1997a) suggests using the following rule for choosing m if $n \leq 5$ and $r \leq 4$:

$$m = \begin{cases} n & \text{if } r_0 > 0 \text{ or } n < 2 \\ n+1 & \text{if } r_0 = 0 \text{ and } n \geq 2 \end{cases}.$$

2.4.3.2 Previous Simulation Results

Simulations for Bierens' nonparametric test have only been presented in the paper by Bierens (1997b) where these tests are proposed. In a small simulation study Bierens employs simulated wage and GNP series to compare the nonparametric test with Johansen's LR test with an unrestricted intercept and a restricted trend term in the error correction representation (LR^+). According to these simulations, the LR test displays higher size distortions, but appears to be much more powerful than the nonparametric test when the size-corrected power is considered. However, Bierens (1997b) refers to simulations by Van Giersbergen (1994) which, in contrast, indicate poor small sample power of the non-parametric BI_{min} test in comparison with Johansen's LR^+_{max}.

Bierens (1997b) points out that in case of a low fit of the cointegration regression the Bierens test shows much lower power than the LR test so that a high deviation of the cointegration rank indicated by the nonparametric test from the cointegration rank found when applying the LR test, hints to misspecification of the error correction model. However, Bierens does not specify what "high deviation" would mean.

For the Bierens test the minimum statistic BI_{min} was advocated by Bierens (1997b) and is, therefore, included in the simulations presented in the following section.

2.5 New Small Sample Simulations

The following section will focus on the comparison of the small sample properties of a large range of different systems cointegration tests. The performance of these tests in small samples is important with respect to their application in empirical analyses. In the sections above small sample comparisons presented in the literature have been summarized in the context of the exposition of the respective tests. Further discussion of previous simulation results and the way in which the simulations are extended in this thesis is provided in Section 2.5.1. The new simulations presented in the Sections 2.5.4 to 2.5.6 compare a range of systems cointegration tests under uniform conditions.

The results from these simulations will also be taken into account in the empirical analysis in Section 3.4.

2.5.1 Previous Simulation Studies

As can be seen from Sections 2.3 and 2.4, simulation studies presented in the literature differ in their focus. Some authors who have proposed modifications of existing tests or who have suggested new testing procedures have also provided limited small sample evidence in favour of their proposals (e.g. Stock & Watson, 1988; Saikkonen & Luukkonen, 1997; Yap & Reinsel, 1995). In other studies only a specific class of tests is compared (e.g. Toda, 1994, 1995), whereas in another group of studies broad ranges of tests are compared (e.g. Reimers, 1991; Haug, 1996, 1992).

As mentioned in Section 2.3.3, Tables 2.3 and 2.4 summarize a large number of simulation studies with respect to the specific test statistics that are considered in this thesis.

To summarize, the simulation evidence available from previous studies of systems cointegration tests is mostly for bivariate or three-dimensional processes with lag orders one or two. In some studies higher dimensional processes have also been used. Toda (1994, 1995) shows that for comparing LR tests, using rather simple DGPs is justified because these tests are invariant to nonsingular linear transformations of the data and, thus, more complicated processes can be reduced to equivalent simple versions. In some studies DGPs derived from real economic data are used (e.g. Ho & Sørensen, 1996; Reimers, 1992; Bierens, 1997b). Moreover, DGPs with moving average components are employed in a number of simulation studies (Boswijk & Franses, 1992; Cheung & Lai, 1993; Yap & Reinsel, 1995; Saikkonen & Luukkonen, 1997; Gonzalo & Pitarakis, 1998; Lütkepohl & Saikkonen, 1999b).

The sample sizes considered in the Monte Carlo studies cover a range of 30 to 10 000 observations. In many cases they are concentrated on sample sizes around 100 to 200 and cover situations often encountered in macroeconometric applications.

Johansen's LR tests or their small sample modifications are included in almost all simulation studies because they may be regarded as benchmark tests with comparatively good performance and wide application in empirical research. Of the other tests discussed in the previous sections, only the Stock & Watson (*SW*) tests have been included in several simulations, e.g., by Haug (1996), Reimers (1992) and Yap & Reinsel (1995) (see the sections above). The simulation evidence for the other tests considered in this chapter is limited. Therefore, one main new contribution of the review paper by Hubrich et al. (2000) is the presentation of small sample simulations for a large number of cointegration rank tests for a number of different DGPs. The simulation evidence in the following sections presents detailed results for further DGPs, dimensions and sample sizes, that have only been summarized in Hubrich et al. (2000).

Although it is not easy to adequately summarize the main findings of previous simulation studies, the following general picture emerges. None of the tests is uniformly superior to all other tests in terms of size and power. However, some of the tests exhibit occasional extreme size distortions.

As can be seen from Section 2.3, a lot of possible problems that may occur when applying LR tests have been addressed in earlier simulation studies. One important issue, as the analyses in Toda (1994, 1995), Gonzalo & Lee (1998) and the papers by Saikkonen & Lütkepohl (see Section 2.3) have shown, is how deterministic terms are taken into account in the testing procedure. In some cases, not accounting for these deterministic terms can lead to spurious cointegration (Gonzalo & Lee, 1998). In other cases, a loss of power is encountered if prior information on trending properties is not taken into account. The present study elaborates on the relevance of the deterministic terms in systems cointegration tests and compares all the tests on the basis of the same DGPs.

Generally, it should be noted that all available studies compare only a few of the tests presented in the review by Hubrich et al. (2000) and in this thesis. In fact, little is known about the relative small sample performance of the LR^{SL}, SW, BY and BI tests in comparison with the original as well as trend-adjusted LR statistics.

Therefore, one aim of the small sample simulations presented in the following sections is to compare the size and power properties of a

Table 2.3: Some Previous Simulation Studies for BY, SW and BI as well as LR Tests

Author(s)	Test	DGP	Sample Size	Seq. Tests	Topics analysed
Stock & Watson (1988)	SW_{ma}, SW_{ta}	VAR(2), 3-dim., VARMA(1,1), 3-dim.	200	no	size, power
Reinsel & Ahn (1992)	LR^{0}, LR^{i0}	VAR(2), 4-dim., $r = 2$	200	no	size, finite sample correlation
Reimers (1991, 1992)	LR^{i0}, LR^{i0}_{RA}, SW_{ma}	RW(2-/3-dim.), VAR(1), 2-dim., VAR(2), 3-dim., databased (German interest rates)	50, 100, 200	no	size, power, lag order, dimension
Boswijk & Franses (1992)	LR^{i}	VARX, 2-dim., VARMAX, 2-dim.	50	no	size, power, lag order
Cheung & Lai (1993)	LR^{i0}, LR^{i0}_{mod}	$\text{VAR}(1)^{H}$, 2-dim., VAR(2), 2-dim., VARMA(1,1), 2-dim.	50-300 50-200 200	no	size, power, lag order, dimension, finite order correction, non-normality, MA component
Toda (1994)	LR^{i}, LR^{PC}	VAR(1), 2-dim.	100, 200, 300, 400	yes	size, power, initial values, innov. corr., determ. terms
Toda (1995)	LR^{i}, LR^{i0}, LR^{*}, LR^{i} & LR^{*}	VAR(1), 2-dim., with drift parameters	100, 200, 300	yes	size, power, initial values, innovation correlation, deterministic terms
Yap & Reinsel (1995)	LR^{i0}_{YP}, SW_{ma}	VAR(2), 3-dim., VARMA(1,1), 3-dim.	200	no	size, power, lag order, MA component
Bewley & Yang (1995)	LR^{i0}, BY	$\text{VAR}(1)^{G}$, 2-dim., VAR(1), 5-dim.	75, 100, 200	no	size, size-adjusted power, innovation correlation
Bierens (1997a, 1997b)	LR^{+}, BI	VAR(8), data based (wages, GNP)	80	yes	size, power, lag order $\alpha = 10\%$
Haug (1996)	LR^{i}, SW_{ma}	$\text{VAR}(1)^{G}$, 2-dim.	100	no	size, (not) size-adjusted power, lag order

Note: H: DGP of Haug (1996); T: DGP of Toda (1994, 1995) ; YR: DGP of Yap & Reinsel (1995); G: DGP of Gonzalo (1994); LR^{i0}_{RA}, LR^{i0}_{YR} and LR^{i0}_{mod}: small sample modifications of LR^{i0}

Table 2.4: Some Previous Simulation Studies of LR Tests

Author(s)	Test	DGP	Sample Size	Seq. Tests	Topics analysed
Ho & Sørensen (1996)	LR^i	4- to 9-dim. data-based DGP (sectorial data), 7-dim. data-based DGP (exchange rates), VAR(p), p=1,2,3 , p_{AIC}, p_{SC}	40	yes	lag order, dimension, finite sample correction, ratio no. of parameters to no. of observations,
Lütkepohl & Poskitt (1998)	LR^i_{RA}	VAR(1), 3-dim. VAR(1)^G, 2-dim.	50, 100, 200	no	size, power, lag order
Saikkonen & Luukkonen (1997)	LR^{i0}, LR^{SL}	VAR(2)^{YR}, 3-dim., VARMA(1,1)^{YR}, 3-dim.	200	no	size, size-adjusted power, lag order, MA component
Lütkepohl & Saikkonen (1999c)	LR^+, LR^{PC}	VAR(1)^T	100, 200	no	size, power, deterministic terms
Saikkonen & Lütkepohl (2000c)	LR^+, LR^{PC}, LR^{LS}_{ta}, LR^{GLS}_{ta}	VAR(1)^T, 2-dim.	100, 200	no	size, power, innovation correlation, deterministic terms
Saikkonen & Lütkepohl (2000a)	LR^i, LM^i, LR^i_{ta}, LR^+, LR^{PC}	VAR(1)^T, 2-dim.	100, 200	no	size, power, deterministic terms, innovation correlation
Lütkepohl & Saikkonen (1999b)	LR^0, LR^i	VAR(2)^{YR}, 3-dim. VARMA(1,1)^{YR}, 3-dim.	100, 200	yes	size, power, lag order, MA component
Gonzalo & Pitarakis (1998)	LR^0	VAR(1), 3-dim., VAR(2), 2-dim., VARMA(0,1), 3-dim.	150-160	no	size, lag order
Gonzalo & Pitarakis (1999)	LR^0	VAR(1), n=2,5,10	30, 90, 150, 400	no	size, dimension
Gonzalo & Lee (1998)	LR^i, LR^*	diff. VAR(1)^G $n=2$ with det. term	100 (1000, 10000)	no	size, lag order, deterministic terms, order of integration, singularity of error covariance, random unit root coefficient

Note: H: DGP of Haug (1996); T: DGP of Toda (1994, 1995) ; YR: DGP of Yap & Reinsel (1995); G: DGP of Gonzalo (1994); LR^i_{RA}: small sample modification of LR^i; LR^0: LR test for $\mu_0 = \mu_1 = 0$; p_{AIC}, p_{SC}: lag order choice on the basis of Akaike and Schwarz criterion

wide range of tests on the basis of the same DGPs. Another focus is to compare the tests systematically with respect to their assumptions regarding the deterministic terms. Tests for the analysis of data without a linear deterministic trend are compared in addition to tests for the analysis of trending data. Alternative test statistics apply depending on whether the constant or the trend parameter enter the cointegrating relation or not. The small sample performance of these test statistics is systematically explored in the new simulations presented below. Additionally, the performance of the tests for near integrated processes, different cointegration ranks, varying innovation correlation and dimensionality will be explored further.

For the new small sample simulations presented in the next section the following issues are important:

The choice of the test statistics included in the simulations below has been based on the results from the previous simulations discussed in Sections 2.3 and 2.4 as well as the simulation results presented in Hubrich et al. (2000). The following simulations will, therefore, focus on LR tests as well as the best performing variants of the BY, SW and BI tests.

The performance picture becomes more diffuse for more complicated processes of higher order or larger dimension. Therefore, the focus here is on simple processes only. A test or class of tests which does not perform well in simple situations under ideal conditions cannot be expected to do well for complicated DGPs in general even if there is simulation evidence to that effect in a previous simulation study. This implies that the favorable performance is at least partly due to the special simulation design in other studies.

The choice of the lag order was found to have an important impact on the test performance in previous simulation studies (see Section 2.3.3). To avoid distortions resulting from inadequate lag order selection the focus is on the properties of the tests when the lag order is specified correctly. The objective is to identify tests which do not work well under ideal conditions.

Initial values were found to have an impact on the test performance (see Toda, 1994, 1995). Since in practice the initial values are unknown, they are chosen randomly in the simulations below by starting the simulated series at zero and discarding the first 50 observations.

Since the deterministic terms of a DGP have a severe impact on the performance of the tests, the simulation results below are structured according to the assumptions for the deterministic terms.

The simulation results displayed in the following sections extend the experiments presented in Hubrich et al. (2000) with respect to the number of underlying DGPs, including different parameter values and sample sizes, DGPs of higher lag order and DGPs with structural breaks. The analysis focusses on a range of tests that are most relevant for applied research in terms of the underlying DGP as well as computational implementation.

2.5.2 Simulation Details

Tables 2.1 to 2.2 (see Sections 2.3 and 2.4) summarize the tests reviewed and compared in this thesis. The assumptions for the deterministic terms of the DGP, $y_t = \mu_0 + \mu_1 t + x_t$, under which the tests are supposed to work are presented together with the references for the tests. For the LR tests the respective model to be used for estimation is presented, whereas for the other tests the reader is referred to the relevant sections of this thesis. The tables are also provided as a reference with respect to the notation used for the test statistics considered in this thesis.

In the presentation of the simulation results the tests considered are grouped according to their assumptions regarding the deterministic terms, i.e. whether the tests allow for a linear trend in the data or not, or whether they allow for a linear trend in the cointegration relation.

The size of the respective tests is analysed first because, in order to control the type I error, a test should not exceed the nominal significance level considerably to be useful in applied work. If the actual size is much smaller than the nominal size, the test is conservative and tends to have little or no power. In the present case, this is a particular problem since the cointegrating rank is usually determined in a sequential procedure starting with the null hypothesis $r_0 = 0$, which will often terminate too early and, hence, indicate fewer cointegrating relations than the true number.[21] On the other hand, if the actual size is much larger than the nominal size, the test procedure tends to overestimate the cointegrating rank which can also result in severe interpretation problems. Strictly speaking the procedure cannot be considered to be a valid test in such a situation because bounding the type I error is an important property of a test.

In order to evaluate the results with respect to their random variation the standard error of the true rejection probability P based on 1000 replications is given by $s = \sqrt{P(1-P)/1000}$. In the case of a 5% nominal

[21] In the following, r always denotes the true cointegration rank whereas r_0 denotes the cointegration rank under the null hypothesis.

significance level, as in the simulations presented below, the standard deviation is $s = 0.007$ and, thus, the two-standard-error confidence interval for P is $[0.036, 0.064]$. A power comparison is performed for those tests which have roughly a correct size.

The performance of the tests will be evaluated on the basis of their behaviour in terms of size and power in response to variations of the key parameters influencing the DGPs considered (such as the autoregressive eigenvalues, the innovation correlation, the cointegrating rank and the deterministic part). DGPs of different dimensions will be employed in the simulations and the impact of the length of the time series on the test performance will be studied.

In the simulations, the correct lag specification is taken as the most favourable situation for the tests with respect to dynamic specification. Samples of sizes $T = 50, 100, 200$ and 400 were generated. The initial value is set to 0 and 50 presample values are discarded to eliminate the influence of the zero initial value on the test results. The first sample values are used for estimation purposes. Simulation results are presented for $T = 100$ first, as empirical analysis in economics is often based on similar sample sizes. These findings are compared with results for other sample sizes.

All programmes are written in GAUSS. The Johansen and Stock & Watson routine are partly adapted from Sam Ouliaris' COINT GAUSS program.[22] The RNDNS function in GAUSS with a fixed seed has been used to generate the pseudo-normal variates. All simulations were performed on a Pentium MMX PC.

The rejection frequencies in the tables are obtained on the basis of asymptotic critical values for a nominal level of 5%. The simulation results presented in Tables 2.5 to 2.14 and Figures 2.1 to 2.13 are based on unconditional tests for the respective cointegrating rank, that is, none of the tests is conditioned on the outcome of some other tests, as would be the case in sequential testing procedures.

2.5.3 The Toda DGP

Because one of the main objectives of this study is to analyse the impact of the trending properties of the DGP on the performance of the tests, a

[22] Version 1, 1991

DGP of the general form

$$w_t = \begin{bmatrix} 0 \\ \delta e_{n-r} \end{bmatrix} + \begin{bmatrix} \Psi_r & 0 \\ 0 & I_{n-r} \end{bmatrix} w_{t-1} + u_t, \quad u_t \sim iidN\left(0, \begin{bmatrix} I_r & \Theta \\ \Theta' & I_{n-r} \end{bmatrix}\right) \tag{2.5.1}$$

is employed, as in Toda (1994).[23] The quantity δ is a nonnegative scalar, e_{n-r} is an $(n-r)$-vector of the form $e_{n-r} = (0, ..., 0, 1)'$, Ψ_r is a diagonal matrix with diagonal elements inside or on the unit circle. The diagonal elements of this matrix are the eigenvalues which determine the number of cointegrating relations and common trends. Toda shows that this type of process may be regarded as a *canonical form* for investigating the properties of LR tests for the cointegrating rank. Other VAR(1) processes of interest can be obtained by nonsingular linear transformations of w_t and, hence, leave the LR tests for the cointegrating rank invariant. The simplicity of the process makes it attractive for the purposes here.

The corresponding two-dimensional VAR(1) DGP ($n = 2$) is of the following form:

$$w_t = \begin{bmatrix} 0 \\ \delta \end{bmatrix} + \begin{bmatrix} \psi_1 & 0 \\ 0 & \psi_2 \end{bmatrix} w_{t-1} + u_t, \quad u_t \sim iid\,N\left(\begin{bmatrix} 0 \\ 0 \end{bmatrix}, \begin{bmatrix} 1 & \theta \\ \theta & 1 \end{bmatrix}\right). \tag{2.5.2}$$

If $\psi_1 = \psi_2 = 1$ in DGP (2.5.2), the cointegrating rank is $r = 0$ and the process consists of two nonstationary components. In this case, the second component has a deterministic linear trend if $\delta \neq 0$ and no linear trend is present if $\delta = 0$. For $\theta = 0$ the two components are independent, whereas they are instantaneously correlated for $\theta \neq 0$. If $\psi_2 = 1$ and $|\psi_1| < 1$ the cointegrating rank is $r = 1$. Again there will be a linear trend in this case if $\delta \neq 0$. If both $|\psi_1| < 1$ and $|\psi_2| < 1$, the process is stationary ($r = 2$). In that case, a nonzero δ cannot generate a linear trend.

Since the properties of some tests depend partly on whether or not μ_1 is zero, but are otherwise independent of the particular values of the deterministic parameters it suffices to vary the deterministic part by varying δ. If $\delta = 0$ the deterministic trend term of the DGP in the representation (2.2.1) is $\mu_1 = 0$. In this case, all tests may be applied that allow for arbitrary values of μ_0 and are derived under the assumption $\mu_1 = 0$. Moreover, tests for arbitrary values of μ_0 as well as μ_1 are applicable.

The initial values w_{10} and w_{20} for the two components of the process w_t determine the mean parameter of w_t. The results of the tests do not

[23]The following exposition is again based on Hubrich et al. (2000).

depend on the initial value of the nonstationary component. In contrast, the mean of the stationary component depends on the initial value with decaying weight and hence the initial value influences the test results. As mentioned in Section 2.5.1, the starting values of the process w_t are chosen randomly in the simulations below by cutting off the first 50 sample observations to eliminate this dependence.

For $\delta \neq 0$ and $r = 1$ with $\psi_2 = 1$, the mean and trend parameters (μ_0^w and μ_1^w) of our process w_t are

$$\mu_0^w = \begin{bmatrix} 0 \\ w_0 \end{bmatrix} \quad \text{and} \quad \mu_1^w = \begin{bmatrix} 0 \\ \delta \end{bmatrix},$$

with $\beta'\mu_1^w = 0$ and w_0 being the initial value of the process. In this case, tests which require zero trend parameters are inappropriate whereas all tests may be applied which allow for a nonzero trend parameter and possibly require $\beta'\mu_1^w = 0$. In the simulations only results for $\delta = 0$ and 1 are reported. The choice of δ has no impact on those tests which allow for a linear trend and are invariant with respect to the values of the trend parameters. Thus, for these tests the value of $\delta \neq 0$ is of no consequence. In studying the small sample behaviour of some tests for which a distinction between $\delta = 0$ and $\delta \neq 0$ is necessary, δ values close to zero give similar results to the case where $\delta = 0$. Accordingly, focussing only on results where δ is equal to 0 and where it is markedly distinct from zero ($\delta = 1$) provides a good picture of the differences in the behaviour of the tests for $\delta = 0$ and $\delta \neq 0$.

The parameter θ in the residual covariance matrix of the process (2.5.2) controls the correlation between the two components of the process. For $\theta = 0$ the two components are independent whereas they are instantaneously correlated for $\theta \neq 0$. In the simulations for the two-dimensional DGP either no innovation correlation ($\theta = 0$) or high innovation correlation ($\theta = 0.8$) is assumed. The simulations are only carried out for nonnegative values of θ because Toda (1995) shows that the LR tests are invariant to the sign of θ.

To understand the relation between the VAR representation (2.5.2) and the EC representation it may be useful to consider the transformation

$$\begin{aligned} y_{1t} &= w_{1t} + w_{2t} \\ y_{2t} &= w_{2t} \end{aligned} \tag{2.5.3}$$

Therefore,

$$\begin{aligned} \Delta y_{1t} &= (\psi_1 - 1)(y_{1,t-1} - y_{2,t-1}) + (\psi_2 - 1)y_{2,t-1} + \epsilon_{1t} \\ \Delta y_{2t} &= \nu_{20} + (\psi_2 - 1)y_{2,t-1} + \epsilon_{2t} \end{aligned} \tag{2.5.4}$$

where $\nu_{20} = \delta$ and

$$\begin{aligned} \epsilon_{1t} &= u_{1t} + u_{2t} \\ \epsilon_{2t} &= u_{2t} \end{aligned} \quad \text{so that} \quad \Sigma_\epsilon = \begin{bmatrix} 2+2\theta & 1+\theta \\ 1+\theta & 1 \end{bmatrix}.$$

Thus, if $\psi_2 = 1$ and $|\psi_1| < 1$ (i.e. $r = 1$), $\psi_1 - 1$ determines the loading coefficient of the cointegrating relation in the system. Moreover, θ determines the instantaneous residual correlation in the EC form. A value of θ close to zero indicates intermediate correlation and a value of θ close to one results in large instantaneous correlation. Furthermore, using the above transformation, the deterministic terms with respect to representation (2.2.1) results in

$$\mu_0 = \begin{bmatrix} w_0 \\ w_0 \end{bmatrix} \quad \text{and} \quad \mu_1 = \begin{bmatrix} \delta \\ \delta \end{bmatrix},$$

with $\beta' \mu_1$=0.

The three-dimensional version of Toda's DGP used in the simulations has the form

$$w_t = \begin{bmatrix} 0 \\ 0 \\ \delta \end{bmatrix} + \begin{bmatrix} \psi_1 & 0 & 0 \\ 0 & \psi_2 & 0 \\ 0 & 0 & 1 \end{bmatrix} w_{t-1} + u_t, \tag{2.5.5}$$

$$u_t \sim iid\, N\left(\begin{bmatrix} 0 \\ 0 \\ 0 \end{bmatrix}, \begin{bmatrix} 1 & \theta_1 & \theta_2 \\ \theta_1 & 1 & 0 \\ \theta_2 & 0 & 1 \end{bmatrix} \right).$$

Here, δ generates the drift in the third component. The third eigenvalue is unity whereas ψ_1 and ψ_2 vary. If $|\psi_1| < 1$ and $|\psi_2| < 1$, the cointegrating rank is $r = 2$. If $|\psi_1| < 1$ and $\psi_2 = 1$, the cointegrating rank is $r = 1$, and the rank is zero if $\psi_1 = \psi_2 = \psi_3 = 1$. θ_1 and θ_2 are the correlations between the first component of the process with the second and third components, respectively.

In addition to the results of the Toda-DGP, small sample simulations of a three-dimensional VAR(2) employed by Yap & Reinsel (1995) have been investigated. Since this DGP is more specific in its structure, it will be presented together with the respective simulation results. In addition to providing simulation results for higher lag order, it has mainly been chosen to facilitate the comparison with earlier simulation studies.

In the next subsection the results from the bivariate DGPs are presented and discussed, followed by results from a three-dimensional DGP.

2.5.4 Two-dimensional VAR(1): The Simulation Results

This section analyses the performance of those tests that allow for a trend in the variables and in the cointegrating relation (see Section 2.3.1.1) for the case of a DGP without a linear trend, and compares their performance in terms of size and power with tests that restrict the deterministic term to take into account that no trend is in the data (see Section 2.3.1.3). It will be analysed whether the finding by Saikkonen & Lütkepohl (1999) that the local power of the tests that apply correct restrictions on deterministic terms will be considerably higher is also true for the power in small samples.

2.5.4.1 Sizes of the Tests

a) DGPs without Linear Trend ($\delta = 0$) Tables 2.5 and 2.6 show empirical sizes of the tests for $T = 100$ and $T = 200$ when the cointegrating rank is $r = 0$ ($\psi_1 = \psi_2 = 1$) or $r = 1$ ($\psi_2 = 1, |\psi_1| < 1$). The first part of Table 2.5 and Table 2.6 shows the tests that allow for a linear trend in the data and in the cointegration relation (μ_0, μ_1 arbitrary). The second part of Table 2.5 and Table 2.6 displays the empirical sizes of the tests which can be applied when it is known that the data exhibit no linear trend (μ_0 arbitrary, $\mu_1 = 0$).

For $r = 0$, the residual correlation represented by θ has no effect on the tests due to the construction of the DGP, but are presented for $\theta = 0$ as well as $\theta = 0.8$ for comparison purposes.

Arbitrary Mean and Trend Term (μ_0, μ_1 arbitrary): The first group of tests considered for this DGP without a linear trend are the tests that allow for arbitrary mean and trend parameters.

For $T = 100$, the size of the LR test LR^+ appears to be reasonable for $r_0 = 0$ whereas it is somewhat conservative for $r_0 = 1$ if the eigenvalue ψ_1 is close to unity and θ is zero. LR_{ta}^{GLS} is less sensitive to a variation in the innovation correlation than LR^+. LR_{ta}^{GLS} has less conservative size properties than LR^+ for $\theta = 0$, but is more conservative than LR^+ for $\theta = 0.8$. In contrast to the LR tests, the SW_{ta} test shows a distorted size for $r_0 = 1$ and $\theta = 0.8$, although it has a correct size for $r_0 = 0$ and $\theta = 0$. Bierens' nonparametric test has correct size for $r_0 = 0$, but the size is extremely conservative for $r_0 = 1$.

The results for sample size $T = 200$ are presented in Table 2.6. These simulation results show that the tests have better size properties than

Table 2.5: Sizes of Tests for 2-dimensional VAR(1) with $r = 0$ or 1 ($\psi_2 = 1$), $\delta = 0$, Sample Size $T = 100$

Test Statistics	Assumptions for Test Statistics	$\psi_1 = 1$ $(r = 0)$ $H_0 : r_0 = 0$	$\psi_1 = 0.9$ $(r = 1)$ $H_0 : r_0 = 1$	$\psi_1 = 0.8$ $(r = 1)$ $H_0 : r_0 = 1$	$\psi_1 = 0.7$ $(r = 1)$ $H_0 : r_0 = 1$
		$\theta = 0$			
LR^+	μ_0, μ_1 arbitrary	0.060	0.008	0.024	0.041
LR_{ta}^{GLS}		0.052	0.018	0.047	0.047
SW_{ta}^{VAR}		0.020	0.005	0.022	0.043
BI		0.050	0.002	0.002	0.003
LR^*	μ_0 arbitrary, $\mu_1 = 0$	0.069	0.017	0.039	0.047
LR^{i0}		0.060	0.023	0.042	0.049
LR^{SL}		0.164	0.088	0.118	0.121
SW_{ma}^{VAR}		0.027	0.016	0.035	0.045
		$\theta = 0.8$			
LR^+	μ_0, μ_1 arbitrary	0.060	0.040	0.065	0.070
LR_{ta}^{GLS}		0.052	0.017	0.031	0.032
SW_{ta}^{VAR}		0.020	0.075	0.138	0.151
BI		0.050	0.000	0.000	0.000
LR^*	μ_0 arbitrary, $\mu_1 = 0$	0.069	0.037	0.055	0.057
LR^{i0}		0.060	0.040	0.053	0.051
LR^{SL}		0.164	0.089	0.091	0.084
SW_{ma}^{VAR}		0.027	0.073	0.095	0.095

Note: Nominal significance level 0.05

for $T = 100$ for most tests as would have been expected. An exception is LR_{ta}^{GLS} that is quite conservative in size for $\theta = 0.8$. The SW test continues to display an empirical size close to 15% for $T = 200$ for a nominal 5% significance level and can therefore not be recommended for applied research. LR^+ and BI show reasonable size properties for $T = 200$. The Bewley-Yang test BY is not included in the tables because appropriate critical values are not available for all cases.

Arbitrary Mean and No Trend Term (μ_0 arbitrary, $\mu_1 = 0$): For a sample size of $T = 100$, LR^{i0} and LR^* reveal reasonable size properties, but are rather conservative for ψ_1 close to 1 and innovation correlation $\theta = 0$. LR^{SL} exhibits a tendency to overreject (i.e., the empirical size is outside the confidence interval of a 5% nominal significance level), and therefore has to be used with caution in empirical work. SW_{ma} displays some size distortions, but the empirical size remains below 10%.

Table 2.6: Sizes of Tests for 2-dimensional VAR(1) with $r = 0$ or 1 ($\psi_2 = 1$), $\delta = 0$, Sample Size $T = 200$

Test Statistics	Assumptions for Test Statistics	$\psi_1 = 1$ ($r = 0$) $H_0 : r_0 = 0$	$\psi_1 = 0.9$ ($r = 1$) $H_0 : r_0 = 1$	$\psi_1 = 0.8$ ($r = 1$) $H_0 : r_0 = 1$	$\psi_1 = 0.7$ ($r = 1$) $H_0 : r_0 = 1$
		$\theta = 0$			
LR^+	μ_0, μ_1 arbitrary	0.059	0.023	0.058	0.058
LR_{ta}^{GLS}		0.037	0.026	0.035	0.035
SW_{ta}^{VAR}		0.039	0.023	0.037	0.043
BI		0.047	0.002	0.000	0.003
LR^*	μ_0 arbitrary, $\mu_1 = 0$	0.057	0.037	0.050	0.054
LR^{i0}		0.053	0.044	0.058	0.059
LR^{SL}		0.121	0.089	0.094	0.095
SW_{ma}^{VAR}		0.045	0.034	0.049	0.050
		$\theta = 0.8$			
LR^+	μ_0, μ_1 arbitrary	0.059	0.057	0.057	0.058
LR_{ta}^{GLS}		0.037	0.006	0.028	0.028
SW_{ta}^{VAR}		0.039	0.137	0.144	0.131
BI		0.047	0.001	0.001	0.002
LR^*	μ_0 arbitrary, $\mu_1 = 0$	0.057	0.061	0.057	0.055
LR^{i0}		0.053	0.064	0.063	0.059
LR^{SL}		0.121	0.090	0.088	0.086
SW_{ma}^{VAR}		0.045	0.115	0.100	0.086

Note: Nominal significance level 0.05

For $T = 200$, LR^*, LR^{i0} and SW_{ma} show reasonable size properties and the tendency of LR^{SL} to overreject is less pronounced.

Comparison: From Tables 2.5 and 2.6 it can be seen that large residual correlation θ lead to better size properties of Johansen's LR tests for $r = 1$. For example, if $T = 100$ LR^* is quite conservative for $\theta = 0$ and ψ_1 close to unity, but displays an empirical size inside the confidence interval for the rejection frequency of a 5% nominal significance level if $\theta = 0.8$. This difference is even more pronounced for LR^+. This outcome has been explained by Toda (1995). He refers to Johansen (1991) who shows that if the true cointegrating rank is $r = 1$, the eigenvalues $\hat{\lambda}_1 > \hat{\lambda}_2$ and the null hypothesis $H_0 : r_0 = 0$ is tested, $\hat{\lambda}_1$ converges to the true value λ_1, while $T\hat{\lambda}_2$ converges to a random variable. Therefore, for Toda's DGP,

$$\hat{\lambda}_1 \xrightarrow{p} \lambda_1 = \frac{1}{1 + (1 - \theta^2)(1 + \psi_1)/(1 - \psi_1)}.$$

It can be seen that the closer $|\theta|$ is to one, the larger λ_1 will be. Thus, the null hypothesis of no cointegration is rejected more easily for $|\theta|$ close to one.

The same dependences cannot be found for the other mean or trend-adjusted LR tests (LR_{ta}^{GLS} and LR^{SL}). Table 2.6 exhibits the opposite development for LR_{ta}^{GLS}. In general, comparing the tests with different assumptions regarding the deterministic terms, the size of the tests for data without a linear trend is less sensitive to variations of the parameters of the DGP than the first group of tests allowing for a linear trend in the data and the cointegration relation.

b) DGP with Linear Trend ($\delta \neq 0$) To illustrate the size performance of the tests that are constructed for a DGP without a linear trend in case of incorrect application, simulations for $\delta = 1.0$ and $T = 100$ are presented in Table 2.7. LR^* and LR^{SL} display severe overrejection whereas LR^{i0} and SW_{ma} are extremely conservative. Therefore, these tests should not be applied if the possibility of a linear trend cannot be excluded. If it is not clear whether the data analysed have a linear trend, tests from the first group in Tables 2.5 and 2.6, that allow for both deterministic components, have to be applied. Their size properties do not depend on the value of δ.

Table 2.7: Sizes of Tests with Misspecified Deterministic Terms, for 2-dimensional VAR(1) with r=0 or 1 ($\psi_2 = 1$), Sample Size $T = 100$, $\delta = 1$

Test Statistics	Assumptions for Test Statistics	$\psi_1 = 1$ $(r = 0)$ $H_0 : r_0 = 0$	$\psi_1 = 0.9$ $(r = 1)$ $H_0 : r_0 = 1$	$\psi_1 = 0.8$ $(r = 1)$ $H_0 : r_0 = 1$	$\psi_1 = 0.7$ $(r = 1)$ $H_0 : r_0 = 1$
		$\theta = 0$			
LR^*	μ_0 arbitrary,	1.000	0.395	0.881	0.998
LR^{i0}	$\mu_1 = 0$	0.028	0.003	0.003	0.007
LR^{SL}		1.000	0.753	0.964	0.997
SW_{ma}^{VAR}		0.026	0.000	0.000	0.000
		$\theta = 0.8$			
LR^*	μ_0 arbitrary,	1.000	0.391	0.832	0.986
LR^{i0}	$\mu_1 = 0$	0.028	0.009	0.007	0.006
LR^{SL}		1.000	0.324	0.503	0.816
SW_{ma}^{VAR}		0.024	0.000	0.000	0.000

Note: Nominal significance level 0.05

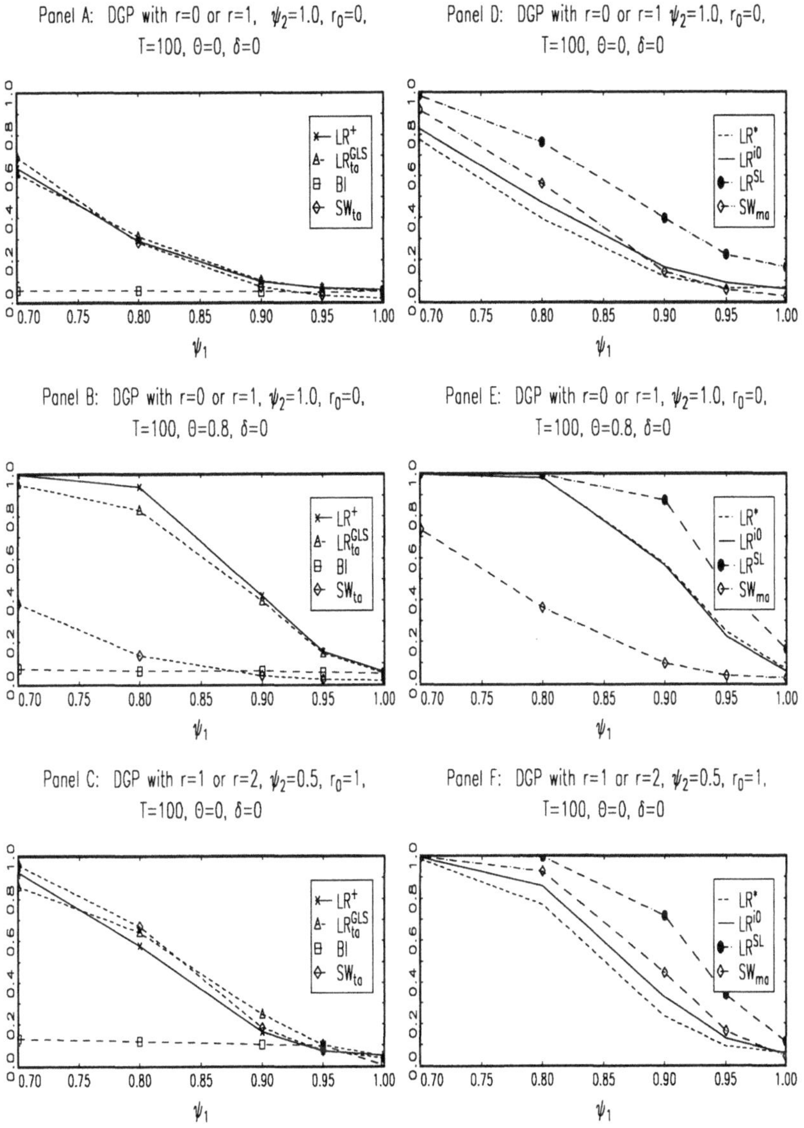

Figure 2.1: Relative Rejection Frequencies for 2-dimensional VAR(1), Assumptions for Test Statistics: μ_0 arbitrary, $\mu_1 = 0$ (Panel A-C), μ_0, μ_1 arbitrary (Panel D-F)

2.5.4.2 Power Performance: DGP without Linear Trend

In the graphs each of the tests has its own combination of line and symbol. The original LR tests proposed by Johansen that are considered as a

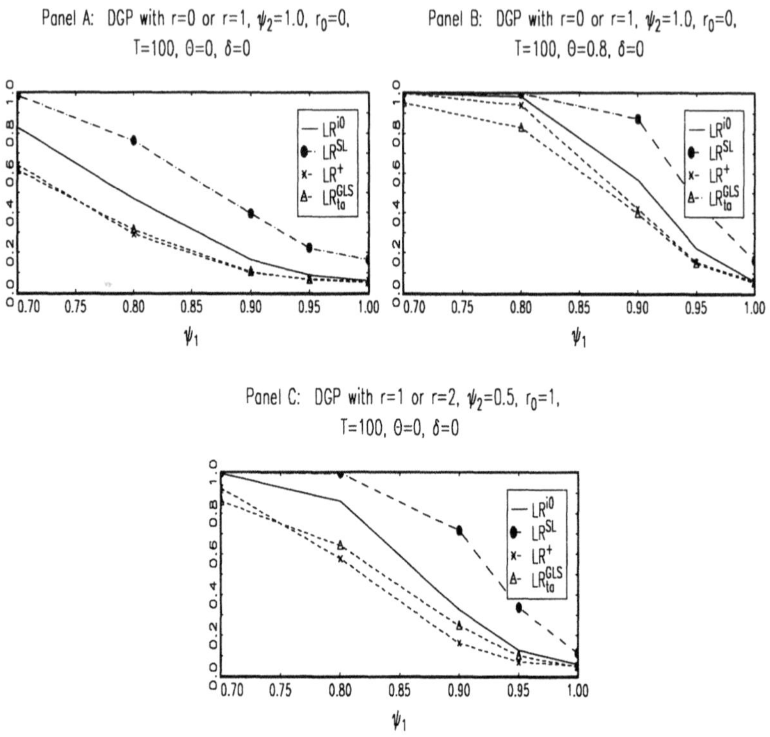

Figure 2.2: Relative Rejection Frequencies for 2-dimensional VAR(1), Comparison of Best Performing Tests of the Respective Groups of Tests Displayed in Figure 2.1

reference for comparison with the other less well known tests always have a solid line (using a different symbol for the respective variant of the test) for easier visual identification. In all graphs, the size is also shown, that is the relative rejection frequency for the true rank tested under the null hypothesis ($\psi_1 = 1$).

Arbitrary Mean and Trend Term (μ_0, μ_1 arbitrary): The power of the tests for arbitrary mean and trend term for a sample size of $T = 100$ are depicted in Figure 2.1, Panels A to C. The performance of the LR tests is rather similar. If the null hypothesis $H_0 : r_0 = 0$ is tested and $\theta = 0.8$ (Panel B), LR^+ performs better than LR_{ta}^{GLS}, whereas for $H_0 : r_0 = 1$, LR_{ta}^{GLS} has larger power for large ψ_1, i.e. near the null hypothesis (Panel C). The SW_{ta} test is outperformed by the LR tests

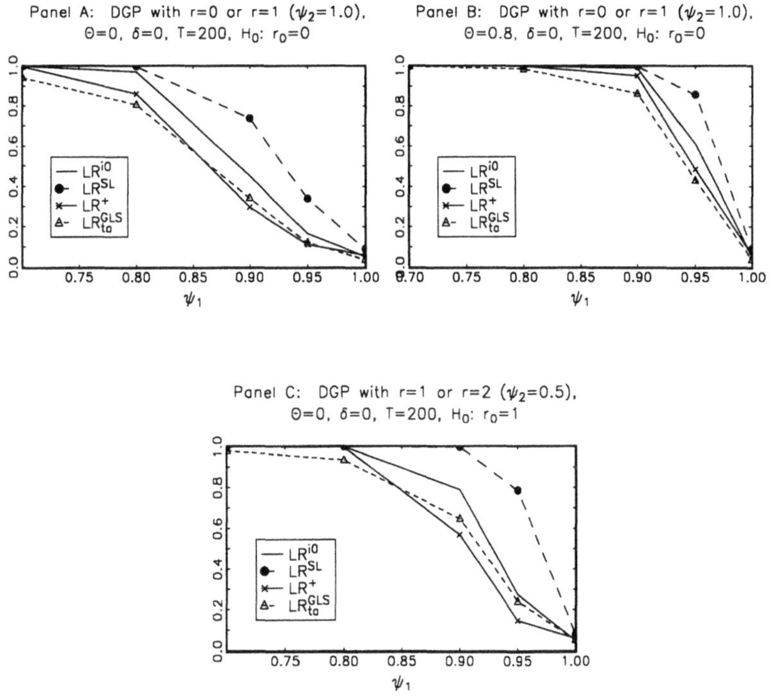

Figure 2.3: Relative Rejection Frequencies for 2-dimensional VAR(1), Sample Size $T = 200$, Assumptions for Test Statistics: μ_0 arbitrary, $\mu_1 = 0$ (LR^{i0}, LR^{SL}), μ_0, μ_1 arbitrary (LR^{+}, LR_{ta}^{GLS}), H_0: $r_0 = 0$ (Panels A and B), H_0: $r_0 = 1$ (Panel C)

in terms of power for $\theta = 0.8$. The Bierens test diplays a power hardly exceeding its size. It can therefore not be recommended for applied research.

Arbitrary Mean and No Trend Term (μ_0 arbitrary, $\mu_1 = 0$): The power of the tests for data without linear trend and a sample size of $T = 100$ is depicted in Figure 2.1, Panels D to F. The graphs show that LR^{SL} clearly outperforms the other tests in terms of power. Although this was to be expected because of the tests distorted size, it should be noted that the difference in power is substantial, especially in case of a cointegration rank of $r = 2$ (Panel F). Saikkonen & Luukkonen (1997) also find that LR^{SL} performs better than other LR tests even if size-adjusted power is considered. LR^{i0} outperforms LR^* in terms of power except in Panel E. Although the SW_{ma} test performs even slightly better than LR^{i0} and LR^* in some cases (Panels D and F), it displays very low power in case of $\theta = 0.8$ and $r_0 = 0$ (Panel E) in comparison with the other tests.

Comparison: A comparison of the best performing tests of both groups of tests considered above is presented in Figure 2.2 ($T = 100$). LR^{SL} clearly outperforms the other tests in terms of power. However, since the test has a tendency to overreject, LR^{i0} might be preferred in applied research. The direct comparison of the performance of LR^{i0} and LR^{SL} with the tests that allow for unrestricted mean and trend terms, LR^+ and LR_{ta}^{GLS}, (see Figure 2.2) for the different parameter constellations considered in Figure 2.1 shows that in case of a DGP without a linear trend it is worth applying tests that incorporate an additional restriction on the trend term since this leads to a considerable gain in the power of the tests.

Figure 2.3 shows the power results of the best performing tests of Figure 2.1 on the basis of $T = 200$ observations. For this higher sample size the power performance of all tests improves as would have been expected. The results for $T = 100$ concerning the relative power performance of the tests are confirmed.

2.5.5 Three-dimensional VAR(1): The Simulation Results

The three-dimensional DGP proposed by Toda (1995) (see Section 2.5.3) was used for further simulations. In this section tests that may be applied in case of trending data are considered. This includes two groups of tests: tests that allow for a trend in the data and in the cointegration relation (see Section 2.3.1.1) as well as tests that allow for a trend in the data, but not in the cointegration relation (see Section 2.3.1.2).

As has been discussed in Section 2.3.1.2 in case of tests constructed for an arbitrary mean and restricted trend term in the DGP (μ_0 arbitrary, $\mu_1 \neq 0, \beta'\mu_1 = 0$), the cointegrating rank of a system can only be $r < n$ due to the restriction $\beta'\mu_1 = 0$, and, therefore, the rank tested under the null hypothesis should be smaller than $n - 1$ ($r_0 < n - 1$). Therefore, testing the null hypotheses $r_0 = 0$ and $r_0 = 1$ is considered for the three-dimensional DGP in the following.

In this section, simulation results for a broader range of sample sizes are presented. The results for the sample size $T = 100$ are considered first to evaluate the relative performance of the tests. These results are then compared with the outcome from simulations based on other sample sizes for those tests that perform best in case of $T = 100$. Further simulations have been carried out for alternative values of the innovation correlation.

2.5.5.1 Size of the Tests

a) DGP with Linear Trend Term ($\delta = 1$)

Arbitrary Mean and Trend Term (μ_0, μ_1 arbitrary): The performance of the first group of tests that are constructed for a DGP with unrestricted trend parameter confirms the findings from the 2-dimensional DGP for this group of tests in that the tests are quite conservative for zero innovation correlation ($\theta_1 = \theta_2 = 0$) in case of $T = 100$. In contrast to LR_{ta}^{GLS} that shows a reasonable size, LR^+ has a tendency to overreject if $\theta_1 = 0.4$ and $\theta_2 = 0.8$ for $T = 100$ (see Table 2.8). The tendency of LR^+ to overreject if $\theta_1 = 0.4$ and $\theta_2 = 0.8$ is also found for other sample sizes, for smaller samples ($T = 50$) as well as larger samples ($T = 200, T = 400$). In contrast, LR_{ta}^{GLS} is somewhat conservative in these cases, especially for ψ_1 near unity (see Tables 2.10 to 2.9). The Stock & Watson test (SW_{ta}) shows considerable variation in its size for sample size $T = 100$, displaying very conservative for some parameter constellations and overrejecting for others. It is therefore not considered for further sample sizes. In case of a sample size of $T = 100$ the Bierens test (BI) again displays a reasonable size for $r_0 = 0$ ($\psi = 1$). However, it is extremely conservative for $r_0 = 1$. Even for $T = 400$ (see Table 2.10) the size of the BI test turns out to be extremely conservative for $r_0 = 1$. In contrast the LR tests, in case of zero innovation correlation, show an empirical size near the 5% nominal significance level for that sample size. Considering its size properties, the Bierens test should not be applied in small samples.

The performance of LR^+ and LR_{ta}^{GLS} is also conservative for $T = 100$ and $\theta_1 = \theta_2 = 0$ (Table 2.8). Further simulations (see Table 2.11) have shown that the tendency of the LR tests to perform very conservative for zero innovation correlations, is less pronounced if one of the innovation correlations is high, i.e. in case of $r = 1$ the innovation correlation between the stationary and the first nonstationary component, θ_1, or between the stationary and the second nonstationary component, θ_2, and the other one is zero. For $T = 50$ the LR tests become even more conservative, but only for zero innovation correlation and $\psi_1 = 0.7$ or 0.8.

Table 2.8: Sizes of Tests for 3-dimensional VAR(1), $r = 0$ or 1 ($\psi_2 = \psi_3 = 1$), $\delta = 1$, Sample Size $T = 100$

Test Statistics	Assumptions for Test Statistics	$\psi_1 = 1$ $(r = 0)$ $H_0 : r_0 = 0$	$\psi_1 = 0.9$ $(r = 1)$ $H_0 : r_0 = 1$	$\psi_1 = 0.8$ $(r = 1)$ $H_0 : r_0 = 1$	$\psi_1 = 0.7$ $(r = 1)$ $H_0 : r_0 = 1$
		$\theta_1 = \theta_2 = 0$			
LR^+	μ_0, μ_1 arbitrary	0.065	0.009	0.018	0.034
LR_{ta}^{GLS}		0.058	0.007	0.017	0.035
SW_{ta}^{VAR}		0.024	0.002	0.012	0.035
BI		0.064	0.000	0.000	0.001
LR^i	μ_0 arbitrary,	0.062	0.011	0.029	0.046
LR_{ta}^i	$\mu_1 \neq 0$,	0.056	0.029	0.049	0.054
BY^i	$\beta'\mu_1 = 0$	0.046	0.014	0.044	0.058
		$\theta_1 = 0.4, \theta_2 = 0.8$			
LR^+	μ_0, μ_1 arbitrary	0.065	0.075	0.080	0.074
LR_{ta}^{GLS}		0.058	0.031	0.037	0.048
SW_{ta}^{VAR}		0.024	0.031	0.074	0.118
BI		0.064	0.000	0.001	0.001
LR^i	μ_0 arbitrary,	0.063	0.092	0.088	0.084
LR_{ta}^i	$\mu_1 \neq 0$,	0.056	0.131	0.091	0.081
BY^i	$\beta'\mu_1 = 0$	0.042	0.119	0.301	0.433

Note: Nominal significance level 0.05

Trending Variables and No Trend in the Cointegration Relation (μ_0 arbitrary, $\mu_1 \neq 0$, $\beta'\mu_1 = 0$): The second group of tests is correctly applied if $\delta = 1$ in the DGP. The LR tests of this group exhibit reasonable sizes, although for $\theta_1 = 0.4$ and $\theta_2 = 0.8$ the tests have a tendency to overreject, especially LR_{ta}^i. This tendency is less pronounced for zero innovation correlations or if $\theta_1 = 0$ and $\theta_2 = 0.8$ or $\theta_1 = 0.8$ and $\theta_2 = 0$. For $T = 50$, LR^i is more conservative than LR_{ta}^i if $\theta_1 = \theta_2 = 0$, whereas for $T = 400$ both tests show reasonable sizes.

In contrast to the LR tests in this group of tests, BY^i displays severe overrejection even if $\theta_1 = 0.4$ and $\theta_2 = 0.8$ (see Table 2.8). The size distortions are clearly too strong to recommend this test for use in practice. Simulations for further sample sizes or parameter constellations have, therefore, not been carried out for this test neither will its power performance be analysed.

Comparison: In general, the comparison of the size of the tests for different sample sizes ($T = 50, 100, 200$ and 400) shows that the dependence on the innovation correlation is less pronounced in large samples

Table 2.9: Sizes of Tests for 3-dimensional VAR(1), $r = 0$ or 1 ($\psi_2 = \psi_3 = 1$), $\delta = 1$, Sample Size $T = 200$

Test Statistics	Assumptions for Test Statistics	$\psi_1 = 1$ ($r = 0$) $H_0 : r_0 = 0$	$\psi_1 = 0.9$ ($r = 1$) $H_0 : r_0 = 1$	$\psi_1 = 0.8$ ($r = 1$) $H_0 : r_0 = 1$	$\psi_1 = 0.7$ ($r = 1$) $H_0 : r_0 = 1$
		$\theta_1 = \theta_2 = 0$			
LR^+	μ_0, μ_1	0.066	0.018	0.042	0.054
LR_{ta}^{GLS}	arbitrary	0.040	0.012	0.035	0.038
LR^i	μ_0 arbitrary,	0.066	0.027	0.052	0.053
LR_{ta}^i	$\mu_1 \neq 0$,	0.047	0.050	0.048	0.045
	$\beta' \mu_1 = 0$				
		$\theta_1 = 0.4, \theta_2 = 0.8$			
LR^+	μ_0, μ_1	0.066	0.087	0.089	0.081
LR_{ta}^{GLS}	arbitrary	0.040	0.032	0.044	0.046
LR^i	μ_0 arbitrary,	0.063	0.080	0.067	0.065
LR_{ta}^i	$\mu_1 \neq 0$,	0.045	0.097	0.079	0.060
	$\beta' \mu_1 = 0$				

Note: Nominal significance level 0.05

(e.g. $T = 400$) whereas for samples of size $T = 50$ (see Table 2.10) it is even stronger than for $T = 100$. In case of $T = 50$, the LR tests (except LR_{ta}^i) become very conservative for $\theta_1 = \theta_2 = 0$ even for a value of $\psi_1 = 0.7$, whereas the Bierens test (BI) is by far too conservative in all situations. There is a tendency of the trend-adjusted LR test LR_{ta}^{GLS} to less variation in size with respect to different innovation correlations and different sample sizes than Johansen's LR test LR^+. However, LR_{ta}^{GLS} shows a more conservative size than LR^+ for $\theta_1 = 0.4$ and $\theta_1 = 0.8$ in case of $T = 100$ and for all innovation correlations in case of larger sample size (see $T = 200$, $T = 400$ in Tables 2.10 and 2.9). It is especially conservative if $\psi = 0.9$.

b) DGP without Linear Trend Table 2.12 shows simulation results for $\delta = 0$. In this case, substantial overrejections occur for LR^i and LR_{ta}^i which is far worse for LR_{ta}^i. LR^+ and LR_{ta}^{GLS} are shown for comparison purposes. They do not depend on the values of μ_0 and μ_1 and, therefore, have exactly the same size (see Table 2.8) and power properties as for $\delta = 1$.

Power results are not presented for this case because of the size distortions of the tests. However, the power of LR^i and LR_{ta}^i is higher than

Table 2.10: Sizes of Tests for 3-dimensional VAR(1), $r = 0$ or 1 ($\psi_2 = \psi_3 = 1$), $\delta = 1$, Sample Sizes $T = 50$ and T=400

Test Statistics	Assumptions for Test Statistics	$\psi_1 = 1$ ($r = 0$) $H_0 : r_0 = 0$	$\psi_1 = 0.9$ ($r = 1$) $H_0 : r_0 = 1$	$\psi_1 = 0.8$ ($r = 1$) $H_0 : r_0 = 1$	$\psi_1 = 0.7$ ($r = 1$) $H_0 : r_0 = 1$
		$T = 50$			
		$\theta_1 = \theta_2 = 0$			
LR^+	μ_0, μ_1 arbitrary	0.084	0.011	0.013	0.020
LR_{ta}^{GLS}		0.061	0.011	0.016	0.021
BI		0.044	0.003	0.001	0.001
LR^i	μ_0 arbitrary, $\mu_1 \neq 0$, $\beta'\mu_1 = 0$	0.080	0.007	0.015	0.024
LR_{ta}^i		0.070	0.025	0.030	0.049
		$\theta_1 = 0.4, \theta_2 = 0.8$			
LR^+	μ_0, μ_1 arbitrary	0.084	0.037	0.084	0.096
LR_{ta}^{GLS}		0.061	0.023	0.037	0.047
BI		0.046	0.001	0.001	0.002
LR^i	μ_0 arbitrary, $\mu_1 \neq 0$, $\beta'\mu_1 = 0$	0.082	0.056	0.092	0.093
LR_{ta}^i		0.071	0.025	0.040	0.056
		$T = 400$			
		$\theta_1 = \theta_2 = 0$			
LR^+	μ_0, μ_1 arbitrary	0.066	0.053	0.064	0.062
LR_{ta}^{GLS}		0.049	0.042	0.049	0.052
BI		0.053	0.000	0.000	0.001
LR^i	μ_0 arbitrary, $\mu_1 \neq 0$, $\beta'\mu_1 = 0$	0.062	0.043	0.051	0.052
LR_{ta}^i		0.050	0.061	0.062	0.061
		$\theta_1 = 0.4, \theta_2 = 0.8$			
LR^+	μ_0, μ_1 arbitrary	0.066	0.074	0.071	0.074
LR_{ta}^{GLS}		0.049	0.029	0.034	0.040
BI		0.053	0.001	0.004	0.005
LR^i	μ_0 arbitrary, $\mu_1 \neq 0$, $\beta'\mu_1 = 0$	0.062	0.066	0.058	0.060
LR_{ta}^i		0.051	0.084	0.055	0.050

Note: Nominal significance level 0.05

in the case of $\delta = 1$, as would have been expected because the size of both tests is too large.

These results lead to the conclusion that tests based on the intercept version of the VAR or EC model should be used with caution if the trending properties are not clear.

Table 2.11: Sizes of Tests for 3-dimensional VAR(1), $r = 0$ or 1 ($\psi_2 = \psi_3 = 1$), $\delta = 1$, Sample Size $T = 100$

Test Statistics	Assumptions for Test Statistics	$\psi_1 = 1$ ($r = 0$) $H_0 : r_0 = 0$	$\psi_1 = 0.9$ ($r = 1$) $H_0 : r_0 = 1$	$\psi_1 = 0.8$ ($r = 1$) $H_0 : r_0 = 1$	$\psi_1 = 0.7$ ($r = 1$) $H_0 : r_0 = 1$
		$\theta_1 = 0$, $\theta_2 = 0.8$			
LR^+ LR_{ta}^{GLS}	μ_0,μ_1 arbitrary	0.065 0.058	0.042 0.026	0.069 0.038	0.071 0.043
LR^i	μ_0 arbitrary, $\mu_1 \neq 0$, $\beta'\mu_1 = 0$	0.063	0.052	0.074	0.074
		$\theta_1 = 0.8$, $\theta_2 = 0$			
LR^+ LR_{ta}^{GLS}	μ_0,μ_1 arbitrary	0.065 0.058	0.045 0.028	0.070 0.035	0.074 0.046
LR^i	μ_0 arbitrary, $\mu_1 \neq 0$, $\beta'\mu_1 = 0$	0.062	0.036	0.063	0.061

Note: Nominal significance level 0.05

Table 2.12: Sizes of Tests with Misspecified Deterministic Terms, for 3-dimensional VAR(1), $r = 0$ or 1 ($\psi_2 = \psi_3 = 1$), Sample Size $T = 100$, $\delta = 0$

Test Statistics	Assumptions for Test Statistics	$\psi_1 = 1$ ($r = 0$) $H_0 : r_0 = 0$	$\psi_1 = 0.9$ ($r = 1$) $H_0 : r_0 = 1$	$\psi_1 = 0.8$ ($r = 1$) $H_0 : r_0 = 1$	$\psi_1 = 0.7$ ($r = 1$) $H_0 : r_0 = 1$
		$\theta_1 = \theta_2 = 0$			
LR^+ LR_{ta}^{GLS}	μ_0, μ_1 arbitrary	0.065 0.058	0.009 0.007	0.018 0.017	0.034 0.035
LR^i LR_{ta}^i	μ_0 arbitrary, $\mu_1 \neq 0$, $\beta'\mu_1 = 0$	0.120 0.096	0.044 0.173	0.080 0.399	0.107 0.655
		$\theta_1 = 0.4$, $\theta_2 = 0.8$			
LR^+ LR_{ta}^{GLS}	μ_0, μ_1 arbitrary	0.065 0.058	0.075 0.031	0.080 0.037	0.074 0.048
LR^i LR_{ta}^i	μ_0 arbitrary, $\mu_1 \neq 0$, $\beta'\mu_1 = 0$	0.120 0.096	0.150 0.776	0.150 0.963	0.147 0.981

Note: Nominal significance level 0.05

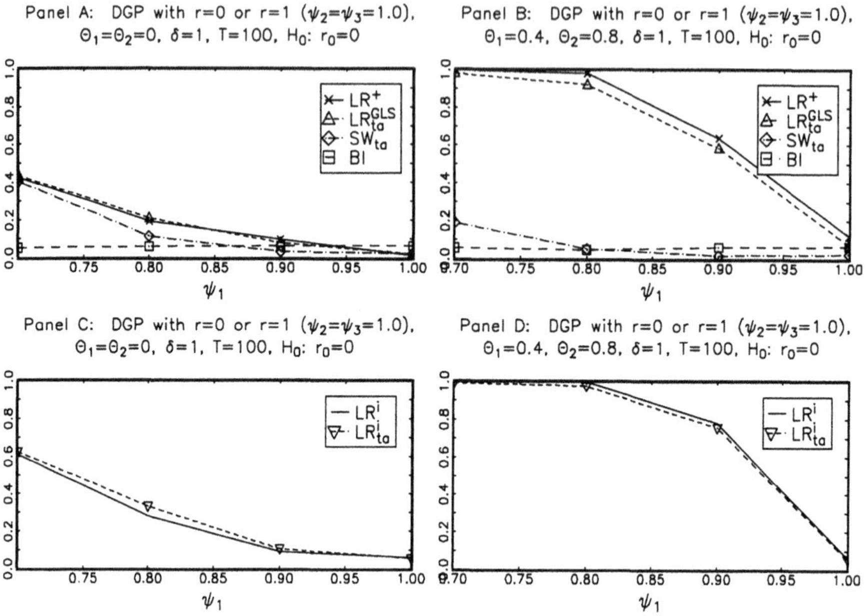

Figure 2.4: Relative Rejection Frequencies for 3-dimensional VAR(1), Sample Size $T = 100$, Assumptions for Test Statistics: μ_0, μ_1 arbitrary (Panels A/B), μ_0 arbitrary, $\mu_1 \neq 0$, $\beta'\mu_1 = 0$ (Panels C/D)

2.5.5.2 Power Performance: DGP with Linear Trend

Figures 2.4 to 2.13 display the power performance of the tests for $T = 50, 100, 200$ and 400 and for the parameter constellations $\theta_1 = \theta_2 = 0$ as well as $\theta_1 = 0.4$ and $\theta_2 = 0.8$, except for Figures 2.6 and 2.7 that display the power performance for a different constellation of innovation correlations. Results for $T = 100$ in Figures 2.4 and 2.5 are discussed first and comparisons with different parameter constellations and sample sizes are presented thereafter. Again, Johansen's original LR tests are presented as a solid line, possibly with some symbols, and in all graphs the relative rejection frequency for the true rank tested under the null hypothesis ($\psi_1 = 1$), that is the size, is shown.

In Figure 2.4 all tests considered in this section are compared for a DGP with $r = 1$ testing $H_0 : r_0 = 0$, first. The LR tests perform best for that situation and are further compared for $r = 2$ testing $H_0 : r_0 = 0$ and $H_0 : r_0 = 1$. They are also compared for different parameter constellations.

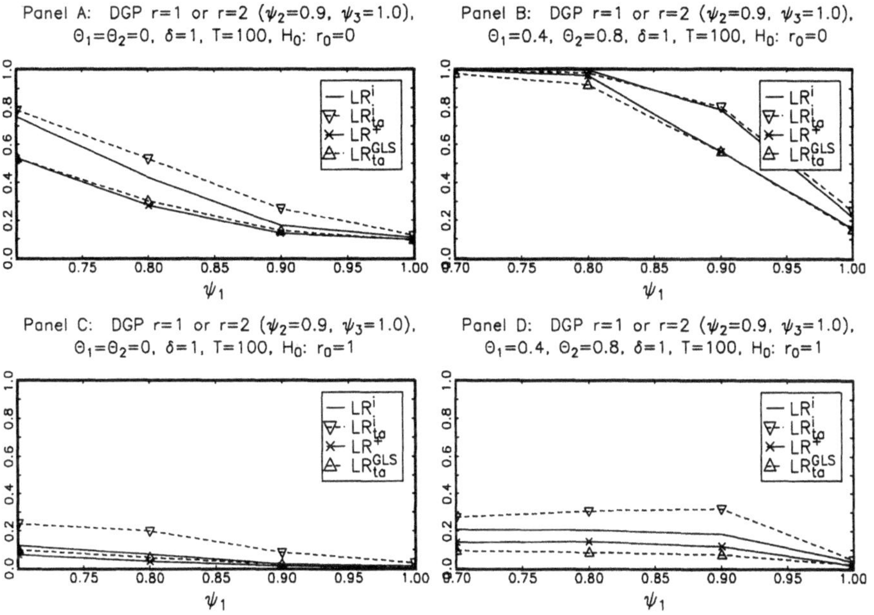

Figure 2.5: Relative Rejection Frequencies for 3-dimensional VAR(1), Sample Size $T = 100$, Panels A/B: Power (and Size) for $H_0 : r_0 = 0$, Panels C/D: Power (and Size) for $H_0 : r_0 = 1$

Arbitrary Mean and Trend Term (μ_0, μ_1 arbitrary): In the first group of tests (see Figure 2.4, Panels A and B and Figure 2.5), LR^+ and LR_{ta}^{GLS} perform best. The SW_{ta} test appears to have lower power than the LR tests even for $\theta_1 = 0.4$ and $\theta_2 = 0.8$ despite large empirical sizes for that parameter constellation. The Bierens test is clearly outperformed by the LR tests in terms of power. In fact, its performance is so poor since its power for this DGP again does hardly exceed its nominal size that its use cannot be recommended.

Trending Variables and No Trend in the Cointegration Relation (μ_0 arbitrary, $\mu_1 \neq 0$, $\beta'\mu_1 = 0$): Figure 2.4, Panels C and D, show the power of the second group of tests for $r_0 = 0$ if the true cointegrating rank is $r = 1$ ($T = 100$). The LR tests perform rather similarly. LR_{ta}^i displays higher power than LR^i if the null hypothesis of a higher rank $H_0 : r_0 = 1$ is tested (Figure 2.5, Panels C and D). The original and the trend-adjusted LR tests are considered in more de-

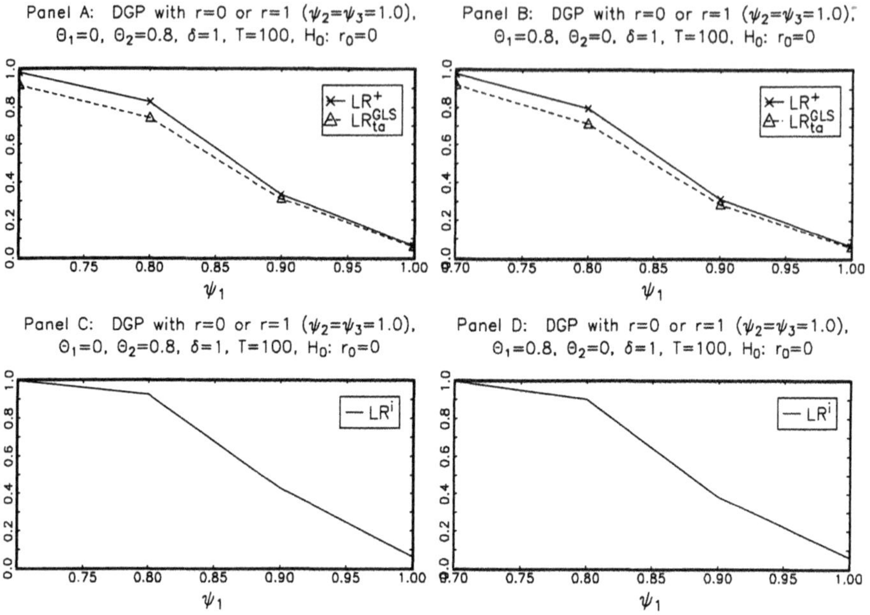

Figure 2.6: Relative Rejection Frequencies for 3-dimensional VAR(1), Sample Size $T = 100$, Different Innovation Correlations, Assumptions for Test Statistics: μ_0, μ_1 arbitrary (Panels A/B), μ_0 arbitrary, $\mu_1 \neq 0$, $\beta'\mu_1 = 0$ (Panels C/D)

tail for other sample sizes below. BY^i is not considered with respect to its power performance because of its heavily distorted size for some parameter constellations.

Comparison for T = 100: When comparing all tests in Figure 2.4 it can be seen that a similar reduction in power is displayed if ψ_1 approaches unity. However, tests that are based on the restriction of the trend parameter $\beta'\mu_1 = 0$ (e.g. see Figure 2.4, Panels C and D), have in most cases substantially higher power. Comparing the power curves in Figure 2.4 clearly reveals that they are steeper in Panels C and D than those of the corresponding tests which allow for a general linear trend in Panels A and B.

Further results of the relative power performance are presented in Figure 2.5. Here, the power is shown for the case where the cointegrating rank of the DGP is $r = 2$ and the null hypothesis $H_0 : r_0 = 0$ (Figure

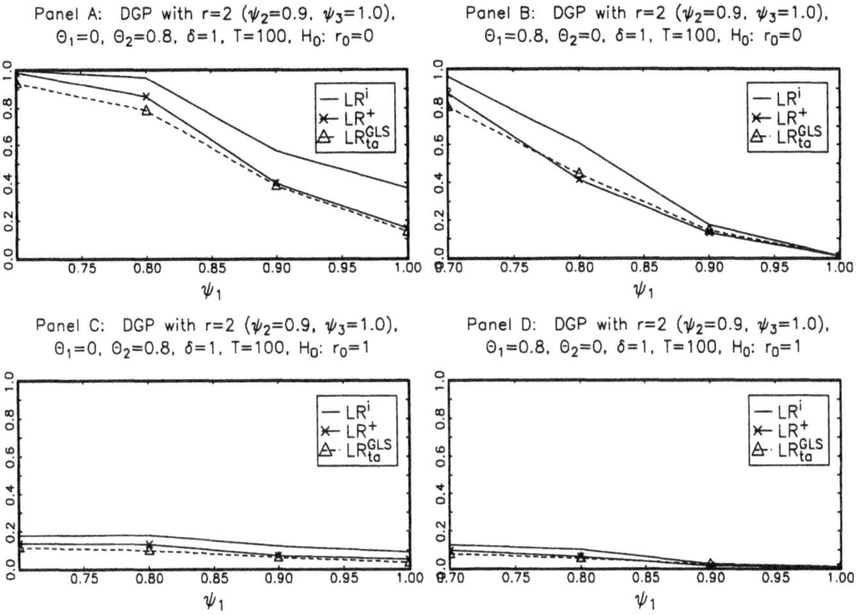

Figure 2.7: Relative Rejection Frequencies for 3-dimensional VAR(1), Sample Size $T = 100$, Different Innovation Correlations, Panels A/B: Power (and Size) for $H_0 : r_0 = 0$, Panels C/D: Power (and Size) for $H_0 : r_0 = 1$

2.5, Panels A and B) as well as $H_0 : r_0 = 1$ (Figure 2.5, Panels C and D) are tested. In these graphs, the results of the tests with low power performance, BI and SW_{ta}, are not presented. However, the power of BI and SW_{ta} has similar characteristics relative to the other tests as in the case $r = 1$ (Figure 2.4).

In Figure 2.5 for the DGP with higher cointegrating rank a similar picture as in Figure 2.4 emerges. The power of the tests based on the restriction of the trend parameter ($\beta'\mu_1 = 0$) is higher than that of the tests that impose no restrictions on the deterministic terms. Further comparisons for both groups of tests show that if $H_0 : r_0 = 0$ is tested, the power is larger for $r = 2$ (Figure 2.5, Panels A and B) than for $r = 1$ (Figure 2.4), as expected. However, if $H_0 : r_0 = 1$ is tested in case of $r = 2$ (Figure 2.5, Panels C and D), the tests have considerably lower power for all values of θ_1 and θ_2 than if the null hypothesis is $H_0 : r_0 = 0$ in case of $r = 1$ (Figure 2.4, Panels A and B).

To generalize, if $r > 1$, then testing higher cointegrating ranks ($r_0 = 1$ in this 3-dimensional system) leads to a loss of power. Of the first group of tests allowing for a trend in the cointegrating relation, LR_{ta}^{GLS} and LR^{+} perform rather similar. Either LR_{ta}^{GLS} or LR^{+} performs somewhat better than the other for different parameter constellations. In the second group of tests, LR^{i} is in most cases outperformed by LR_{ta}^{i}.

Different Parameter Constellations Figures 2.6 and 2.7 display power results for the best performing tests for different constellations of the innovation correlations (θ) if $T = 100$. The following general picture emerges: If one innovation correlation is high and the other zero, the power performance is not as good as if $\theta_1 = 0.4$ and $\theta_2 = 0.8$, but is much better than if both correlations are zero, that is $\theta_1 = \theta_2 = 0$ (Figures 2.4 and 2.5). For $r = 1$ (Figure 2.6), results do not differ substantially whether the innovation correlation between the first and the second component or between the first and the third component is zero and the other correlation is high, because in both cases the correlation innovation is between a stationary and a nonstationary component.

However, for $r = 2$, Figure 2.7, the power performance is better if $\theta_1 = 0$, i.e. the innovation correlation between the two stationary components is zero, than if $\theta_2 = 0$, i.e. the innovation correlation between the stationary and the nonstationary component is zero.

Different Sample Sizes Further power graphs for the best performing tests in the respective group of tests, LR^{i}, LR_{ta}^{i}, LR^{+} and $LR_{ta(2)}^{GLS}$ are presented for $T = 50$ (Figures 2.8 and 2.9), $T = 200$ (Figures 2.10 and 2.11) and $T = 400$ (Figures 2.12 and 2.13). In general, the power results for different sample sizes confirm the relative performance of the tests found for $T = 100$. Figures 2.8 and 2.9 for $T = 50$ provides evidence for the extraordinary loss of power for a sample size less than $T = 100$, i.e. in a sample size often encountered in empirical work using macroeconomic time series. If $r = 2$ (see Figures 2.8 and 2.9) neither of the tests has hardly any power for certain parameter constellations.

If the sample size is $T = 200$, both groups of tests for trending data perform rather similar for $r = 1$, but the tests that do allow for a linear trend in the cointegration relation, still perform better for some parameter constellations (see Figure 2.10) and clearly outperform the more general tests if $r = 2$ (see Figure 2.11). Within this group of tests, LR_{ta}^{i} seems to outperform LR^{i} in most parameter constellations, whereas for LR^{+} and LR_{ta}^{GLS} each of the tests outperforms the other in some situations.

For $T = 400$, both groups of LR tests (with and without linear trend in the cointegration relation) show a similar performance in some parameter constellations (e.g. Figure 2.12, Panels B and D or 2.13 Panels A and B, $\psi_1 < 0.9$). However, the first group of tests allowing for a linear trend in the data and not in the cointegration relation still has higher power than the second group (with linear trend in the cointegration relation) for many parameter constellations, especially if a higher rank is tested and the true rank is larger than one (e.g. Figure 2.13, Panels C and D). It should be noted that the Bierens test, although not presented here still shows extremely low power even for $T = 400$.

Comparing the power LR^{+} and LR_{ta}^{GLS} for different sample sizes, both tests perform rather similar, but LR^{+} performs better for $\theta_1 = 0.4$ and $\theta_2 = 0.8$ if higher ranks are tested (e.g. Figure 2.13, Panel D) and in smaller samples (e.g. Figure 2.9, Panel B).

To sum up the results for different sample sizes, the graphs show a considerable loss of power for $T = 50$ whereas they display improvement of the test performance for $T = 200$ over the test performance for $T = 100$, except for values of ψ_1 near unity. If the sample size is $T = 400$, the LR tests have high power even for $|\psi_1| = 0.9$.

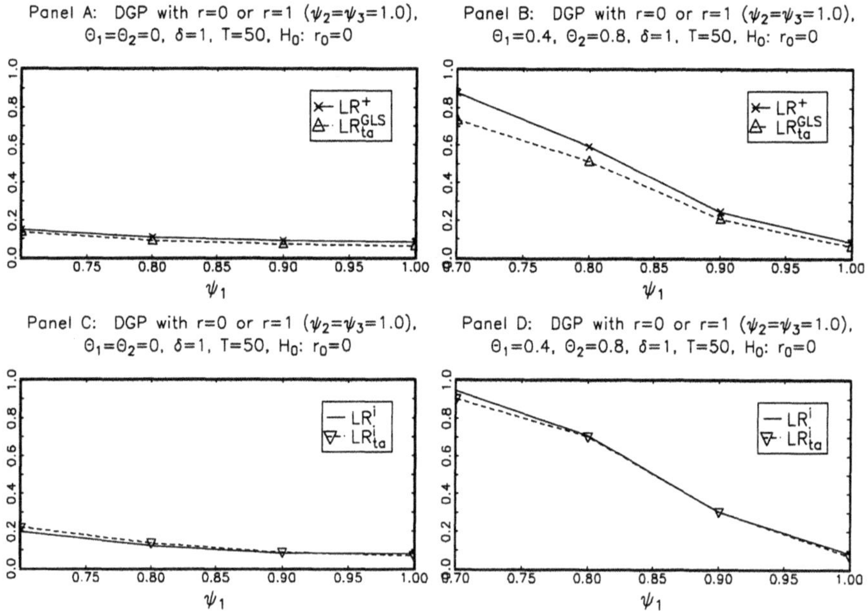

Figure 2.8: Relative Rejection Frequencies for 3-dimensional VAR(1), Sample Size $T = 50$, Assumptions for Test Statistics: μ_0, μ_1 arbitrary (Panels A/B), μ_0 arbitrary, $\mu_1 \neq 0$, $\beta'\mu_1 = 0$ (Panels C/D)

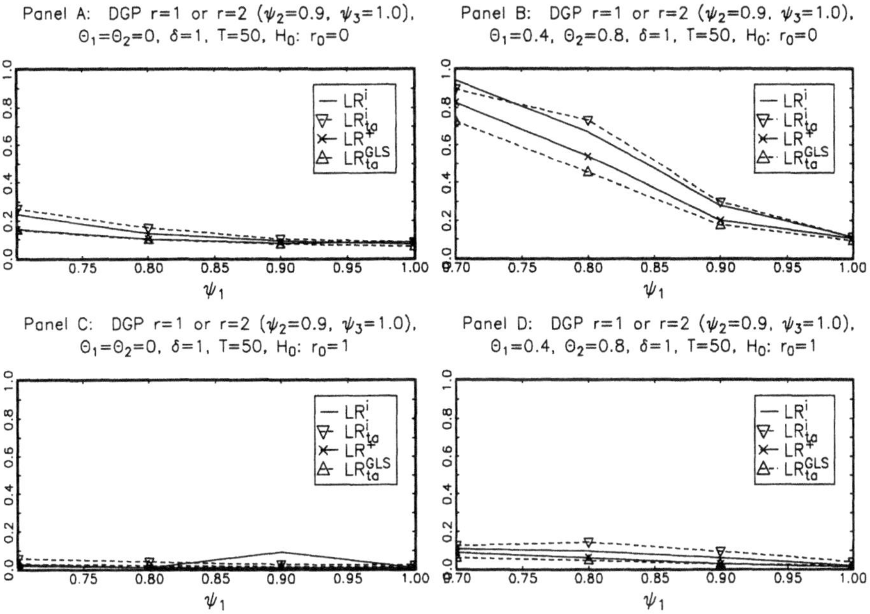

Figure 2.9: Relative Rejection Frequencies for 3-dimensional VAR(1), Sample Size $T = 50$, Panels A/B: Power (and Size) for $H_0 : r_0 = 0$, Panels C/D: Power (and Size) for $H_0 : r_0 = 1$

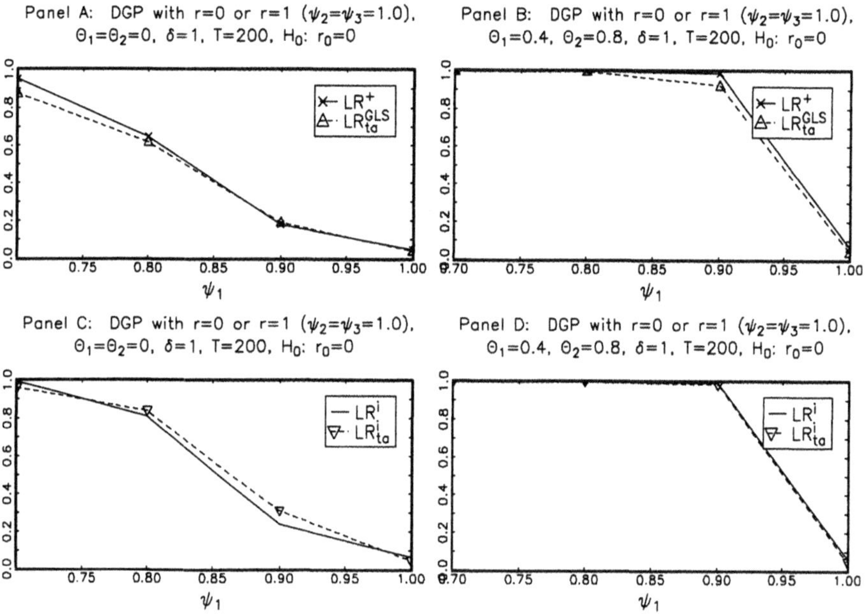

Figure 2.10: Relative Rejection Frequencies for 3-dimensional VAR(1), Sample Size $T = 200$, Assumptions for Test Statistics: μ_0, μ_1 arbitrary (Panels A/B), μ_0 arbitrary, $\mu_1 \neq 0$, $\beta'\mu_1 = 0$ (Panels C/D)

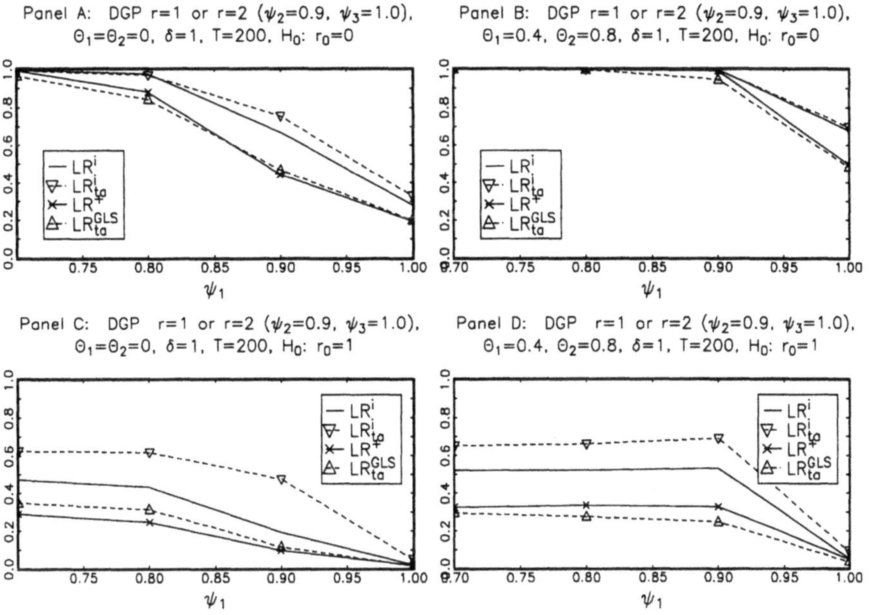

Figure 2.11: Relative Rejection Frequencies for 3-dimensional VAR(1), Sample Size $T = 200$, Panels A/B: Power (and Size) for $H_0 : r_0 = 0$, Panels C/D: Power (and Size) for $H_0 : r_0 = 1$

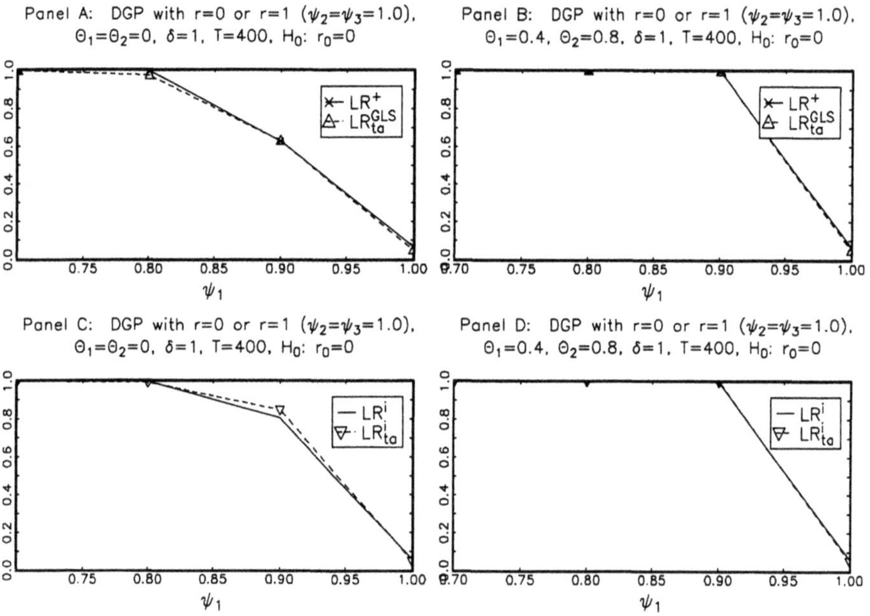

Figure 2.12: Relative Rejection Frequencies for 3-dimensional VAR(1), Sample Size $T = 400$, Assumptions for Test Statistics: μ_0, μ_1 arbitrary (Panels A/B), μ_0 arbitrary, $\mu_1 \neq 0$, $\beta'\mu_1 = 0$ (Panels C/D)

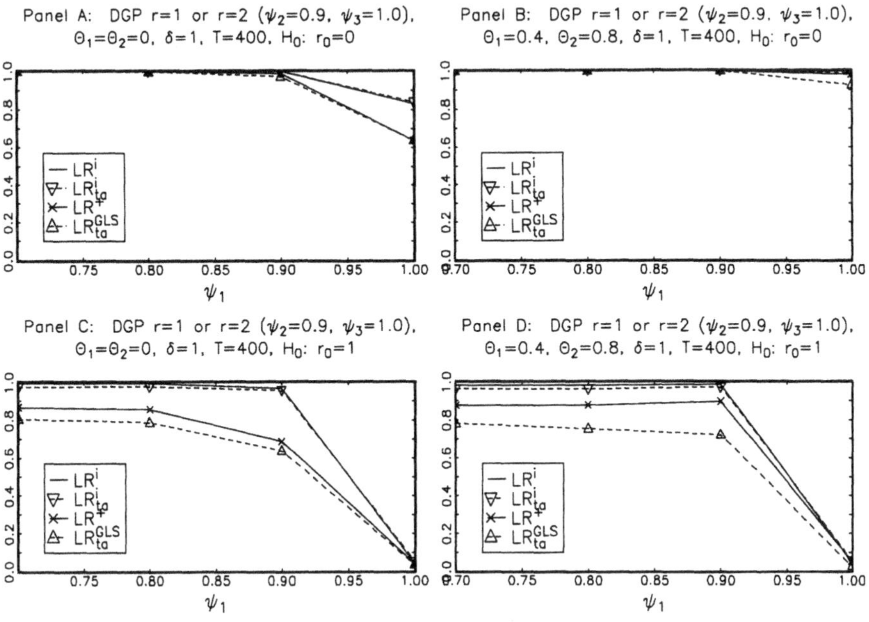

Figure 2.13: Relative Rejection Frequencies for 3-dimensional VAR(1), Sample Size $T = 400$, Panels A/B: Power (and Size) for $H_0 : r_0 = 0$, Panels C/D: Power (and Size) for $H_0 : r_0 = 1$

2.5.6 Three-dimensional VAR(2): DGP and Simulation Results

Simulations for the three-dimensional VAR(2) proposed by Yap & Reinsel (1995) have also been carried out to learn about the performance of the tests for a DGP with higher lag order. The DGP has the following form:

$$\Delta y_t = P^{-1}(\Lambda - I_3)Py_{t-1} + D\Delta y_{t-1} + \varepsilon_t \tag{2.5.6}$$

with

$$\Lambda = \begin{pmatrix} \lambda_1 & 0 & 0 \\ 0 & \lambda_2 & 0 \\ 0 & 0 & \lambda_3 \end{pmatrix},$$

$$P = \begin{bmatrix} -0.29 & -0.47 & -0.57 \\ -0.01 & -0.85 & 1.00 \\ -0.75 & 1.39 & -0.55 \end{bmatrix}, \qquad D = \begin{bmatrix} 0.15 & -0.20 & 0.45 \\ 0.19 & -0.08 & 0.30 \\ 0.11 & -0.05 & 0.32 \end{bmatrix}$$

$$\text{and} \quad \varepsilon_t \sim \text{iid}N\left(\begin{bmatrix} 0 \\ 0 \\ 0 \end{bmatrix}, \begin{bmatrix} 0.47 & . & . \\ 0.20 & 0.32 & . \\ 0.18 & 0.27 & 0.30 \end{bmatrix} \right)$$

where Λ is the matrix of eigenvalues of this DGP. Table 2.13 presents the different constellations of eigenvalues considered in the simulations. All cases denoted (a) correspond to the situation under the null hypothesis, whereas cases denoted (b) and (c) are constellations of eigenvalues under the alternative. In case 1(a), for example, two eigenvalues are smaller than one, thus the threedimensional system has a true cointegration rank of two. Simulations for testing the null hypothesis of $r_0 = 2$ result in the empirical size of the test for this parameter constellation. In cases 1(b) and 1(c) all eigenvalues of the respective system are smaller than one, i.e. the true cointegration rank is three. Simulations for testing the null hypothesis of rank $r_0 = 2$ result in the empirical power of the tests considered. The systems for case 2 and 3 are constructed analogously, but for a true cointegration rank of one and zero testing a rank of $r_0 = 1$ and $r_0 = 0$, respectively.

This DGP has been modified by adding a constant term to the EC representation in 2.5.6 to allow for a linear trend in the data for simulations for tests that are constructed for data with a linear trend. Thus, in the simulations presented for this DGP the deterministic terms are always correctly specified.

Table 2.13: Characteristics of DGPs

		λ_1	λ_2	λ_3	$H_{(0)}$	$H_{(A)}$
Case	1(a)	1.0	0.8	0.7	$r_0 = 2$	$r_A = 3$
	1(b)	0.9	0.8	0.7	$r_0 = 2$	$r_A = 3$
	1(c)	0.8	0.8	0.7	$r_0 = 2$	$r_A = 3$
Case	2(a)	1.0	1.0	0.7	$r_0 = 1$	$r_A = 2$
	2(b)	1.0	0.9	0.7	$r_0 = 1$	$r_A = 2$
	2(c)	1.0	0.8	0.7	$r_0 = 1$	$r_A = 2$
Case	3(a)	1.0	1.0	1.0	$r_0 = 0$	$r_A = 1$
	3(b)	1.0	1.0	0.9	$r_0 = 0$	$r_A = 1$
	3(c)	1.0	1.0	0.8	$r_0 = 0$	$r_A = 1$

Since likelihood based tests have been found to perform better than other tests in the foregoing simulations, the simulations for this DGP are only carried out for this class of tests.

The results for $T = 100$ and $T = 200$ (see Table 2.14) mainly confirm the findings from the two- and three-dimensional VAR(1) processes. Tests allowing for arbitrary μ_0 and μ_1, LR^+ and LR_{ta}^{GLS}, have in most cases lower power than the tests assuming $\mu_1 = 0$ in the DGP, LR^{i0} and LR^{SL}, or with $\mu_1 \neq 0$, $\beta'\mu_1 = 0$, LR^i and LR_{ta}^i (see cases 1b-3b and 1c-3c). Further, LR^{i0} is outperformed by LR^{SL} in terms of power, although it has to be noted that the size of LR^{SL} is outside the interval of 2 standard errors (cases 2a and 3a). LR^i is outperformed by LR_{ta}^i in terms of power and LR_{ta}^i even displays better size properties.[24] These results are found for $T = 100$ as well as for $T = 200$.

Comparing the tests allowing arbitrary μ_0 and μ_1, LR^+ and LR_{ta}^{GLS}, for $T = 100$, LR^+ outperforms the other in terms of power if $r_0 = 0$ is tested, whereas LR_{ta}^{GLS} displays the better power if $r_0 = 2$. Therefore, no clear recommendation concerning the choice between these two tests can be drawn from the results for this DGP in samples of $T = 100$. For $T = 200$, however, LR_{ta}^{GLS} is outperformed by LR^+ in terms of power.

[24] Again, only $r_0 = 0$ and $r_0 = 1$ are tested here as the DGP cannot have three stationary components because at least one component has a trend (see Section 2.3.1.2).

Table 2.14: Relative Rejection Frequencies of Tests for 3-dimensional VAR(2)

Test Statistics	Assumptions for Test Statistics	1(a) $r_0 = 2$ $r = 2$	2(a) $r_0 = 1$ $r = 1$	3(a) $r_0 = 0$ $r = 0$	1(b) $r_0 = 2$ $r = 3$	2(b) $r_0 = 1$ $r = 2$	3(b) $r_0 = 0$ $r = 1$	1(c) $r_0 = 2$ $r = 3$	2(c) $r_0 = 1$ $r = 2$	3(c) $r_0 = 0$ $r = 1$
		$T = 100$								
LR^+	μ_0, μ_1	0.027	0.043	0.102	0.088	0.076	0.169	0.242	0.169	0.290
LR_{ta}^{GLS}	arbitrary	0.024	0.031	0.065	0.183	0.068	0.105	0.328	0.169	0.232
LR^i	μ_0 arbitrary,	-	0.058	0.087	-	0.148	0.148	-	0.359	0.342
LR_{ta}^i	$\mu_1 \neq 0$, $\beta'\mu_1 = 0$	-	0.077	0.070	-	0.241	0.165	-	0.550	0.390
LR^{i0}	μ_0 arbitrary,	0.033	0.052	0.099	0.244	0.111	0.144	0.516	0.244	0.303
LR^{SL}	$\mu_1 = 0$	0.05 0.059	0.080	0.091	0.879	0.268	0.177	0.972	0.487	0.352
	$T = 200$									
LR^+	μ_0, μ_1	0.060	0.066	0.087	0.863	0.346	0.284	0.977	0.826	0.727
LR_{ta}^{GLS}	arbitrary	0.034	0.029	0.040	0.696	0.322	0.238	0.806	0.719	0.695
LR^i	μ_0 arbitrary,	-	0.069	0.074	-	0.577	0.371	-	0.977	0.849
LR_{ta}^i	$\mu_1 \neq 0$, $\beta'\mu_1 = 0$	-	0.053	0.049	-	0.694	0.395	-	0.946	0.868
LR^{i0}	μ_0 arbitrary,	0.054	0.055	0.074	0.985	0.486	0.356	1.0	0.995	0.910
LR^{SL}	$\mu_1 = 0$	0.070	0.086	0.104	1.0	0.770	0.500	1.0	0.995	0.910

Note: Sample sizes $T = 100$ and $T = 200$, nominal significance level 0.05; the deterministic terms are correctly specified in all tests, i.e. simulations for LR^{i0} and LR^{SL} are carried out for the VAR(2) without a linear trend, LR^i, LR_{ta}^i, LR^+ and LR_{ta}^{GLS} for the VAR(2) with a linear trend

2.5.7 Conclusions from Simulations

Comparing Different Classes of Tests The simulation study presented in this chapter aims at comparing a wide range of tests on the basis of the same DGPs. The results of the simulations for relatively simple DGPs show that some of the previous favourable simulation results are due to the specific DGP used.

From the results it becomes apparent that the tests suggested by Stock & Watson (1988) as well as the canonical correlations tests proposed by Yang & Bewley (1996) have in many cases empirical sizes considerably in excess of the nominal size. For the SW tests, this confirms findings by other authors (e.g. Reimers, 1992; Yap & Reinsel, 1995). Therefore, these tests cannot be recommended for applied research, especially as they are also outperformed by LR tests in terms of power. While the Bierens test has correct size for some parameter constellations, it is extremely conservative in other cases, even in relatively large samples. Furthermore, its power hardly exceeds the nominal size of the test. Although this test allows for a more general DGP than the other tests, this test is therefore not recommended for applied work.

Deterministic Terms The assumptions regarding the deterministic terms underlying the different tests have been one main focus in this chapter. As has also been shown in the studies by e.g. Toda (1995), Gonzalo & Lee (1998) and Doornik, Hendry & Nielsen (1998) as well as in the local power analysis by Saikkonen & Lütkepohl (1999), it is very important to specify the deterministic terms correctly. Systems cointegration tests can be classified with respect to the deterministic terms assumed for the underlying DGP. One group of tests allows for a trend in the data and in the cointegration relation. Another group of tests is constructed for trending data, but does not allow for a linear trend in the cointegration relation. Finally, a third group of tests can be applied if the data do not have a linear trend.

If at least one of the time series in the system analysed has a linear trend, then the tests that allow for an arbitrary mean and trend term are available, which allow for a linear trend in the cointegration relation in addition to a linear trend in the data. In this group of tests, the application of original and trend-adjusted LR tests, LR^+ and LR_{ta}^{GLS}, is recommended. However, the simulations have shown that the tests that do not allow for a trend in the cointegration relation have considerably higher power than the more general tests. It is not known a priori whether a linear trend is in the cointegration relation. One possibility would be to test whether a linear trend enters the cointegration relation using LR tests as suggested by Johansen (1994, 1995, p.162). Furthermore, this decision can be considered as a model selection problem, as e.g. in Pesaran & Smith (1998), who apply model selection criteria to choose between a range of models with different lag lengths and different deterministic terms. However, it has also been argued that the inclusion of a linear trend in the cointegration relation should be decided a priori on the basis of economic theory (see e.g. Doornik et al., 1998). This will be further discussed with respect to the empirical analysis of Chapter 3.

If a linear trend can be excluded from the cointegration relation, the researcher might apply tests for the situation μ_0 arbitrary, $\mu_1 \neq 0$, $\beta'\mu_1 = 0$. From the above simulations, the LR tests LR^i and LR^i_{ta} can be recommended. It should be noted, however, that LR^i_{ta} has higher power than LR^i in many situations, but also shows slight size problems in some situations.

If the data do not exhibit a linear deterministic trend, tests can be applied that take this additional restriction ($\mu_1 = 0$) into account. In such a situation, the gain in power in comparison to the tests that do not restrict this deterministic term is even higher than for the tests that exclude the linear trend from the cointegration relation. The suggestion by Johansen (1992) to apply $LR^*\&LR^i$ (see Section 2.3.1.2) to test for a linear trend in the data has to be considered with some care, since it often fails to detect the presence of a linear trend (Toda, 1995). Considering the simulation results from the previous sections, LR^{i0} and LR^{SL} can be recommended in case of non-trending data. LR^{SL}, suggested by Saikkonen & Luukkonen (1997), is superior because it outperforms all other tests constructed for such data in terms of power, although it has a slight tendency to reject too often if the null hypothesis is true.

Some further topics have been analysed in the simulation study and the results are summarized in the following.

Eigenvalues Close to Unity Generally, the size of all tests becomes more conservative, if the DGP has near integrated components. This leads to lower power of the tests. Exceptions are the LR^{SL}, LR^i_{ta} and the LR^{GLS}_{ta} tests, which even perform quite well if an eigenvalue is near unity. In this respect, the original LR tests are outperformed by these recently suggested tests. In applied research, where the true properties of the DGP underlying the data are unknown, this implies that neither the original nor the trend-adjusted LR tests can be unambiguously preferred.

Testing Different Cointegrating Ranks For testing higher cointegrating ranks, either the LR_{ta}^{GLS}, or LR^{+} have a power advantage in some cases, whereas LR_{ta}^{i} displays higher power than LR^{i}, and the power advantage of LR^{SL} over LR^{i0} becomes even more pronounced. According to simulation studies based on sequential testing procedures it is difficult for standard LR tests to find the correct rank if the cointegrating rank is greater than one (see e.g. Toda, 1994, 1995). Therefore, it may be worth applying one of the aforementioned tests for testing large cointegrating ranks as alternatives to carrying out standard LR tests. However, in a sequential testing procedure, LR tests with prior trend adjustment may be inferior to the LR tests if the true cointegration rank is large, as they have lower power if $r_0 = 0$ is tested.

Dimensionality and Sample Size Further important determinants of the performance of systems cointegration tests are the dimension of the system analysed as well as the size of the sample on which the analysis is based. A higher dimension of a system leads to a more conservative size of the cointegrating rank tests for some parameter constellations. Therefore, there is also a tendency to lower power. A direct comparison of the power of, for example, the LR^{+} test for the two- and for the three-dimensional Toda-DGPs in Figure 2.2, Panel A, and Figure 2.4, Panel A, shows a power of 0.6 in case of the two-dimensional DGP and of about 0.4 in case of the three-dimensional DGP for an eigenvalue of ψ_1=0.7 if the null hypothesis $r_0 = 0$ is tested. Simulations for different sample sizes have shown that increasing the sample size from $T = 50$ to $T = 100$ in non-sequential tests does not improve the performance of the LR tests markedly, whereas most LR tests are more reliable for $T = 200$. In the 3-dimensional VAR of order two (Table 2.14) the power gain from $T = 100$ to $T = 200$ is even more substantial than in the 3-dimensional DGP of order one (e.g. Figures 2.4 and 2.10). However, other studies have found that in sequential testing procedures it is still difficult, even for LR tests, to find a cointegration rank greater than 1 using samples of size $T = 200$. For the Bierens test, even a sample size of $T = 400$ is not large enough for a reasonable performance for the DGP considered here. However, the availability of long time series in applied work is often limited by regime changes. Therefore, to keep the ratio of parameters to observations reasonably low, the number of variables included in the analysis should be kept relatively low.

2.6 Further Deterministic Terms: Dummy Variables

The objective of the simulations in Section 2.5 has been to compare a broad range of tests in a relatively simple setting. The focus is on the specific case where the deterministic part of the DGP consists of mean and linear trend terms. In applied work, however, there may also be additional deterministic terms.

Many economic time series exhibit a seasonal pattern that might be modelled by seasonal dummy variables. To avoid consequences for the asymptotic properties of Johansen's tests for the cointegration rank centered seasonal dummies are included in the system. Johansen (1995, p.84) recommends to orthogonalize the seasonal dummies on the constant term. Consequently, a centered seasonal dummy sums to zero over a year, i.e. for 4 quarters it is (0.75, -0.25, -0.25, -0.25) (Doornik & Hendry, 1997a, p.30).

Furthermore, real world data underlying empirical research often exhibit structural breaks. Several procedures have been presented in the unit root and cointegration literature to detect unknown breaks in the deterministic trend of the time series (see e.g. Maddala & Kim, 1998, Part IV).

However, in many empirical applications the time of the structural break is known, for example the structural break of German reunification in German time series (see Section 3.4). Therefore, the question arises how a known structural break can best be modelled.

Single-equation procedures that allow for smooth nonlinear changes in the mean of a dependent series or in the cointegration relationship, classified as smooth transition regression (STR) models, have been suggested by Teräsvirta (see e.g. Granger & Teräsvirta, 1993; Teräsvirta, 1998; Lin & Teräsvirta, 1994). In the multivariate context, STR models or other multivariate methods to test for the form of a break in the deterministic terms are, to the knowledge of the author, not yet available. However, known structural breaks can in many cases be modelled including dummy variables in the system analysed. Alternative dummy variables possibly included in a system are impulse dummies of the form

$$di_t = \begin{cases} 1, & t = T_1 \\ 0, & otherwise \end{cases},$$

as well as step dummies (sometimes also called shift dummies) of the form

$$ds_t = \begin{cases} 0, & t < T_1 \\ 1, & t \geq T_1 \end{cases} .$$

Furthermore, step dummies that are one for some periods, but go back to zero at some point in time, could be introduced in a model. They take the form

$$ds_t^i = \begin{cases} 1, & T_1 \leq t \leq T_2 \\ 0, & otherwise. \end{cases}$$

These dummies can also be considered as impulse dummies extended over more than one period. This is indicated by the superscript i.

The presence of specific dummy variables might change the asymptotic distribution of some of the systems cointegration tests considered in this thesis. Bierens (1997b) considers seasonal dummy variables whereas Bewley & Yang (1995), Yang & Bewley (1996) and Stock & Watson (1988) do not consider either seasonal dummies nor step dummies. In contrast, the different LR tests discussed in Section 2.3 are extended to allow for different dummy variables.

The inclusion of an impulse and a step dummy in the present framework leads to a DGP of the form

$$y_t = \mu_0 + \mu_1 t + \delta_0 di_t + \delta ds_t + x_t, \qquad t = 1, 2, \ldots, \tag{2.6.7}$$

where μ_0 and μ_1 are again mean and trend parameters, t the linear trend and δ_0 and δ are the parameters of the impulse and step dummies (di_t and ds_t), respectively.[25]

Similarity of inference with respect to the parameter of interest is of great importance, i.e. that the null-distribution of the test statistic is invariant with respect to nuisance parameters (Kiviet & Phillips, 1992). In the group of LR tests, LR^+ and LR_{ta}^{GLS} are similar tests with respect to mean and trend term. However, LR^+ is, in contrast to LR_{ta}^{GLS}, not invariant to the inclusion of certain dummy variables.

The introduction of certain dummy variables changes the asymptotic distribution of Johansen's LR tests for the cointegration rank. The asymptotic distribution with respect to dummy variables has been discussed by Johansen & Nielsen (1993). They show that the asymptotic distribution under the null hypothesis in the case of a step dummy restricted to the cointegration relation depends on the timing of the structural shift, i.e. it depends on the breakpoint relative to the sample. If T_1 is a

[25] Seasonal dummies are not included here for ease of exposition. However, they are included in the presentation of Appendix A.

known break point, then critical values can be simulated with the program DisCo (Johansen & Nielsen, 1993). The asymptotic distribution of the rank test is also changed by a break in the slope of a linear trend. The introduction of an impulse dummy does not influence the asymptotic distribution of the test statistic since it only excludes a single oberservation from the sample.

Saikkonen & Lütkepohl (2000b) extend the trend-adjusted LR tests described in Section 2.3.1.1, suggesting that all deterministic terms in (2.6.7) including dummy variables should be estimated first, be subtracted from the time series y_t and the cointegration tests should be applied to the adjusted data.

This approach can be extended to include more than one step and impulse dummy as well as seasonal dummies (see Appendix A for an extension of the framework given in Saikkonen & Lütkepohl (2000b) to a model including two impulse and two step dummies as well as seasonal dummies). The resulting test statistics have the same limiting null distributions as the LR_{ta}^{GLS} statistic in Section 2.3.1.1.

It should be noted that Johansen derives his LR test from the EC representation $\Delta y_t = \nu_0 + \nu_1 t + \delta D_t + \alpha\beta' y_{t-1} + \varepsilon_t$ (for lag order 1), where D_t includes all dummy variables possibly included. This has implications for the way how the structural break is modelled in this test. In the representation underlying the trend-adjusted LR tests, the structural break is modelled as a strict break in the levels. In contrast, Johansen's LR tests allow for a break in the levels that is somewhat smooth.

The purpose of this section is mainly to sketch the consequences of introducing dummy variables in a system, since this will be of interest for the empirical analysis in Section 3.4. In the following, a small simulation study is presented to obtain an impression of the change in the performance of cointegration rank tests due to the introduction of dummy variables.

To the knowledge of the author, the only available small sample simulation study including dummies has been carried out by Doornik et al. (1998). They analyse the impact of different possibilities to include impulse dummies (restricted or unrestricted) in the model for estimation on the performance of the LR tests for either DGP. Additionally, they analyse the performance of the tests if dummies are not included to model a structural break in the DGP. However, these simulations focus on impulse dummies only. In contrast, not only impulse but also step and seasonal dummies are considered in the following simulation results, since a step dummy is introduced in the analysis in Section 3.4 to model German reunification.

The simulations are carried out for LR^+ and LR_{ta}^{GLS}. These tests have been chosen because they perform best among the tests that do allow for arbitrary mean and trend term but no dummy variables, and because both tests can be extended to include dummy variables.[26]

Simulation Results for a Data-Based DGP In the following, the results from a simulation experiment based on a DGP derived in a bootstrap procedure as described below are presented to compare the performance of Johansen's original LR test with LR_{ta}^{GLS} for such a situation.[27] To derive the bootstrap data, the following EC model has been estimated in a first step on the basis of Johansen's representation (Johansen, 1995, p.70). German data have been used to estimate the EC model based on a five-dimensional VAR(2) including the variables real money, real GNP, the inflation rate, a long-term and a short-term interest rate (for details on the data, see Section 3.4.1.1):

$$\begin{aligned}\Delta y_t &= \nu + \alpha(\beta' y_{t-1} - \tau t - \theta_1 ds_{1,t} - \theta_2 ds_t^i) \\ &\quad + \Gamma_1 \Delta y_{t-1} + \gamma_{01,0} di_{1,t} + \gamma_{02,0} di_{2,t} \\ &\quad + \gamma_{s1} sd_{1,t} + \gamma_{s2} sd_{2,t} + \gamma_{s3} sd_{3,t} + \varepsilon_t.\end{aligned} \tag{2.6.8}$$

The dummy variables included in model (2.6.8) account for German reunification and other special factors influencing the monetary regime in the sample period considered.[28] The model includes a step dummy of the form

$$ds_t = \begin{cases} 0, & t < 1990(3) \\ 1, & t \geq 1990(3) \end{cases}$$

as well as a step dummy that goes back to zero after a few periods (i.e. an extended impulse dummy)

$$ds_t^i = \begin{cases} 1, & 1994(3) \leq t \leq 1995(4) \\ 0, & otherwise. \end{cases} .$$

Furthermore, the following two impulse dummies enter the system

---

[26] Johansen's LR tests that do not allow for a linear trend in the cointegration relation, LR^* and LR^i, are also available if dummy variables are included. The trend-adjusted LR test, however, is only available for the case with arbitrary mean and trend term considered here.

[27] For reviews of bootstrap methods for small sample inference in general, see e.g. Efron & Tibshirani (1993) or Maddala & Kim (1998, Chapter 10).

[28] A more detailed discussion of the dummy variables included in the system can be found in Section 3.4.1.3.

$$di_t = \begin{cases} 1, & t = 1990(3) \\ 0, & otherwise \end{cases} \quad \text{and} \quad di_t = \begin{cases} 1, & t = 1993(3) \\ 0, & otherwise \end{cases}.$$

Additionally, seasonal dummies $sd_{i,t}$ for $i = 1, 2, 3$ account for the seasonality in the data are included in the model. The data include 76 sample values, 1979(1) to 1997(4), and 2 presample values.

In a second step, $T = 78$ residuals have been drawn randomly with replacement from the residuals ε_t of the estimated model. Using these newly created residuals, new data are successively generated based on the estimated parameter matrices of model (2.6.8) under the assumption of the cointegration rank of $r = 3$ that has been estimated from the data initially.[29] The resulting sample of size $T = 76$ is the bootstrap sample underlying the following simulations.

Table 2.15: Rejection Frequencies for a Data-based Simulation Experiment, $T = 76$, $r = 3$

H_0: rank=r_0	LR_{ta}^{GLS}	LR^+
$r_0 = 0$	0.967	1.000
$r_0 = 1$	0.426	0.990
$r_0 = 2$	0.138	0.723
$r_0 = 3$	0.021	0.134
$r_0 = 4$	0.001	0.014

Note: Critical values are the 95% quantiles of the asymptotic distribution of LR_{ta}^{GLS} (tabulated by Lütkepohl & Saikkonen (1999c, Table 1)) and of LR^+ (simulated with the program DisCo (Nielsen, 1994))

The simulation experiment is based on these newly generated data with a cointegration rank of $r = 3$. The simulations are carried out assuming a correctly specified five-dimensional model (VAR(2)) and the results are presented in Table 2.15. These results show that LR_{ta}^{GLS} correctly rejects the cointegration rank $r_0 = 2$ only in about 14% of all

[29] Note that the assumption that the residuals are independently identically distributed is fulfilled due to the bootstrap design. However, the problem might arise that the distribution of the bootstrapped residuals might not reflect the distribution of the actual residuals. Another possibility would be to generate the DGP with normally distributed residuals, since deviation from normality might also affect the performance of the tests.

cases whereas LR^+ displays a power of about 0.72 if $r_0 = 2$. Such a large difference in power can partly be explained by the empirical size of the tests for this DGP. LR^+ shows a tendency of overrejection, whereas LR_{ta}^{GLS} displays reasonable size, although it is somewhat conservative (see $H_0 : r_0 = 3$). However, this difference in size cannot explain the poor performance of LR_{ta}^{GLS} alone. It seems that the performance of the LR_{ta}^{GLS} test is more strongly affected by the inclusion of dummy variables as well as by the higher dimension of the system than LR^+.[30] However, a more detailed simulation analysis taking these aspects as well as the possible impact of deviations from the normal distribution into account would have to be carried out to draw more general conclusions. The results presented here are meant to help to evaluate the empirical results of the rank tests presented in Chapter 3.

2.7 Recommendations for Applied Research

The findings of the simulations for DGPs that do not require dummy variables show that the application of LR tests can be recommended. Original and trend-adjusted LR tests have some strengths in certain situations. Regarding the comparative performance of LR^+ and LR_{ta}^{GLS} it has been found that results of the LR_{ta}^{GLS} in higher dimensional systems with dummy variables have to be considered with some caution as this test tends to find too low a cointegration rank. However, further research has to be carried out to explore the relative strengths and weaknesses of the tests in the presence of structural shifts.

Regarding the deterministic terms, the conclusion is that it is important to specify these terms correctly as the tests may reject far too often or have substantially reduced power in case of misspecification. With respect to the specification of the deterministic terms, the trending properties of the data have to be accounted for. The exclusion of deterministic terms might be tested. Alternatively, model selection criteria can be applied to choose the specification of deterministic terms. In some cases, it might be desirable to decide the deterministic specification on the basis of economic considerations. To enhance the understanding of the effects of dummy variables on the performance of the tests, further research is necessary.

[30] Simulations on the basis of a data-based DGP generated according to representation (1.3) in Appendix A instead of (2.6.8) let to similar results.

Since the LR tests have been found to perform best in small samples in comparison with other systems cointegration tests, the findings of previous and new small sample simulations concerning the sensitivity of the performance of these tests with respect to model selection, non-normality, dimension, sample size and the specification of deterministic terms have to be taken into account in empirical applications.

Prior to testing for the cointegration rank, model selection criteria should be applied to choose the lag order since such a procedure leaves the asymptotic distribution of the LR rank tests unchanged. Furthermore, misspecification tests should be carried out to evaluate the chosen specification.

The applied researcher should be aware that a large number of variables included in the system influences the test performance negatively, especially in rather small samples. This might be an argument for restricting the number of variables included in the system and analysing comparatively simple models.

Chapter 3

A Cointegrated Monetary System for Germany

3.1 Introduction

One important precondition for the policy of monetary targeting by the Bundesbank is the stability of German money demand for a period including German reunification. Therefore, a central issue of an empirical analysis of German monetary policy is testing an economically plausible money demand relationship. Apart from its monetary target M3, the Bundesbank monitors a number of economic variables in the financial as well as the real sector (see e.g. Schich, 1996; König, 1996). The term structure plays an important role in the context of German monetary policy since it serves the Bundesbank as an indicator for inflationary expectations. Inflationary expectations are essential for the transmission mechanism of monetary policy. Transmission channels include an expectations channel as well as an aggregate demand channel. The expectations channel works via the effect of monetary policy on inflation expectations that will with some lag affect inflation via the wage- and price-setting behaviour in the economy (see Svensson, 1998a). Further, monetary policy affects aggregate demand with some lag via its effect on long real interest rates (and possibly the availability of credit). Thus, the term structure of interest rates as well as the long-run Fisher equation, possibly implying a stationary real interest rate, might be determinants in the transmission channel of monetary policy. They are therefore tested in the empirical study in this chapter in addition to a long-run money demand function.

The aim of the following section is to set the empirical analysis presented in this chapter in perspective to the controversy on monetary policy strategies with respect to the decision of the ECB on its monetary policy strategy and, in that context, the discussion of German monetary policy. Furthermore, the relevance of the stability of the demand for money is highlighted. Central banks in countries of the European Union have followed three different monetary strategies: monetary targeting, inflation targeting and exchange rate targeting. The following discussion will focus on monetary versus inflation targeting, since these have been the two options considered as a viable strategy for the ECB. Section 3.3 reviews the economic theory underlying the long-run relationships considered in the empirical study on Germany in Section 3.4. Additionally, recent empirical analyses for Germany and, briefly, for other countries based on these theories are summarized. Section 3.4 presents the results of the empirical analysis of a German monetary system.

3.2 Monetary Policy Strategies and the ECB

The discussion with respect to the design of monetary policy has undergone some change in recent years. The focus has shifted from the controversy whether monetary policy should follow a rule or a discretionary path to a discussion on how to balance transparency of a central bank's action with its flexibility. Moreover, the focus of the arguments has shifted from the discussion which target variable a central bank should choose to the question which target variable should be given priority in the process of screening a broad range of indicators. These two aspects of the discussion on monetary policy strategies will be analysed in the following sections in the context of the monetary policy strategy of the Bundesbank and the decision of the ECB on its future monetary policy strategy.[1]

3.2.1 Inflation Targeting versus Monetary Targeting

The decision process with respect to the monetary policy strategy of the ECB has led to an increased discussion about the choice of the target variable for an intermediate target strategy. This section focusses on the main arguments and tries to clarify some terminology. A broad discussion

[1]For a more detailed discussion of monetary strategies, see e.g. Leiderman & Svensson (1995), König (1996), von Hagen & Neumann (1996), King (1996), Issing (1997), Bernanke & Mishkin (1997) and Svensson (1997, 1998), among others.

of different concepts of monetary policy strategies of central banks is beyond the aim and scope of this thesis, however.[2]

From the perspective of monetary policy practice, the discussion on whether a central bank should pursue a monetary targeting strategy or, rather, an inflation targeting strategy is to some extent a question of names rather than implementation. The actual question seems to be how the key elements of monetary policy are combined and the importance that is attributed to the respective elements. In the discussion on the Bundesbank's actual policy strategy Bernanke & Mishkin (1997), for example, consider the Bundesbank's policy as "inflation targeting as a framework" in contrast to the strategy followed by the Bank of England, referred to as "direct inflation targeting" (Mishkin & Posen, 1997; King, 1996) or "explicit inflation targeting" (Svensson, 1997). A strategy of direct inflation targeting implies the publication of an inflation forecast, but no other intermediate target is published. In contrast, inflation targeting as a framework implies that the final target of the central bank is inflation, but an intermediate target is published, which in case of the Bundesbank is a money growth target.[3]

With respect to the ECB's monetary policy the concepts of *inflation targeting* as well as *monetary targeting* have been discussed. The main ideas of these strategies are outlined in the following.

In evaluating the suitability of both monetary policy strategies, four main criteria should be taken into account: the stability of the relationship between the target of the monetary policy strategy and price developments, the control by the central bank over the target, the flexibility of the monetary policy strategy as well as its transparency and, thereby, the accountability of the central bank. Two preconditions with respect to the stability of the relation between monetary aggregates and prices have to be fulfilled in a monetary targeting regime: the stability of the demand for money as well as a close relationship between money and inflationary pressure. In contrast, inflation targeting does only rely on a close relationship between the inflation forecast and the actual inflation rate. Svensson (1997) argues that an inflation forecast is superior over

[2] An overview of issues like instrument rules, targeting rules, intermediate targeting, inflation and monetary targeting, the role of transparency as well as technical and political problems with the implementation of the ECB's monetary policy can be found, e.g., in Svensson (1998a).

[3] With respect to the role of instrument rules, Svensson (1998a) argues that target rules are more stable than instrument rules and that they are easier to motivate and to verify. In practice, no central bank follows instrument rules (e.g. a Taylor rule), either implicitly or explicitly, but they might be taken as a frame of reference for the actual policy and its evaluation.

other intermediate targets, since the inflation forecast is most correlated with the final goal, the inflation rate.[4]

With respect to the control of the central bank over its monetary policy target it is easier to control money by monetary policy actions than to control inflation directly. Whereas money stock can be observed with a short time-lag (e.g. von Hagen & Neumann, 1996), the central bank has imperfect control over inflation as a "control lag" occurs between the instrument change and the effect on inflation.

The success of a monetary policy strategy also depends on the degree of flexibility with which the central bank reacts to deviations from its target. Pragmatic monetary targeting (as has been implemented by the Bundesbank in Germany) displays a high degree of flexibility since it allows for deviations from target under specific circumstances, a target corridor is implemented and a range of economic variables are monitored in addition to the monetary aggregate. The same is true for an inflation forecasting strategy, where a measure of uncertainty for the inflation forecast is published additionally.

Furthermore, the issues of transparency and accountability are of great importance for the evaluation of a monetary policy strategy. The intermediate target should guide the public's monetary policy and inflation expectations. Under a monetary targeting regime deviations from the monetary target might be difficult to explain, raising the question what the central bank is really targeting. Svensson (1998a) has therefore criticized the rhetoric inconsistency of a monetary targeting strategy. In contrast, an essential argument in favour of inflation targeting emphasizes that the inflation rate is easy to monitor by the public. Missing the target would, therefore, mean a reduction in prestige of the central bank and its managers. Thus, inflation targeting provides appropriate incentives for central bankers to achieve the announced target.[5] However, the evaluation of deviations between an inflation forecast and the actual inflation might be difficult for a broad public.

The success of the Bundesbank's policy over the last 20 years and its high credibility has led to the adoption of a monetary policy by the ECB characterized by the announcement of a reference value of the broad monetary aggregate. An inflation forecast is not published, probably to avoid confusing the public in case of conflicting signals from the inflation forecast and money growth. However, the final target of the ECB's

---

[4]Haldane (1997) assesses the effects of inflation targeting in the countries where it has been introduced and concludes that the introduction of an inflation targeting regime has most likely induced lower inflation expectations.

[5]See e.g. King (1996).

monetary policy is, of course, inflation, and the practice of future policy will display the targets or indicators that are given priority by the ECB.

3.2.2 'Discretion versus Rule' or 'Flexibility versus Transparency'

Severe uncertainties remain concerning the link between money and inflation in the euro area. Euro-wide measures of inflation and money have been constructed, but an interpretation of these numbers is not straightforward. Furthermore, the relationship between money and inflation after the introduction of a single currency, most probably followed by deeper integration of financial markets, is hard to predict. The links between interest rates, output and inflation in the euro area are also unclear, especially because countries start EMU at different stages of their economic cycle. This means that some countries need higher and others lower interest rates. Additionally, changes in interest rates have different effects on the economies of the euro area due to differences in the speed of the transmission process as well as the strength of the impact of interest rate changes on the economy. The effects of the monetary policy measures are determined by the countries' institutional and financial structure as well as the behaviour of agents in the respective economies. The uncertainties with respect to the beginning of EMU lets the introduction of discretionary elements in monetary policy seem advisable. However, most of the recent literature argues in principle for a rule bound monetary policy. Three main problems with discretionary policy, i.e. a policy approach based on the central bank's case-to-case evaluation of the respective circumstances, have been pointed out in the literature (e.g. Issing, 1997). First, variable time lags of monetary policy make fine-tuning of economic activities rather difficult. Second, monetary policy in the longer term affects only inflation not real activity. And third, a time inconsistency problem[6] might arise. A central bank following no pre-specified policy rule might have an incentive to act inconsistently with earlier plans and announcements if agents anticipate its policy. This implies a tendency of higher inflation.[7]

In practice, central bankers should aim at a correct mix of rules and discretion (König, 1996). In the context of the ECB's monetary policy strategy the need for flexibility in a transition period is undoubted. The stability-oriented strategy of the ECB takes the uncertainties of the trans-

[6] See Kydland & Prescott (1977)

[7] For a discussion of this "inflation bias", see e.g. Green (1996).

ition period into account. The ECB has defined price stability as a "year-to-year increase in the Harmonized Index of Consumer Prices (HICP) of the euro area of below 2%" (European Central Bank, 1998) and has made clear that this is a medium-term objective. Further, the policy of the ECB is based on "two pillars": A quantitative reference value for the growth of the monetary aggregate M3[8] and the broadly based assessment of the price developments and the risks to price developments (European Central Bank, 1999a). By the announcement of a quantitative reference value for the growth of the broad monetary aggregate M3, that is 4.5 % for 1999, the ECB gives a signal to the public with respect to its future policy (European Central Bank, 1999a). However, the ECB has also pointed out that it will not mechanistically adjust monetary policy towards short-run deviations of money growth from the reference value. This is also the argument why the ECB announces a reference value of money growth rather than a monetary target. Furthermore, the ECB does announce a reference value rather than a reference corridor, since it argues that a corridor might be falsely interpreted by the public as implying an automatic change in interest rates to deviations from the corridor (European Central Bank, 1999a). As mentioned above, the ECB will also look at a broad range of indicators to assess economic and price developments allowing for some flexibility in the policy reaction. One of the indicators will be an inflation forecast which will, however, not be published.

Obviously, the constitution of the ECB as well as its policy have been designed in many respects according to the blue print of the German Bundesbank. The aim is to carry over some of the Bundesbank's credibility and reputation to the ECB.[9] However, the ECB has also learned from the Bundesbank's experience that missed its target in about 50% of all years (Issing, 1997) which led to criticism of the Bundesbank's strategy and to the question what the Bundesbank was really targeting. Furthermore, although the ECB has emphasized the medium-term horizon of the monetary policy strategy aiming at stability as well as transparency, the strategy allows to react to unforeseen short-term developments and volatility. The ECB's monetary policy allows considerable flexibility taking into account the uncertainties of the transition to EMU. Uncertainties remain in many respects, e.g. whether the ECB actually can control its monetary target in EMU, whether there is a causal relationship between

[8] M3 in EMU is broader than M3 in Germany as it also includes e.g. money market papers and debt securities (European Central Bank, 1999a).

[9] See Barro & Gordon (1983) and Rogoff (1985), for example, on the role of the credibility and reputation of a central bank.

money and prices and with respect to the stability of the underlying economic relationships. The reference value is announced to communicate aims and decisions of the ECB to the public to achieve transparency[10] of its actions and decision process. However, since the reference value will hardly ever be met exactly it is questionable whether the degree of transparency of such a strategy will be very high. To conclude, the ECB has made clear by the decision on its future monetary policy that it will follow a rule-bound policy aiming at transparency, but allowing short-term flexibility. The next years will show how short-term and medium-term objectives can be balanced.

Since the ECB has decided to adopt most of the main features of the Bundesbank's policy, the implementation of the Bundesbank's policy is discussed next, with special emphasis on the role of the stability of money demand which will be one main focus of the empirical analysis in Section 3.4.

3.2.3 German Monetary Policy: Monetary Targeting and the Stability of the Demand for Money

According to the statute of the Bundesbank the aim of its policy is "safeguarding the currency" (Bundesbank Act, Art. 3). This is interpreted to mean that price stability should be achieved (Issing, 1997). This objective has been imposed on the ECB. Another characteristic of the Bundesbank, namely its strict independence from government, is even more pronounced in the ECB. In the following, the Bundesbank's monetary strategy is more closely reviewed.[11]

The Money Growth Target The Bundesbank follows a strategy of monetary targeting since 1974.[12] The aggregate targeted since 1988 is the chosen monetary aggregate M3. Between 1975 and 1987 the target of the monetary policy of the Bundesbank was the central bank money stock which included currency, sight deposits, time deposits and savings deposits weighted with their minimum reserve requirements in 1974. Since such a weighting scheme assigned too much weight to currency

[10]For the role of transparency in monetary policy, see e.g. Svensson (1998a). For a discussion of the ECB's monetary policy options, see also Svensson (1998b).

[11]For a detailed discussion of the different elements of monetary policy of the Bundesbank, see for example Issing (1995, 1997) and König (1996).

[12]In December 1974 the Bundesbank published the annual target for the broad monetary aggregate for the first time.

in the late 1980's, M3 was chosen as a more appropriate aggregate for monetary targeting, adding the individual components unweighted.

The Bundesbank has chosen a broad monetary aggregate as it's monetary target because in countries with a highly developed financial market a large-scale switching between currency, sight, time and savings deposits might occur. If a narrow aggregate would be used as the target for monetary policy, this would, on the one hand, necessitate a highly volatile reaction by the central bank although the relevant money demand might not have changed. Further, deviation of a highly volatile money growth from the official target would be difficult to explain to the public. Additionally, the reaction of the central bank would necessarily have to be more volatile instead of focusing on the medium term.

The annual money growth target is derived on the basis of the quantity equation $M \cdot V = P \cdot Y$, stating that the product of money (M) and velocity (V) is equal to the product of prices (P) and real GNP (Y). Taking logarithms as well as first differences and rearranging this equation results in a rule for deriving the money target:

$$\Delta\overline{m} = \Delta\overline{p} + \Delta\hat{y}^* - \Delta\hat{v}^*$$

where $\Delta\overline{m}$ is the targeted money growth, $\Delta\overline{p}$ is the normative inflation, $\Delta\hat{y}^*$ is the estimated growth of the production potential and $\Delta\hat{v}^*$ is the estimated rate of change in the velocity of circulation (Issing, 1992). The normative rate of inflation is taken to be 2% since 1987[13] to allow for inaccuracy in the measurement of inflation.[14] On the other hand, the normative inflation has to be low enough not to lead to allocative distortions in the economy.

Since 1979 the Bundesbank is announcing a four-quarter target based on the average of the fourth quarter rather than on the end-of-year value in order to minimize random effects. A further change in the Bundesbank's strategy in 1979 was the decision to formulate a target corridor for each year to give the Bundesbank more flexibility.[15] However, the target has only been adapted in 1991 following German reunification.

By its mid-year revision of its target the Bundesbank allows a kind of feedback rule (Issing, 1997). Issing (1997, p.72) considers the policy of the

[13]For details on the normative inflation rate since 1974, see e.g. Clarida & Gertler (1996, Table 1).

[14]The objective is to allow for a possible overstatement of inflation due to imperfect adjustment for quality improvements in the price index. For a discussion of the problems of accurate measurement of inflation, see e.g. Hoffmann (1998).

[15]Since 1985 securities repurchase agreements have served as the main tool of the Bundesbank to control short-term money market rates (see e.g. Nautz, 1995).

Bundesbank "a successful synthesis of a theoretical basis and practical implementation". This attitude is mirrored by the design of the ECB policy. However, the feature of a target corridor has not been taken up by the ECB's monetary policy concept so far although it might be reasonable given the uncertainties with respect to developments during the first years of EMU.

It has often been criticized that the Bundesbank has missed its target in nearly 50 % of the years.[16] In contrast, it can be argued that only the success in reaching the aim of price stability should be considered as a measure of success.

Critics have argued in accordance with Goodhardt's law (Goodhart, 1975, p.5) that a central bank which decides to rely on a statistical link between the money stock and its ultimate goal, the inflation rate, by following a monetary targeting strategy would consequently have to expect this link to break, since the instrumentalization changes the underlying relationships. However, Issing (1997) points out that the instability of economic relationships can be avoided if the authorities behave according to a consistent policy reaction function. He attributes the success of the Bundesbank's policy to the steadiness and medium-term orientation of the monetary targeting strategy stabilizing market participants' expectations thereby reinforcing the stability of monetary relationships, i.e. the preconditions of the policy itself.

As mentioned above, Bernanke & Mishkin (1997) distinguish between inflation targeting as a rule and inflation targeting as a framework. They consider the policy of the Bundesbank as inflation targeting, not interpreted as a discretionary rule, but as a framework within which different targets are considered and credibility is to be achieved. Svensson (1998a) also considers the Bundesbank as an inflation targeter. He argues that the Bundesbank has missed it's monetary target in 50% of the years because it has given priority to the implicit inflation target.[17] The Bundesbank, of course, has always emphasized the importance of its monetary target.

However, the question how the Bundesbanks' strategy should be classified is of minor importance. It might be helpful to follow the convention to call a policy that publicly announces a money growth target a "monetary targeting strategy", noting that this could also imply further implicit

[16]Issing (1997, Table 1) displays the targets set by the Bundesbank since 1975 and whether the target was achieved.

[17]Cabos, Funke & Siegfried (1998) analyse the controllability of the monetary aggregate M3 in Germany empirically and find that control problems involved in targeting broad money are larger than for direct inflation targets.

targets as have been monitored by the Bundesbank and that will receive even more attention by the ECB.

The Stability of the Demand for Money The stability of the demand for money, which will be one of the central issues in the empirical analysis presented in Section 3.4, is a precondition for any intermediate targeting strategy followed by a central bank (von Hagen & Neumann, 1996). A stable long-run money demand relation linking money to income, interest rates and inflation is the basis for the predictability of the transmission of changes in monetary policy instruments to inflation via the monetary aggregate in the economy.

In contrast to other countries as the UK and the US, money demand in Germany has still been found stable in most empirical studies. Even German reunification does not seem to have led to a permanent instability in the relationship between the relevant macroeconomic variables. Two main factors have facilitated this stability: early liberalization of the financial markets and minor relevance of new financial products in recent years (see Issing, 1997). With respect to the ECB's policy, however, central bankers have to be aware that with higher integration of financial markets within the EMU area the behaviour of agents will probably change. It remains an open question to what extent and how soon money demand behaviour in Germany will change and/or whether it will dominate the agents' behaviour in other EU countries as suggested for the period before the start of the EMU by some studies on European money demand (e.g. Wesche, 1997).

3.3 Long-Run Economic Relations Influencing the Monetary Transmission Mechanism

The empirical analysis in Section 3.4 focusses on testing long-run monetary relationships suggested by economic theory. In this section, the relevant economic theories are reviewed to motivate the choice of variables that enter the system and to derive the specification of long-run relationships to be tested.

3.3.1 The Demand for Money

3.3.1.1 Theories on Money Demand

There are two fundamentally different approaches to a theory of money demand: One line of analysis is set within the usual approach to demand theory considering a utility function. In contrast, theories that separate money from other goods emphasize two characteristics of money. First, money is universally acceptable as a means of exchange for goods and services. Second, the market value of money is relatively stable or at least predictable over the short-term.

However, these two approaches to the theory of the demand for money are not necessarily contradictory, but can be viewed as complementary. Therefore, the alternative theoretical models outlined below include approaches set in a utility framework as well as those focusing on the motives of the demand for money.

Economic theories of money demand suggest two main motives for holding money: Money is held for transaction purposes as well as a part of a portfolio. In the following, a brief overview of the ideas underlying the different theoretical approaches to the demand for money is given.[18] Concluding from that exposition, it is highlighted which variables should be included in an empirical analysis of the demand for money according to the respective theory.

The Classical Quantity Theory The origin of the theories of the demand for money can be traced back to the work of Irving Fisher who first introduced the concept of a "transactions velocity of circulation for money", the rate at which money passes from hand to hand, in his book "The Purchasing Power of Money" (1911). In the classical quantity theory of money originating in Fisher's work the transactions velocity of money is assumed to be constant. Therefore, the classical quantity theory can be stated in the following form:

$$M_S V_T = PT,$$

where M_S is the quantity of money in the economy, V_T is the transactions velocity, P is the price level and T is the volume of transactions. If V_T and T are assumed constant, the equilibrium price level moves in strict proportion to the quantity of money. This original quantity theory derived under strong assumptions, especially the constancy of the velocity

[18]For further details on the various lines of research in the theory of the demand for money, see e.g. Laidler (1993) which served as the basis of this summary.

of money which Fisher assumes to be given by behavioural, technical and institutional conditions in the economy, has later been modified by Friedman (see below).

From Fisher's question of what determines the amount of money an economy needs to carry out a given volume of transactions, the focus of analysis then shifted to the question what determines the amount of money an individual agent would wish to hold. Therefore, the choice-making behaviour of individuals became the center of interest.

Keynes' Motives of Holding Money Keynes' work is an extension of the ideas introduced in the work of Marshall and Pigou. Keynes provides the first indepth analysis of the motives that lead people to hold money, especially in Keynes (1936). Keynes (1930) was the first to identify three distinct motives for holding money. One possibility is to hold money for transaction purposes to bridge the gap between receipt of income and planned regular expenditure. Further, there might be precautionary money demand for the case of unexpected expenditure which depends on the level of income. Also, money can be held for speculative purposes. The amount of money held for speculative purposes is influenced by interest rates as opportunity costs of holding money. High interest rates lead to expectations of decreasing interest rates and increasing value of bonds, which in turn lead to an increase in money holdings.

Friedman's Version of the Quantity Theory of Money Friedman is the most prominent proponent of an approach to the analysis of holding money referred to as the "modern quantity theory". Friedman's focus is on the analysis of the factors rather than the motives that determine peoples' demand for money. His work builds on the quantity theory of money, but does assume that the velocity of money changes over time.

One important factor for holding money is, according to Friedman (1956), wealth. He not only considers present income as a determinant of money demand, but also future labour income (human wealth) as well as an individual's assets (nonhuman wealth) which can be accumulated or sold in the future and generate income additional to labour income. Further essential factors in Friedman's theory are interest rates and the expected inflation rate that enter as opportunity costs of holding money.

The Demand for Money as a Means of Exchange According to the transaction motive that is central to the *Baumol-Tobin model*, money is held as a medium of exchange as well as an inventory to balance the time gap between income and expenditures (Baumol, 1952; Tobin, 1956). In the Baumol-Tobin model it is assumed that transactions are regular and completely foreseen. The amount of money held by the agent is determined by real income as well as the costs of holding money in terms of interest rates representing opportunity costs of holding money as well as the real costs of turning bonds into cash.

Another branch of the money demand literature emphasizes the *precautionary motive* of money holding, i.e. the uncertainty about the timing and amount of inflows and outflows. According to these models agents hold money for precautionary reasons. Restricted substitutability of money and bonds is assumed because of transaction costs of selling bonds if higher liquidity is needed.[19]

Further, the so-called *shopping time model* has been introduced in the literature, e.g., by McCallum & Goodfriend (1987).[20] The aim of the shopping time model is to analyse the demand for money by taking explicit account of its role as a means of exchange in markets for goods and services. The main argument of the shopping time model is that barter is much less efficient than trade with money. Therefore, money saves shopping time. This time can be used for leisure (increasing utility) or for working to get additional earnings. The more money is spent on shopping, the more time is saved. The theoretical considerations result in a carefully derived money demand function which encompasses Friedman's ideas, but yields additional insight as the money demand function is more precisely formulated. The utility maximising behaviour of the agent is modelled, which takes into account current behaviour as well as future plans (intertemporal model). The role of money as a means of exchange is emphasized.

The Demand for Money as an Asset In a broader sense, the demand for money can be considered as a part of a *portfolio decision* (Tobin, 1958; Friedman, 1956), where assets are allocated within a portfolio with the aim of profit maximization. In this case, holding money is considered as one alternative to allocate assets.

The *Tobin model* (Tobin, 1958) deals with optimization of a portfolio under uncertainty. Reallocation of a portfolio can be due to an increase in interest rates which means an increase in opportunity costs of holding money. A decrease in interest rates is expected to be accompanied by an increase in the value of bonds in the future. One central focus of the

[19]Details on the development of this approach and on its proponents can be found in Patinkin (1989), Chapter 4.

[20]See also McCallum (1989), Chapter 3.

Tobin model is on the risk the agent is willing to take regarding the value of a bond.

In the *overlapping generations model*, originally suggested by Samuelson (1958) and mainly developed by Sargent & Wallace (1988), money is interpreted as a store of value between periods as well as generations. All generations gain from the introduction of money because each generation is able to smooth its consumption over time. Additionally, money allows for the possibility of intergenerational trade. Therefore, the demand for money as an asset rather than a means of exchange is emphasized in this class of theories.

The Choice of Variables on the Basis of Theoretical Propositions Economic theory of money demand suggests two main motives for holding money: As mentioned before, money is held for transaction purposes and as part of a portfolio. According to the transaction motive, money is held as a medium of exchange and as an inventory to balance the time gap between income and expenditures. In a broader sense, the demand for money can be considered as a part of a portfolio decision, where assets are allocated within a portfolio with the aim of profit maximization. In this case, holding money is considered as one alternative to allocate assets.[21]

Different theories have emphasized different aspects of the demand for money. The identification of separate and stable money demand functions for narrow money and for time deposits (see e.g. Laidler,1966; Goldfeld,1973) indicates that narrow money is held as a means of exchange. It has also been shown that the degree of substitutability between narrow money and other assets is limited. These results lead to the view that narrow money is held for transactions purposes and not as an asset.

Laidler (1993, p.180) argues that asset demand theories do not give a satisfactory explanation of the demand for money, since asset motives do not lead the public to hold sight and savings deposits if there are perfect substitutes that pay more interest. At least, asset motives do not dominate the demand for money. However, in the context of the empirical analysis in Section 3.4 asset motives might be important for savings included in the broad monetary aggregate in Germany. In contrast, it seems extremely implausible, as pointed out by Laidler (1993, p.183), to

[21] Barr & Cuthbertson (1991) state that to a certain extent it suffices for empirical work to specify a money demand function without being concerned with the role money plays in an economy. However it leads to further insight to take account of the motives of holding money stemming from the money's role as a means of exchange.

consider money as a pure store of value as in the overlapping generations models.

For the empirical analysis in Section 3.4 a broad monetary aggregate has been chosen. Therefore, different motives of holding money should be considered as the theoretical approaches can to some extent be complementary in explaining the demand for broad money in an economy.[22]

All theories except the Tobin model suggest to include some kind of income variable in an empirical analysis. Some theories focus on labour income or human wealth whereas others also suggest that non-human wealth, e.g. unearned income and inherited assets, also play an important role (Friedman; shopping time model). Models focusing on the precautionary motive of holding money as well as the shopping time model suggest to additionally include (consumption) expenditure. Further, all theories of money demand imply the incorporation of interest rates in an empirical analysis. In addition, the inflation rate as well as the expected inflation rate should be introduced in a money demand analysis according to the shopping time model, whereas Friedman suggests only to include the expected rate of inflation. Some further variables have been focussed on by some of the studies. The Baumol-Tobin model as well as models based on the precautionary motive propose wages as a proxi of the liquidation costs of bonds (Baumol-Tobin model) or assets in general (precautionary models). In the Tobin model the uncertainty over the development of asset values can be modelled by the volatility of a bond price.

Neither wealth nor a wage variable is incorporated in the German monetary system in Section 3.4. Wealth is not included because for Germany only data on financial wealth are available, where financial wealth includes M3, i.e. the variable to be explained. Expected inflation in Germany is difficult to measure. However, the current inflation rate can be considered as an approximation of inflationary expectations. An income variable is included in the system, but the real side of the economy is not explicitly modelled, as the analysis concentrates on monetary long-run relationships within a system of variables.[23] The wage rate as a proxi for costs of asset liquidation is not incorporated either.

---

[22]Barnett (1980) has introduced the use of the Divisia Index to generate a monetary aggregate where each component of the aggregate is weighted by the difference of its own rate of return and a representative rate of interest. However, such an aggregate is not employed in the empirical analysis in this chapter (see Section 3.3.1.2 for an explanation).

[23]For a study on Norwegian money demand explicitly taking the labour market into account, see e.g. Eitrheim (1998).

On the basis of the theories discussed, real money demand $M3^r$ can be considered to be mainly a function of real income (y^r) and of opportunity costs of holding money, i.e. long-term interest rate (r^l) and inflation (Δp), as well as an own (short-run) interest rate of money (r^s):

$$M^r = f(y^r, r^l, r^s, \Delta p),$$

where $\frac{\partial M^r}{\partial y^r} > 0$ and $\frac{\partial M^r}{\partial r^s} > 0$, i.e. higher income and an increase in the own rate of M3 lead to higher demand for real money. In contrast, an increase in the long-term interest rate as well as the inflation rate will lead to decreasing demand for real money, i.e. $\frac{\partial M^r}{\partial r^l} < 0$ and $\frac{\partial M^r}{\partial \Delta p} < 0$. These variables enter the system presented in the empirical analysis in Section 3.4. The income variable can be taken as a proxi for the influence of the volume of transactions on the demand for money. The long-term interest rate represents the opportunity costs of holding money with respect to holding other financial assets, whereas the short-term interest rate represents the own rate of return of M3. The inflation rate can be interpreted as opportunity costs of holding money compared to investments into real capital.[24]

3.3.1.2 Recent Empirical Literature of the Demand for the Monetary Aggregate M3 in Germany

The focus of many empirical studies on German monetary policy has been on the money demand function, since a stable money demand for M3 is a precondition for a policy of monetary targeting as pursued by the Bundesbank. In other countries, such as the US and the UK, targeting monetary aggregates has been abandoned because financial innovations led to instabilities in the demand for money. Financial innovations have not played a very important role in Germany so far, but the question has been raised whether money demand is still stable after German reunification. There have been a number of money demand studies for Germany. During the last years, cointegration methodology has become a standard tool for the analysis of the demand for money. Several authors analyse German money demand for M3 before German reunification using a cointegration approach, for example von Hagen & Neumann (1988), Gaab & Liedtke (1992), and Biefang-Frisancho Mariscal & Trautwein (1994). A number of studies have been presented analysing German demand for the monetary aggregate M3 for a sample period including German reunification. Most of these studies place their emphasis on single equation mod-

[24] Wolters & Lütkepohl (1997) show how the inflation rate influences the long-run demand for real money even if it is assumed that no opportunity costs of investment into real capital enter the nominal money demand function (see also Section 3.4.1.1).

elling, as the Monthly Report of the Bundesbank (Deutsche Bundesbank, 1995b), Issing & Tödter (1995), Kole & Meade (1995), Tullio, de Souza & Giucca (1996), Gaab (1996), Gaab & Mullineux (1996), Scharnagl (1996), König (1996), Wolters & Lütkepohl (1997) and Wolters, Teräsvirta & Lütkepohl (1998).[25] The main focus of the studies cited varies, but all find that German money demand for M3 is stable if they model German reunification by including dummy variables.

A number of papers on German money demand have concentrated on a comparison of the stability of money demand functions for simple-sum M3 and Divisia monetary aggregates (e.g. Gaab & Mullineux, 1996; Gaab, 1996; Tödter, 1994) with a special emphasis on the influence of financial innovations. These studies conclude that Divisia are better suited to account for financial innovations. However, in Germany the difference in comparison with simple-sum aggregates is not sufficiently distinct to justify a change in the intermediate target for monetary policy. Therefore, the empirical analysis in Section 3.4 concentrates on the simple-sum aggregate M3.

To test for the cointegration rank, Johansen's maximum likelihood rank test is applied in some of the studies for German M3 cited above. In contrast to the present study, the authors usually derive a cointegration rank of one and proceed to carry out their analysis within a single equation error correction framework. Very few studies present a test for weak exogeneity of the variables of the money demand function to justify their single equation approach, e.g. Hansen & Kim (1995), Wolters et al. (1998) and Beyer (1998a, b). Wolters et al. (1998) test weak exogeneity in a three-variable system including money, income and inflation, find that weak exogeneity of the inflation rate is clearly rejected, but nevertheless proceed with a single-equation analysis arguing that long-run coefficients will still be estimated superconsistently. In contrast, Beyer (1998a) finds that not only weak but also super exogeneity holds for the parameters in an M3 money demand model in his analysis of a five-variable system using seasonally adjusted data. Scharnagl (1998) applies the fully modified approach suggested by Phillips & Hansen (1990) that is asymptotically equivalent to systems procedures.

The first study on German monetary policy which extensively tested within the Johansen procedure is Juselius (1996). In contrast to her work, the paper by Hubrich (1999) considers the EMS period and includes the weighted own rate of M3 rather than a deposit rate. A linear time trend is not included in the cointegration relation here. These differences

[25] For a more detailed overview of the literature on German money demand, see for example Scharnagl (1996).

have important implications for the long-run relationships found in the analysis. One important difference is that no structural break in 1983 is found. Juselius (1996, 1998) concludes from her analysis that the break in 1983 marks the liberalization of capital markets in Europe. However, due to the fact that capital markets in Germany have largely been liberalized at the beginning of the 1970s (see also Issing, 1997), such finding appears to be rather implausible. The analysis in Hubrich (1999) confirms these doubts by finding a stable money demand over a sample period from 1979(1) to 1994(2), including the 1980s.

A further systems approach on German monetary policy based on the same variables as Juselius (1996), but using seasonally adjusted data is presented by Beyer (1998a). He also finds three stable cointegration relationships and extends the analysis of the long-run by modelling the dynamics of the system. In contrast to Juselius (1996, 1998) he finds no break in 1983, in that respect confirming the results of Hubrich (1999). Section 3.4 will elaborate on the implications of the differences in specification in an empirical analysis based on Hubrich (1999), but employing an extended sample.

The studies by Juselius (1996, 1998), Beyer (1998a) as well as Hubrich (1999) analyse the question of stability of the demand for M3. This is a necessary condition for a policy of monetary targeting. However, additional conditions have to be fulfilled, i.e. the monetary aggregate has to be controllable by the central bank and a causal link between money and prices, i.e. the intermediate and the final target of the monetary targeting strategy, should exist. These conditions have been analysed in Lütkepohl & Wolters (1998). Their methodological approach differs from the studies discussed above as well as from the analysis presented in Section 3.4 since their system analysis starts from a money demand equation derived in a single-equation procedure. The variables included in the system are the same as those that enter the system analysed in Section 3.4, but an import price index is added as an exogenous variable. The system is estimated using a three stage least squares procedure where the long-run money demand equation enters the system as the only cointegration relation. On the basis of the resulting model an impulse response analysis to investigate dynamic interdependencies between the variables and the transmission mechanism is carried out. They find no strong influence of money growth on inflation, but considerable effects of shocks in the inflation rate on money growth. This main result of the study allows some doubt about the strength of the causal link between money growth and inflation that is a precondition for a strategy of monetary targeting.

However, these problems go beyond the empirical analysis of Section 3.4 that aims at the analysis of long-run monetary relationships in Germany.

3.3.1.3 Estimation of Money Demand Systems for other Countries

Systems analyses of money demand have, of course, been carried out for other countries than Germany, as well. Hendry & Doornik (1994) have presented an analysis for the UK, whereas Hoffman & Rasche (1996) analyse US data. Hendry & Doornik (1994) find two stable cointegration vectors, a money demand relation as well as an output relation (deviation of output from trend). Hoffman & Rasche (1996) analyse 3-,4- and 5-dimensional systems for the US. In their 5-dimensional system they include similar variables as in Hubrich (1999) and in Section 3.4 of this thesis and find very similar cointegration relations: a money demand relation, an interest rate spread and a Fisher relation. Johansen & Juselius (1990) test for long-run money demand in Finland and Denmark. Juselius (1998) presents analyses for systems of Germany, Denmark and Italy, drawing on papers on the single countries, e.g. on Gennari & Juselius (1998) analysing a money demand system for Italy using the Johansen procedure. Juselius (1999) presents a structured VAR for Denmark where the money demand relation is one focus.[26]

3.3.2 The Term Structure of Interest Rates

With respect to the transmission of the monetary policy the relation between short- and long-term interest rates is of importance. A stable long-run relation between short-and long-term interest rates makes the transmission of changes in monetary policy conditions easier to predict. In this context the long-run influence of the relation between the short- and long-term interest rates on the money demand function is important, where the short-term interest rate might be interpreted as own interest of money and the long-term interest rate as the interest of alternative

[26] In contrast to *structural* VARs (SVAR) where the identification restrictions are e.g. imposed on the covariance matrix of the residuals, a *structured* VAR has identifying restrictions on the long-run as well as the short-run coefficients of a VECM. The growing literature of empirical analyses using a SVAR framework is not reviewed here due to its different methodological approach and because the focus of this thesis is on long-run monetary relationships. However, it should be noted that German monetary policy has been analysed within an SVAR framework, e.g. by Bernanke & Mihov (1997) and Clarida & Gertler (1996).

assets. A long-run one-to-one relationship between long-term and short-term interest rates is implied by the expectations theory of the term structure that is discussed in the following.

3.3.2.1 The Expectations Theory of the Term Structure

The expectation hypothesis of the term structure originates in the work of Fisher, e.g. Fisher (1930).[27] It can be formulated in a linearized form as follows:

$$R_t^{(k)} = \frac{1}{k}\sum_{i=0}^{k-1} E_t R_{t+i}^{(1)} + \phi_{k,t}.$$

Here, $R_t^{(k)}$ is the yield on a discount bond with k periods to maturity. The model states that the yield on a k-period bond is given by the average of expected future one-period rates up to $k-1$ periods in the future (E_t denotes the conditional expectation in period t). The symbol ϕ_k reflects a term premium, i.e. the predictable excess return on the k-period bond over the one-period bond held in k periods. ϕ_k depends on time to maturity k and is assumed to be stationary in the following. The expectations theory of the term structure presented here is based on the hypothesis of rational expectations, as in Campbell & Shiller (1991).

The expectations theory of the term structure describes the relationship between interest rates of different maturities and is based on the assumption that bonds are homogeneous. Also, the theory is confined to bonds with fixed interest and is, therefore, restricted to the term structure in time. The underlying conjecture of the expectations theory is that there are no arbitrage opportunities due to differences in interest rates, because arbitrage would lead back to equilibrium.

Assuming interest rates are I(1), it can be shown that according to the expectations hypothesis of the term structure every possible spread between two interest rates with different maturities is stationary. The stationarity of the spread is derived from the expectations theory of the term structure as follows (see Wolters, 1998): $R_t^{(k)}$ can be rewritten as

$$R_t^{(k)} = \frac{1}{k}\sum_{i=0}^{k-1} E_t R_{t+i}^{(1)} + \phi_{k,t} = \frac{1}{k}[E_t(R_t^{(1)} + R_{t+1}^{(1)} + R_{t+2}^{(1)} + \ldots + R_{t+k-1}^{(1)})] + \phi_{k,t}. \tag{3.3.1}$$

$R_{t+i}^{(1)}$ results from the sum of $R_t^{(1)}$ and the changes in $R_t^{(1)}$ from one period

[27] For an exposition and applications of the model, see Shiller (1990) and Campbell & Shiller (1991), among others.

to another.

$$R^{(1)}_{t+i} = R^{(1)}_t + [R^{(1)}_{t+1} - R^{(1)}_t] + [R^{(1)}_{t+2} - R^{(1)}_{t+1}] + \ldots + [R^{(1)}_{t+k-1} - R^{(1)}_{t+k-2}] + \phi_{k,t} \tag{3.3.2}$$

Equation (3.3.2) substituted into (3.3.1) gives equation (3.3.3):

$$R^{(k)}_t - R^{(1)}_t = \frac{1}{k}\left[E_t \Delta R^{(1)}_{t+1} + E_t \Delta R^{(1)}_{t+2} + \ldots + E_t \Delta R^{(1)}_{t+i}\right] + \phi_{k,t}. \tag{3.3.3}$$

As ΔR_{t+i} ($i = 1, \ldots, k$) and $\phi_{k,t}$ are stationary, $R^{(k)}_t - R^{(1)}_t$ must be stationary as well. The implicit cointegration relation is (1,-1), i.e. the expectations theory of the term structure postulates a long-run one-to-one relationship between long-term and short-term interest rates. This implication will be tested in Section 3.4.[28]

The term structure is considered as an essential indicator of monetary policy. Especially, the term structure can be employed as an indicator for the expected inflation rate. If the individuals would expect the inflation rate to rise, this would lead to higher long-term interest rates.[29] This, in turn, would mean an increase in the spread and vice versa.

3.3.2.2 Cointegration Analysis of the Term Structure of Interest Rates

An extensive literature on the term structure of interest rates presents empirical analyses of the expectations hypothesis of the term structure for a large number of different countries.[30] Shiller (1990) presents a survey on the term structure literature.

Yet, the focus of the term structure literature varies. Some studies rather concentrate on the long-run relationship between short-term and long-term interest rates. Some other papers analyse the predictive performance of the spread for the development of the short-term and/or the long-term rate. A number of studies also analyse the predictive power of the term structure for growth (e.g. Estrella & Mishkin (1997) for Europe and the US and Plosser & Rouwenhorst (1994) for Germany, the US and the UK).[31]

[28]It is the aim of this analysis to test the necessary condition, i.e. that there is a (1,-1) cointegration relationship between any pair of interest rates of different maturities.

[29]See also Section 3.3.3 for an exposition of the Fisher effect.

[30]See e.g. Fama (1984, 1990) and Campbell & Shiller (1987, 1991), Mishkin (1992), among others, for an analysis of the US term structure.

[31]Further studies suggest that interest rate dynamics are nonlinear and apply a threshold model to the term structure, e.g. Pfann, Schotman & Tschernig (1995).

Alternatively, the predictive performance of the term structure for the development of the inflation rate (e.g. Tzavalis & Wickens, 1996, for the US) or the market expectations with respect to future inflation (e.g. Schich, 1996; Gerlach, 1997; Kirchgässner & Savioz, 1995, for Germany) is analysed. This is highly relevant for the policy of the Bundesbank as the conduct of monetary policy relies on the development of indicators of current and expected future macroeconomic conditions. The Bundesbank monitors the development of the term structure as an indicator for inflationary expectations (see e.g. Schich, 1996).[32]

The focus of the empirical analysis in Section 3.4 is on long-run monetary relationships. Therefore, the studies investigating the long-run relationships between different interest rates are of special interest. Cointegration methodology has been used in recent studies in a single-equation as well as systems context.[33]

There is mixed evidence with respect to the expectations hypothesis tested on German term structure data. The different results of studies cited below indicate sensitivity of the analysis to the periodicity of the data. Analysing monthly data, Hassler & Nautz (1998) and Wolters (1995b) do not find empirical evidence for a long-run (1,-1) relationship between short-term and long-term rates as suggested by the expectations theory of the term structure, neither for the capital market nor for a spread between money market and capital market. An exception are the stationary long-run spreads in the money market (Wolters, 1995b).

Wolters & Hassler (1998) investigate the expectations hypothesis of the German money market for the period after German reunification and find pairwise cointegration relationships between the interest rates in a four-dimensional system. Nautz & Wolters (1996) find that long-term credit rates are cointegrated with long-term bond rates of the same maturity, whereas the long-run relationship between interest rates of different maturity suggested by the expectations theory of the term structure is rather weak. Analysing the term structure in the German bond market, Wolters (1998) finds cointegration between interest rates of different maturities analysing monthly data, but only between three interest rates and not a (1,-1) relationship as predicted by the expectation theory.

In contrast, a cointegration relationship between the bond rate and the three months money market rate has been found by Hansen (1997), Juselius (1996) and Beyer (1998b) using quarterly data in higher dimen-

[32] An analysis of the relationship between the term structure of interest rates and monetary policy can be found in Kugler (1996).

[33] Wallace & Warner (1993), for example, employ the Johansen procedure to test for the term structure of interest rates and the long-run Fisher effect using US data.

sional systems including additional long-run relationships.[34]

The interest rate data employed, the dimension of the system as well as the sample period analysed in the mentioned studies vary, but only Wolters et al. (1998) test the same data as in the present study for a similar sample period and find a stationary spread between the bond rate and the weighted own interest rate of M3 using an ADF test.

To conclude, evidence for a stationary spread between a short- and a long-term interest rate as a necessary condition for the expectations hypothesis of the term structure to hold for Germany, can be found in quarterly but not in monthly data.

3.3.3 The Fisher Effect

3.3.3.1 Is the Real Interest Rate Stationary?

The Fisher equation, originating in Fisher's (1930) work, states that the nominal interest rate r_t is given by

$$r_t^m = r_{r,t}^m + \pi_t^m - \epsilon_t,$$

where $r_{r,t}^m$ denotes the *ex ante* real interest rate for period t to $t+m$, π_t^m is the inflation rate from time t to $t+m$ and the forecast error $\epsilon_t = \pi_t^m - E_t\pi_t^m$ (i.e. the inflation rate for m periods ahead minus the expectation of the inflation rate m periods ahead based on information up to t) under rational expectations is white noise and therefore must be stationary.[35] Assuming $m = 1$, results in an *ex-post* real interest rate represented as $r_t - \pi_t$ that can be tested. If the *ex-post* real interest rate $r_t - \pi_t$ is found to be stationary, the *ex ante* real interest rate $r_{r,t}$ is stationary, as the above equation for $m = 1$ can be reformulated to $r_{r,t} = r_t - \pi_t + \epsilon_t$ (see e.g. Mishkin, 1992).

The relationship between the inflation rate and the interest rate considered in the present analysis is Fisher's original weak form which implies that markets do not suffer from money illusion but from fiscal illusion.[36]

---

[34]Hardouvelis (1994) analyses the term structure of the Group of Seven (G7) countries using quarterly data. He concludes that the empirical findings , except for the US, do not contradict the expectations hypothesis. Therefore, he also finds evidence for the expectations hypothesis for Germany.

[35]The ex ante real interest rate can thus be rewritten as $r_t^m = r_{r,t}^m + \pi_t^m - \epsilon_t = r_{r,t}^m + \pi_t^m - (\pi_t^m - E_t\pi_t^m) = r_{r,t}^m + E_t\pi_t^m$.

[36]Some studies on the Fisher effect have also accounted for the effects of taxes on financial returns, e.g. Darby (1975). The tax-adjusted Fisher equation (assuming a full Fisher effect) can be represented as $r_t = \frac{1}{1-\tau}r_{r,t} + \frac{1}{1-\tau}\pi_t - \frac{1}{1-\tau}\epsilon_t$, where the coefficients exceed unity since $0 < \tau < 1$ (τ: tax rate). For details, see e.g. MacDonald & Murphy (1989).

However, due to specific features of the German tax system as well as to tax evasion it is difficult to adequately account for the effects of tax on interest income.[37] Therefore, tax effects have not been considered in the empirical analysis in Section 3.4.

Mishkin (1992) also pointed out that empirical evidence supports the existence of a long-run rather than a short-run Fisher effect as has already been suggested by Fisher (1930). Further, arguments have been brought forward in the literature for a Fisher relation between the short-term yield and the inflation rate as well as the long-term interest rate and the inflation rate. The theoretical arguments to consider long-term as well as short-term interest rates in the Fisher equation are presented in Wallace & Warner (1993). They basically argue that if the expectations hypothesis of the term structure holds and the real short-term rate is stationary, then the long-term real interest rate must also be stationary. In the empirical analysis in Section 3.4, the Fisher equation of the form

$$r_{r,t} = r_t - \pi_t$$

will be tested separately as well as together with the interest rate spread and the money demand equation.[38]

The stationarity of real interest rates is relevant for the transmission process of monetary policy because it is an important determinant of investments and savings. Furthermore, stationarity of real interest rates is consistent with theories of financial market behaviour such as the consumption based capital asset pricing model (CCAPM) (Rose, 1988; Crowder & Hoffman, 1996). The predictive power of nominal interest rates for the inflation rate (e.g. Fama, 1975) is also relevant in the context of monetary policy. The behaviour of the real interest rate may also mirror a regime shift in monetary policy. In that context, Garcia & Perron (1996) and Canzoneri & Dellas (1998) have analysed whether changes in the operating procedure of a central bank have affected the real interest rate.

3.3.3.2 Recent Empirical Evidence for the Fisher Effect

Numerous empirical studies of the Fisher equation have been presented in the literature. During the past decade, empirical analyses have

[37] An analysis focusing on tax effects on interest rates can be found in, e.g., Stehle, Jaschke & Wernicke (1998).

[38] The model of the Fisher relation is set up between the inflation and interest rate based on the same horizon. However, this aspect is difficult to take into account in the context of the empirical analysis in Section 3.4, since both the long- as well as the short-term interest rate are weighted interest rates.

been carried out in the framework of cointegration methodologies. For example, the Fisher effect has been analysed and tested by MacDonald & Murphy (1989) for the US, Belgium, Canada and the UK within the single-equation procedure suggested by Engle & Granger (1987). They find some evidence of cointegration with respect to the Fisher equation for the fixed exchange rate period, but no evidence for the floating exchange rate period. Mishkin (1992) finds mixed results for the US employing the Engle-Granger procedure, as the existence of the Fisher effect depends on the sample period considered. In contrast, the study by Wallace & Warner (1993) applies the Johansen procedure and finds strong evidence of a long-run Fisher effect within a two-dimensional system for the US and Japan, and also for Germany. Rose (1988) concludes from his empirical analysis that the real interest rates in the US are nonstationary. This result has been questioned by Crowder & Hoffman (1996), who have carried out an extensive empirical analysis of the US Fisher relation. Crowder & Hoffman (1996) also review the analysis by Evans & Lewis (1995) who apply the Dynamic OLS (DOLS) method for cointegration analysis suggested by Stock & Watson (1993). Crowder & Hoffman (1996) ask why the projection of interest rates on inflation yields vastly different conclusions than the projection of inflation on interest rates in Evans & Lewis (1995). They criticize that the single-equation procedure used by these authors depends on the normalization prior to estimation. In contrast, Crowder & Hoffman (1996) illustrate the advantage of using Johansen's maximum likelihood approach in this context by a series of Monte Carlo experiments.

Furthermore, Hoffman & Rasche (1996) find a Fisher relation simultaneously with a money demand relation and an interest rate spread within a system of five variables, applying the Johansen procedure to US data.

For Germany, Kirchgässner & Wolters (1990, 1993) do find rather weak empirical evidence for the Fisher effect in an analysis based on monthly data and set into a single-equation context. In contrast, Yuhn (1996) has tested the Fisher relation for the short-term as well as the long-term interest rate for several countries in a multivariate framework using the Johansen procedure. For German data, he finds evidence for the stationarity of the real interest rate. Overall, it seems that empirical evidence for the Fisher relation is more likely to be found in a systems approach rather than in a single-equation framework. Following the findings of Crowder & Hoffman (1996), the systems approach is considered to be the appropriate methodological choice to deliver plausible results.

3.4 A Cointegrated System: Empirical Analysis of Long-Run German Monetary Relations

In this section, long-run relationships between the variables of a monetary system for Germany as suggested by economic theory (see Section 3.3) and their stability are tested. The empirical analysis is similar to Hubrich (1999), but is based on an extended sample period, i.e. the sample period is 1979(1) to 1997(4) instead of 1979(1) to 1994(2).[39] The results for the extended period will be compared with the results presented in Hubrich (1999) to demonstrate the robustness of the specification with respect to a variation of the sample.

The initial VAR comprises the variables real money M3, real GNP, the inflation rate, a long-term and a weighted short-term interest rate. The sample of the present study covers the period of the European Monetary System (EMS), i.e. it starts in 1979(1) and ends in 1997(4).

The variables are chosen to allow an identification of a money demand function to analyse the stability of money demand.

For the analysis of the time series properties, the Perron test (Perron, 1989) is applied in addition to the Augmented Dickey Fuller (ADF) test as the structural break of German reunification has to be taken into account. In contrast to most comparable analyses, multivariate tests of the order of integration of the variables are applied additionally. The univariate procedures test the null hypothesis of nonstationarity, whereas stationarity of the variables is tested under the null within the multivariate approach.

The aim of this chapter is to analyse long-run relationships between variables that influence the conduct and transmission process of German monetary policy. Therefore, a systems cointegration approach that allows for more than one cointegration relationship and for testing restrictions on the cointegration space is applied.

Johansen's LR test as well as the trend-adjusted LR tests suggested by Saikkonen & Lütkepohl (2000b) are carried out to test for the cointegration rank. These tests have been found to perform best in small sample simulation comparisons with a broad range of recently suggested systems cointegration tests in Chapter 2. As the inclusion of the step dummies

[39] In contrast to the present study, the analysis in Hubrich (1999) is based on GNP data constructed from preliminary biannual data.

changes the asymptotic distribution of Johansen's LR test statistic, new critical values have been simulated.[40]

Johansen's multivariate approach of cointegration analysis has been chosen to analyse the long-run relationships further as it facilitates testing for weak exogeneity of the variables and also allows to test overidentifying restrictions on the cointegration vectors. Economic theory suggests three long-run relationships between the variables of the monetary system: a money demand relation, an interest rate spread and a Fisher relation. Stationarity of these long-run relationships essential for monetary policy is simultaneously tested and not rejected for a period including German reunification. In that context, it is of considerable importance whether the structural break of German reunification can be modelled by dummy variables. The analysis extends studies on German monetary policy presented in the literature that concentrate on one of the long-run relationships considered in this thesis. The robustness of the cointegration vectors found for the EMS period with respect to a variation of the sample as well as model specification is analysed.

3.4.1 The initial VAR

3.4.1.1 Data

This study is based on quarterly data covering the sample period from 1979(1), when the European Monetary System was founded, to 1997(4), thereby including German reunification.[41] As the Bundesbank announces targets for M3 (since 1988), this monetary aggregate has been taken as a proxi for the money stock. Real money in logarithms is denoted as m^r.

Further variables are included to capture the notion of money demand for transaction purposes as well as the demand for money as a part of portfolio choice decisions (see Section 3.3.1). The real GNP (in prices of 1991) is taken as a transaction or income variable and its logarithm is denoted as y^r; the logarithm of the deflator of GNP (nominal GNP divided by real GNP multiplied by 100), denoted p, represents the development of the prices.

Both a long-term and a short-term interest rate are employed in the analysis. The long-term interest rate is an average long-term interest rate for bonds in circulation (*Umlaufsrendite inländischer Inhaberschuldvers-*

[40] In Hubrich (1999) empirical critical values have additionally been generated using a bootstrap procedure to account for the small sample analysis. These are presented for comparison.

[41] The end of the sample is determined by the availability of data at the time when the analysis was carried out.

chreibungen), representing opportunity costs for holding money. The short-term interest rate is a constructed interest rate representing the own rate of M3. The interest rates on the individual components of M3 are weighted according to their respective contribution to M3. For the period 1979(1) - 1990(2) the yield on time deposits is weighted by 0.25 while the yield on saving deposits is weighted by 0.41. For the period 1990(3) - 1997(4) the weights are 0.30 and 0.33, respectively. The interest rates of currency and sight deposits are assumed to be zero. The weighted interest rate is employed rather than the three-months FIBOR which has often been used in earlier studies on German money demand. However, the three-months FIBOR does not really represent the own rate of M3 and can lead to an implausible sign of the coefficient. The interest rates, denoted r^l and r^s, are the same as those used by Wolters et al. (1998). However, in the present analysis they enter the model separately to be able to test the cointegration relationship between the interest rates in the multivariate framework.[42]

The inflation rate (Δp) is incorporated in the model. This variable may represent opportunity costs of holding money with respect to investments in real capital.[43] No currency substitution term is introduced into the model, as the Deutsche Bundesbank (1995a) finds very little evidence for currency substitution for a sample period including German reunification. Our own analyses, not presented here, for a sample until 1994(2) with various terms to represent the substitution between domestic and foreign currency, confirm this result.

The data are taken from the data bases of the Bundesbank and the German Institute for Economic Research (DIW).[44] Quarterly seasonally unadjusted data are employed in the analysis. Fig. 3.1 and 3.2 graphically display the time series and their differences. Fig. 3.1 clearly shows the structural break of German reunification in real money M3 and real GNP. This is taken into account in testing for unit roots as well as in the system's analysis.

[42]Issing & Tödter (1995) also use a weighted short-term interest rate, but their weights of the interest rates on the different components of M3 do not change after German reunification.

[43]Wolters & Lütkepohl (1997, Appendix A) show that the inflation rate could possibly influence the long-run demand for real money even if it is not assumed to influence desired nominal money demand, i.e. if opportunity costs of investment in real capital are assumed not to exist. Under such an assumption, the inflation rate can be interpreted as an indicator for the adjustment process whether it might be in nominal or real terms.

[44]For further details on the data, see Appendix B.

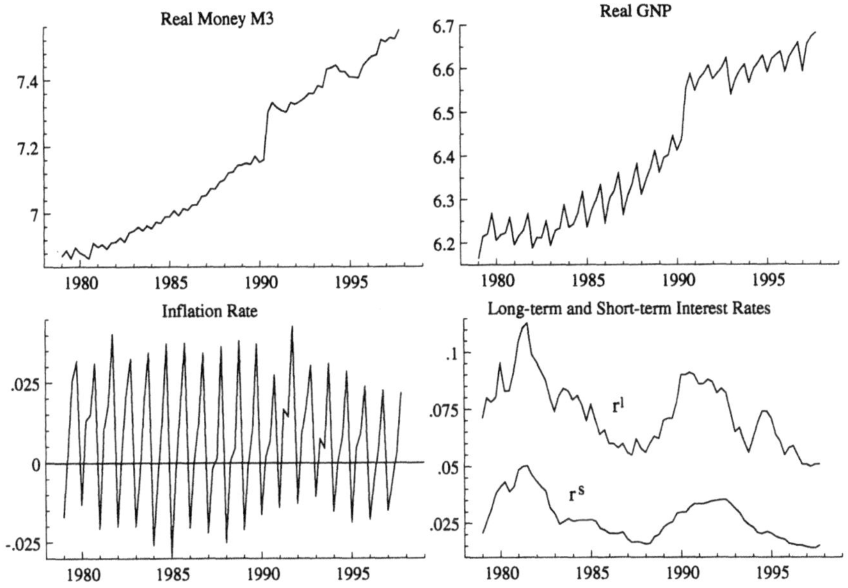

Figure 3.1: Data in Levels

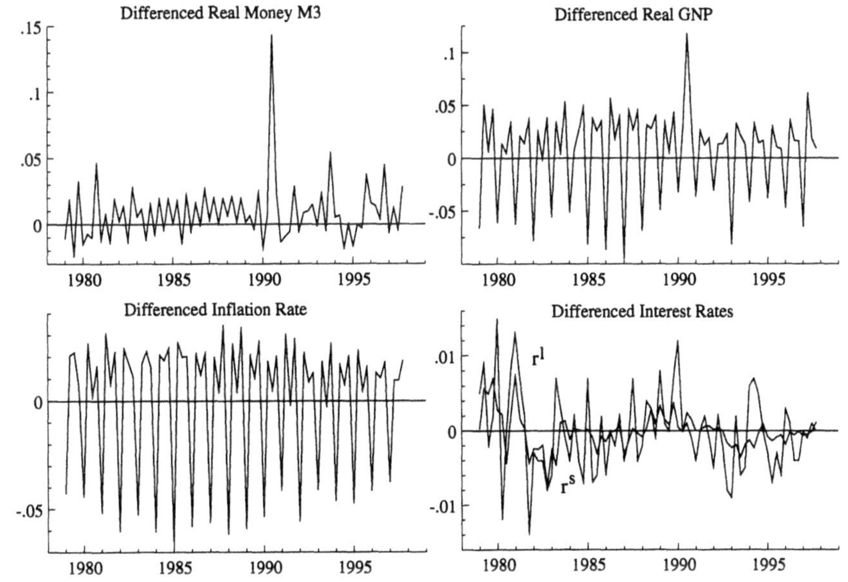

Figure 3.2: Data in Differences

3.4.1.2 Univariate Tests for Unit Roots

Univariate tests for unit roots can also be considered within the framework set up in Section 2.2. In this context, y_t is a one-dimensional process. Therefore,

$$y_t = \mu_0 + \mu_1 t + x_t, \qquad t = 1, 2, \ldots, \tag{3.4.1}$$

where μ_0 is the mean, μ_1 the slope parameter and t a linear trend. The quantity x_t is again an unobservable process with zero mean that is assumed to be of finite order and can be represented as

$$\Delta x_t = \rho x_{t-1} + \sum_{j=1}^{p-1} \gamma_j \Delta x_{t-j} + \varepsilon_t, \qquad t = 1, 2, \ldots. \tag{3.4.2}$$

In this framework, different procedures to test for a unit root in a time series can be considered.

A standard method of testing for a unit root in an observed time series is the Augmented Dickey Fuller (ADF) test. To construct a similar test, i.e. a test that is independent of unknown nuisance parameters,[45] a constant and/or trend has to be included depending on the time series tested. Three different models can be considered to test for a unit root (see Fuller, 1976; Dickey & Fuller, 1979). The null hypothesis of nonstationarity, i.e. $\rho = 1$ is tested against the alternative of stationarity ($\mu_0 = \mu_1 = 0$ in (3.4.1)), stationarity around a mean (μ_0 arbitrary, $\mu_1 = 0$ in (3.4.1)) as well as trend-stationarity (μ_0, μ_1 arbitrary in (3.4.1)). Lagged differences are included when testing for unit roots to avoid autocorrelation in the error term. The t-type test statistic is $(\hat{\rho}-1)/\hat{\sigma}_{(\hat{\rho})}$ and has a non-standard distribution depending on the deterministic terms.[46] Critical values, originally computed by D.A. Dickey, are reported in Fuller (1976), Banerjee et al. (1993) or MacKinnon (1991), for example.

Other unit root tests have been suggested, e.g. the nonparametric procedure proposed by Perron (1988) and Phillips & Perron (1988),[47] or a test for the null of stationarity by Kwiatkowski, Phillips, Schmidt & Shin (1992).[48]

---

[45] For the concept of similar tests, see Kiviet & Phillips (1992).

[46] According to Monte Carlo studies presented in Dickey, Bell & Miller (1986) the t-type statistic tends to display better size properties than the statistic $T(\hat{\rho} - 1)$.

[47] This procedure suggests to correct for the autocorrelation applying a nonparametric correction to standard statistics.

[48] An overview of various unit root tests is presented, e.g. in Banerjee et al. (1993), Hassler (1994) and Hamilton (1994).

A large number of simulation studies has presented mixed evidence. For example, the simulation evidence presented in Schwert (1989) shows that nonparametric unit root tests might perform very poorly in some cases. In general, no unit root test seems to outperform the others in all situations. However, the ADF test is most commonly used in applied research and will be applied in the following to test for a unit root in the variables (except for m^r and y^r, see below).

However, as can be seen from Figures 3.1 and 3.2 German reunification represents a clear structural break in the real money series as well as in real GNP, an extension of the Augmented-Dickey-Fuller methodology suggested by Perron (1989) has to be applied to account for this structural break. The underlying model can be written as follows:

$$y_t = \nu_0 + \nu_1 t + \rho y_{t-1} + \delta_1 Dstep_t + \delta_2 DT_t + \sum_{i=1}^{p-1} \gamma_i \Delta y_{t-i} + \varepsilon_t. \qquad (3.4.3)$$

$Dstep_t$ is a step dummy which is zero before the breakpoint T_1 and one thereafter. DT_t is a trend dummy, i.e. a linear trend is multiplied with $Dstep_t$.

Perron (1989) considers three different types of structural breaks using the following models: Model (A) allows for a shift in the level of the series (δ_2=0 in (3.4.3)), model (B) for a break in the trend of the series (δ_1=0 in (3.4.3)) and model (C) allows for both a shift in the level as well as a break in the trend of the series ($\delta_1 \neq 0, \delta_2 \neq 0$ in (3.4.3)). The critical values, tabulated in Perron (1989), do not only depend on the characteristics of the break in a series, but also on the time of the breakpoint relative to the sample length considered.[49]

To test for the null hypothesis of non-stationarity of the real monetary aggregate and of the GNP, an auxiliary regression is carried out where m^r and y^r are regressed on a constant (c), a linear deterministic trend (t), a step dummy ($Dstep90$ is 1 after 1990(2) and 0 otherwise) and seasonal dummies (SD). This approach corresponds to model (A) in Perron (1989)) which allows for an exogenous change in the level of the series under the null hypothesis.[50]

The critical values for these tests are taken from Perron (1989) for $\lambda = 0.6$ where λ is the time of the break in the series relative to the total sample period.

[49] The critical values of the Perron test are larger in absolute terms than the critical values of the standard ADF test since the additional dummy variables are taken into account.

[50] For both time series, real money as well as real GNP, it is assumed that only a shift in the level of the series has occurred.

Table 3.1: Perron Test / Augmented Dickey Fuller Test, Sample Period 1979(1)-1997(4)

variable (in log)	auxiliary regression	k	t-statistic	critical value (5%)
m^r	$c, t, Dstep90, SD$	1	−2.61	$-3.76^{(1)}$
y^r	$c, t, Dstep90, SD$	5	−1.99	$-3.76^{(1)}$
Δp	c, SD	4	−1.57	−2.90
r^l	c	4	−2.01	−2.90
r^s	c	5	−2.57	−2.90
Δm^r	$c, D903i, SD$	1	−8.0**	−2.90
Δy^r	$c, D903i, SD$	4	−3.21*	−2.90
$\Delta\Delta p$	c, SD	3	−59.5**	−2.90
Δr^l	c	1	−7.38**	−2.90
Δr^s	c	5	−5.04**	−2.90

Notes: k : is the number of lagged differences included in the DF/ADF test (according to the highest significant number of lags with a maximum of 5 lags); ** and *: significance at a 1% and 5% level; critical values from MacKinnon (1991), except for (1): critical value of Model(A) in Perron (1989), $\lambda = 0.60$, c: constant, t: linear trend, $Dstep90$: step dummy (1 after 1990(2), 0 otherwise, $D903i$: impulse dummy (1 in 1990(3)), SD: seasonal dummies

Table 3.1 presents the results of the unit root tests.[51] A maximum of five lags has been chosen. k denotes the longest significant lag according to the t-statistic. A constant, seasonal dummies as well as an impulse dummy that is one in 1990(3) to account for the outlier due to German reunification (see Figure 3.2) have been included in the ADF test for the differenced series Δm^r and Δy^r. The introduction of an impulse dummy does not change the asymptotic distribution of the test statistics. A constant and seasonal dummies have been included when applying the ADF test for the inflation rate and the change in the inflation rate, whereas for the interest rates only a constant has been incorporated.

Long-run price homogeneity of the money demand has been assumed in this study, since the demand for money is a demand for real balances

[51] PcGive 9.0 and PcFiml 9.0 by Doornik & Hendry (1997a, 1997b) have been used for the computations presented in this Chapter, except for the trend-adjusted LR test in Section 3.4.2 that has been implemented in GAUSS.

(see e.g. Laidler, 1993, pp 160–163). Other studies, e.g. Gaab (1996), have found a price elasticity close to one using Johansen's maximum likelihood procedure. Wolters et al. (1998) also assume long-run price homogeneity of the demand for money. Therefore, the following analysis has been carried out under the working assumption of long-run price homogeneity of money demand.

The null hypothesis of non-stationarity is not rejected for the level of all time series, but is rejected for the differenced series. Thus, for all variables included in the empirical analysis presented here, i.e. real money, real income, the inflation rate and the long- as well as the short-term interest rate, the unit root tests suggest that they are I(1).

The multivariate tests presented later clearly reject stationarity of the level variables, thereby confirming these results.

3.4.1.3 Model Specification

Known Structural Breaks Several procedures have been presented in the unit root and cointegration literature to detect breaks in the deterministic trend of time series. However, in the empirical analysis presented here, German reunification represents a known structural break. Therefore, the question arises how this structural break can best be modelled.

Tests against smooth transition regression (STR) models, as suggested by Teräsvirta (see Section 2.6), have been applied by Wolters et al. (1998) for the set of variables included in the empirical analysis in this chapter. In a single-equation framework, they find no evidence for non-linearity with respect to the break of German reunification, but that the break can be modelled using dummy variables. On the basis of these results and since multivariate STR models are not yet available, the structural break of German reunification has been modelled including dummy variables in the system analysed below.

In a first step, an unrestricted vector autoregressive model (VAR) in levels, including the variables m^r, y^r, r^l, r^s and Δp, is estimated. The deterministic terms include a constant and seasonal dummies and the model is estimated with as well as without a linear deterministic trend. Results for model selection, misspecification and stability tests are very similar for the model with and without trend. In the following two sections the results presented are on the basis of a model without a linear trend. An impulse dummy ($D903i$), which is one in 1990, third quarter, and null otherwise has been introduced into the VAR model to account for the structural break of reunification. Furthermore, a step dummy

(*Dstep*90), which is zero until 1990, second quarter, and one thereafter has been introduced to allow for a change in the velocity trend.

An additional impulse dummy, *D*933*i*, which is one in 1993, third quarter, and zero otherwise, has been included to account for the effects of the turbulences within the European Monetary System in the summer of 1993 which led to the widening of the currency bands from ±2.25% to ±15.0% on August 2nd. To model negative money growth, which occured for the first time in the period from 1994(3) to 1995(4), as well as a steep increase in long-term interest rates relative to short-term interest rates, a step dummy (*D*9495) is introduced, which is one from 1994(3) to 1995(4) and zero otherwise.[52] Although this dummy variable improves the model, it should be noted that the results presented in the following sections also hold without this variable.

Model Selection As discussed in Chapter 2, model selection criteria should be applied to choose the lag order in a first step before testing for the cointegration rank. Since none of the criteria can be considered to be generally optimal, the results for different order selection criteria are presented.

Table 3.2: Lag Order Selection

	Schwarz Criterion	Hannan Quinn Criterion	Akaike Criterion
VAR(4)	−47.451	−50.029	−52.429
VAR(3)	−47.945	−50.063	−51.498
VAR(2)	−48.868	−50.525	−51.996
VAR(1)	−49.171	−50.368	−51.875

The Schwarz (SC), the Hannan-Quinn (HQ) and the Akaike (AIC) criterion have been applied for the system considered in this empirical analysis (see Table 3.2). With a maximum lag length of $k = 4$, the Schwarz criterion indicates a VAR order of $k = 1$, the Hannan-Quinn

[52] A similar dummy variable multiplied with the spread of the interest rates has been employed by Wolters & Lütkepohl (1997) and Lütkepohl & Wolters (1998).

criterion selects a VAR order of $k = 2$, whereas the Akaike criterion suggests a lag order of $k = 4$. A lag order of four is not considered for further analysis, since the number of parameters relative to the sample size would be very large. As misspecification tests show high autocorrelation for the VAR(1) and as an F-test of model reduction rejects the reduction of a VAR(2) to a VAR(1) model at a 1 % significance level, a VAR order of $k = 2$ is chosen.

Table 3.3: Single Equation Misspecification Tests, VAR(2), 1979(1)-1997(4)

Test	AR 1-4	Normality	ARCH 4
m^r	0.851	0.209	1.757
	[0.52]	[0.90]	[0.15]
y^r	6.155**	1.509	3.078*
	[0.0001]	[0.47]	[0.02]
r^l	2.377	5.381	0.733
	[0.50]	[0.272]	[0.38]
r^s	1.125	15.414**	0.431
	[0.36]	[0.0004]	[0.79]
Δp	2.237	0.455	0.369
	[0.06]	[0.80]	[0.83]

Note: p-values in brackets; ** and * denote the significance at a 1% and 5% level, AR 1-4: autocorrelation tests from lags 1 to 4, ARCH 4: tests for autoregressive conditional heteroscedasticity with order 4

3.4.1.3.1 Misspecification and Stability Tests. Misspecification tests are carried out for the VAR(2) chosen as the basis for further analysis. The misspecification tests presented include single equation misspecification tests (LM tests for autocorrelated residuals (Harvey, 1990), tests for normality (Doornik & Hendry, 1997a), LM tests for autocorrelated squared residuals (ARCH test Engle, 1982)) and vector tests as described in Doornik & Hendry (1997a) (vector error autocorrelation test, vector normality test).[53]

[53] Tests for normality are chi-square tests, the other tests are in F form.

Table 3.4: Vector Tests, VAR(2), Sample Period 1979(1)-1997(4)

Test	test statistic	p-value
AR 1-4	1.319	0.053
Normality	22.16*	0.014

Note: * denotes significance at a 5% level, AR 1-4: autocorrelation tests from lags 1 to 4

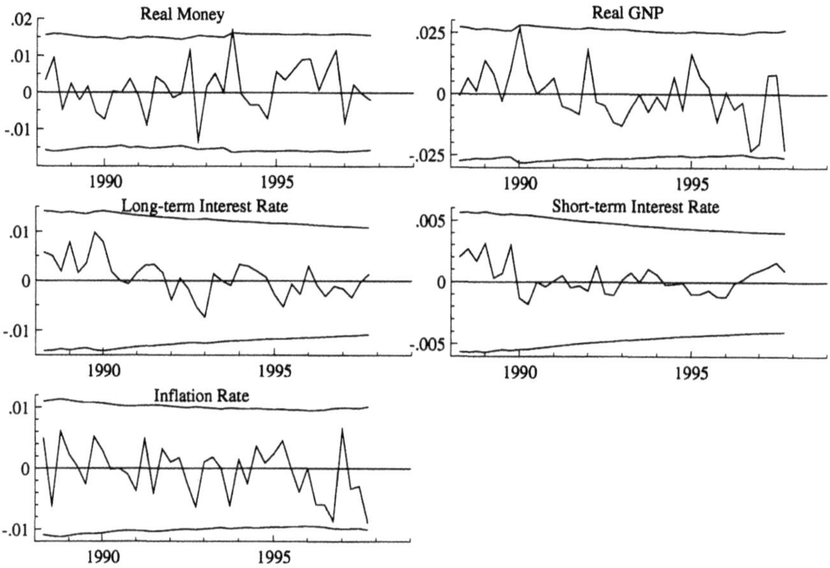

Figure 3.3: 1-Step Residuals (Recursive Estimation Statistics)

Single equation misspecification tests for the VAR(2) reveal no misspecification except some autocorrelation in the income equation and rejection of normality with respect to the short-term interest rate equation at a 5% significance level (see Table 3.3). The autocorrelation problem in y^r probably occurs because the real side of the economy is not sufficiently modelled in the system. However, this study concentrates on monetary relationships. Also, the number of variables should be held small as the power of cointegration tests is reduced considerably for a large parameter to observations ratio Ho & Sørensen (1996, and Chapter

2 of this thesis). The vector tests for misspecification do not exhibit any autocorrelation, but normality is rejected at a 5% significance level (see Table 3.4). Since the Johansen procedure does not strictly depend on the normality assumption (Lütkepohl, 1991, p.359), however, the VAR(2) is taken as the basis for further analysis.[54]

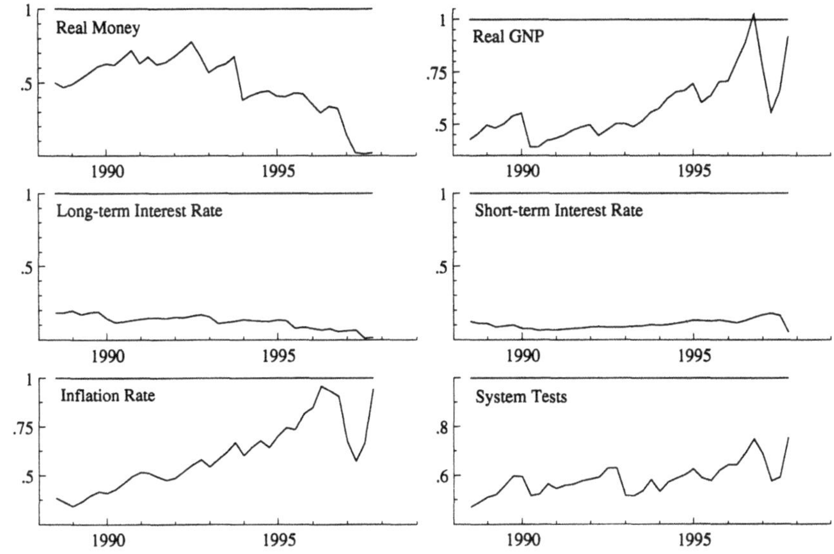

Figure 3.4: Break-point Chow Test (1.0: 5% significance level)

For the investigation of the parameter constancy, the 1-step residuals and the break-point Chow test (Chow, 1960) based on recursive estimation have been computed. For these recursive procedures the coefficients of the dummy variables are fixed at the full sample values (Doornik & Hendry, 1997a, p.30). The 1-step residuals (Fig. 3.3) only indicate a slight problem in the money equation in the end of 1993. This is probably due to the special factors, e.g. changes in tax regulations, that have led to an increase of money demand during the winter of 1993 (see Deutsche Bundesbank, 1994). Introducing an additional impulse dummy for 1993(4) does not improve the fit of the VAR substantially and has not been included in the model presented. The break-point Chow tests are scaled by the critical values of the 5% significance level and none of their

[54] Alternative suggestions in case of a non-normal distribution are reviewed in Hubrich et al. (2000).

values exceeds unity (Fig. 3.4) except a slight problem in the income equation in the end of 1996. Thus, the VAR is considered to be stable.

Furthermore, the recursive eigenvalues of the VAR have been calculated. They are derived by solving the eigenvalue problem as, for example, in (2.3.5) in Chapter 2 for each sample $t = M, \cdots, T$ recursively, where M is the size of the initial sample of the recursive estimation (see Doornik & Hendry (1997a, p.226) and Hansen & Johansen (1993)). Again, the coefficients of the dummy variables are fixed at the full sample values. These recursive eigenvalues are depicted in Fig. 3.5. All recursive eigenvalues are reasonably stable over time, which is a further indication for the stability of the system. The graphs show that there are at least three cointegration vectors. The last eigenvalue is nearly zero, whereas the fourth eigenvalue is not much smaller than the third. We come back to this result in the context with the evaluation of the cointegration rank tests.

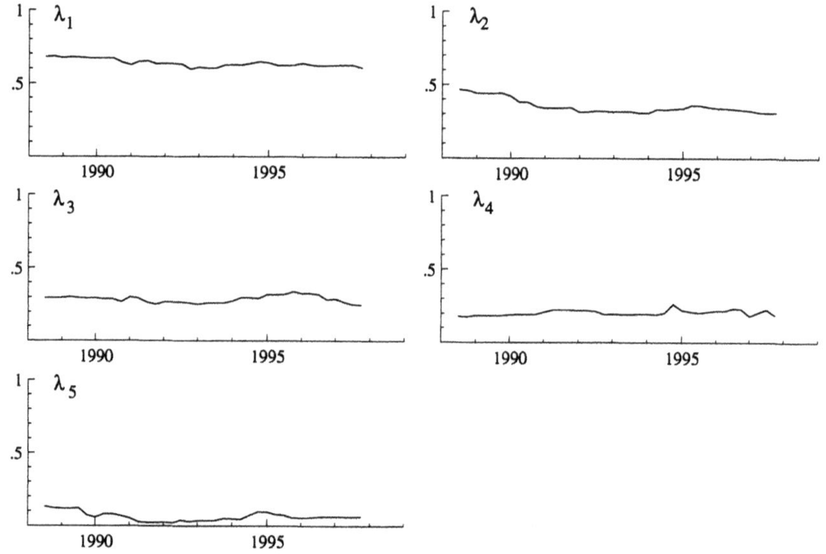

Figure 3.5: Recursive Eigenvalues

3.4.2 Tests for the Cointegration Rank

A wide range of different cointegration rank tests have been presented in Chapter 2 and have been compared with respect to their small sample performance. The likelihood ratio rank test proposed by Johansen and the trend adjusted likelihood ratio test suggested in a series of papers by Saikkonen and Lütkepohl have been found to perform best. Therefore, these tests are employed in the following.

Most of the simulation comparisons presented in Chapter 2 have focussed on the specific case where the deterministic part of the DGP consists of mean and linear trend terms because of their particular importance for the asymptotic theory and for the small sample performance of systems cointegration tests. However, seasonal dummy variables have to be included in a model when working with seasonally unadjusted data and shift dummies might be introduced in a system to account for structural breaks in the time series.

As considered in Section 2.6, Johansen & Nielsen (1993) show that the asymptotic distribution of the maximum likelihood trace tests changes in the presence of dummy variables in the cointegration relation. Therefore, Nielsen (1994) provides the program DisCo for the simulation of asymptotic critical values for very general specifications of deterministic terms. In contrast, Lütkepohl & Saikkonen (1999c) and Saikkonen & Lütkepohl (2000c) provide LM type and LR tests where the series are adjusted for deterministic terms before carrying out tests for cointegration (see Section 2.3). They extend their approach to allow for dummy variables in addition to a constant and a trend (see Saikkonen & Lütkepohl, 2000b, see also Section 2.5.7).

This approach is applied in the following in addition to the Johansen test. In the present empirical study dummy variables, i.e. impulse dummies, step dummies as well as seasonal dummies, have been introduced into the system.[55]

In Section 2.6, the likelihood ratio tests favoured from the broad simulation comparison of tests allowing for arbitrary mean and trend parameter in the DGP have been compared in a small sample comparison on the basis of a DGP that is generated from the system analysed empirically in this chapter. The results show considerably lower power of the trend-adjusted LR test in comparison with Johansen's original LR test. This difference in performance also becomes apparent in the empirical results presented below.

[55]The extension of the framework given in Saikkonen & Lütkepohl (2000b) to a model including two impulse and two step dummies as well as seasonal dummies is presented in Appendix A.

3.4.2.1 The Johansen Rank Test

The results of Johansen's LR^+ test based on the VAR(2) for the sample period 1979(1) - 1997(4) and the underlying eigenvalues are presented in Table 3.5.

The impulse dummy $D903i$ is included in the EC representation unrestrictedly. Therefore, $D903i$ accounts for the outlier in the differenced series due to the structural break of reunification and also for the structural break in the long-run relationships between the levels of the variables. In addition, a step dummy ($Dstep90$), which is zero until 1990, second quarter, and one thereafter, has been included in the VAR model. This step dummy is restricted to enter the long-run relationship in the cointegration analysis, allowing for different changes in y^r and m^r after German reunification and, therefore, a change in velocity trend.[56]

Table 3.5: Johansen's LR Test, 5-dimensional VAR(2), Det. Terms: Constant, Linear Trend, SD, $D903i$, $D933i$, $Dstep90$ and $D9495$, Estimation Period: 1979(1)-1997(4)

eigenvalues	H_0: rank=r_0	LR^+ trace statistic	95% (critical values without dummies$^{(1)}$)	95% (critical values with dummies$^{(2)}$)
0.61	$r_0 = 0$	166.30	87.3	107.4
0.35	$r_0 = 1$	93.88	63.0	79.2
0.30	$r_0 = 2$	61.45	42.2	54.8
0.24	$r_0 = 3$	34.33	25.3	34.4
0.16	$r_0 = 4$	13.61	12.3	17.2

Note: critical values are the 95% quantiles of the asymptotic distribution: (1) Osterwald-Lenum (1992), (2) simulated with the program DisCo (Nielsen, 1994)

The trace test supports a cointegration rank of four if the critical values from Osterwald-Lenum (1992) are applied.[57] However, as available

[56] The terminology restricted/unrestricted has been used in this context in accordance with Johansen (1995, p.214-216) and Doornik & Hendry (1997a, p.281).

[57] Small sample corrections of the test statistics as suggested by Ahn & Reinsel (1988) have not been applied here, because it was found in a simulation study by Cheung & Lai (1993) that these modifications are inadequate in parts of the parameter space (see also Section 2.5.1).

asymptotic critical values are not appropriate because step dummies are restrictedly included in the model, the program DisCo by Nielsen (1994) has been used to simulate the 95% quantiles of the asymptotic distribution of the test statistic where a constant enters the model unrestrictedly and the two step dummies as well as the linear trend are restricted to the long-run.[58]

As would have been expected, the simulated critical values displayed in Table 3.5 are higher than the critical values from the asymptotic distribution that does not account for the dummy variables. Therefore, $r_0 = 3$ is not rejected if these critical values are applied. It should be noted, however, that the test statistic for $r_0 = 3$ is very close to the critical value so that $r_0 = 3$ is nearly rejected.[59]

3.4.2.2 Trend-adjusted LR Tests

It has been pointed out in Section 2.6 that the asymptotic distribution of the trend-adjusted LR statistic is invariant with respect to the introduction of dummy variables, as these are estimated and subtracted from the data before computing the test statistic. The trend-adjusted LR test based on Saikkonen & Lütkepohl (2000b) allows for a constant and linear trend in the DGP in addition to dummy variables.

In contrast to the original LR^+ test, the trend-adjusted LR statistic, LR_{ta}^{GLS}, indicates a cointegration rank of $r = 1$ (see Table 3.6).[60] This result for LR_{ta}^{GLS}, i.e. a lower rank than found with Johansen's LR^+ test, might not be that surprising considering the simulation results in Section 2.6. Furthermore, lower power of the trend-adjusted tests than Johansen's LR tests in sequential procedures based on small samples has been found by Müller (1998). In any case it can be argued that the higher cointegration rank of $r = 3$ should be chosen for further analysis on the basis of both test results.

---

[58]Simulations have been based on 10000 replications and 400 observations. Impulse dummies are not included in the simulations because they do not change the asymptotic distribution of the test statistic.

[59]Note, that PcFiml handles any deterministic terms, e.g. dummy variables, that are restricted to the long-run by including them unlagged in the cointegration relation (Doornik & Hendry, 1997a, p.226).

[60]A similar result is found if a dummy variable that is one from 1994(2) to 1995(3) is included instead of $D9495_t$, that is one from 1994(3) to 1995(4). That approach is comparable to an unlagged inclusion of $D9495_t$ in the Johansen test.

Table 3.6: Trend-adjusted LR Test, 5-dimensional VAR(2), Det. Terms: Constant, Linear Trend, *SD*, *D903i*, *D933i*, *Dstep90* and *D9495*, Estimation Period: 1979(1)-1997(4)

H_0: rank=r_0	LR_{ta}^{GLS} trace statistic	95% (asymptotic)
$r_0 = 0$	71.15	65.7
$r_0 = 1$	38.51	45.1
$r_0 = 2$	21.40	28.5
$r_0 = 3$	9.69	15.9
$r_0 = 4$	6.13	6.8

Note: critical values are the 95% quantiles of the asymptotic distribution, Lütkepohl & Saikkonen (1999c), Table 1

3.4.2.3 Rank Test for a Model without a linear Trend

Model selection criteria can be applied to choose between models with different deterministic terms (see Chapter 2). Applying the model selection criteria *SC*, *AIC* and *HQ*, different models with and without a linear trend and with as well as without different dummy variables are compared. LR tests for a linear trend have also been applied.[61] Since the results from the model selection criteria and the LR tests provide mixed evidence with respect to the inclusion of the trend, Johansen's rank test is carried out for a model without trend in the cointegration relation as well.[62] Here, again a cointegration rank of $r = 3$ is found if the critical values allowing for the step dummies are applied (Table 3.7). This shows that the result $r = 3$ of Johansen's rank test is even robust with respect to the exclusion of the deterministic trend term. In contrast to the LR^+ test allowing for a linear trend, the result of a cointegration rank of three is not ambiguous. A result of $r = 3$ is also in accordance with economic theory that suggests three possible hypotheses for cointegration vectors.[63]

[61] If the step dummy *Dstep90* is included, an LR test rejected the exclusion of a linear trend from the system. However, if the step dummy was excluded from the system, restricting the linear trend to zero is not rejected.

[62] The trend-adjusted LR test is not available for deterministic terms including constant and dummy variables, but no linear trend.

[63] The largest cointegration rank tested is $r_0 = n - 2 = 3$ because a linear trend in the data is allowed by the specification of the model. This excludes the possibility of $n = r$, i.e. n stationary variables. Therefore, $r_0 = n - 1$ is not a reasonable null

Table 3.7: Johansen's LR Test, 5-dimensional VAR(2), Det. Terms: Constant, *SD*, *D903i*, *D933i*, *Dstep90* and *D9495*, Estimation Period: 1979(1)-1997(4)

eigenvalues λ_i	H_0: rank=r_0	LR^i trace statistic	95% (without dummies[1])	95% (with dummies[2])
0.605	$r_0 = 0$	141.00	68.5	87.5
0.310	$r_0 = 1$	70.50	47.2	62.4
0.248	$r_0 = 2$	42.28	29.7	40.9
0.188	$r_0 = 3$	20.60	15.4	22.9

Note: critical values are the 95% quantiles of the asymptotic distribution: (1) Osterwald-Lenum (1992), (2) simulated with the program DisCo (Nielsen, 1994)

Table 3.8: Johansen's LR test, 5-dimensional VAR(2), Det. Terms: Constant, *SD*, *D903i*, *D933i* and *Dstep90*, Estimation Period: 1979(1)-1994(2)

H_0: rank=r_0	LR^i trace statistic	95% (asymptotic/ with dummy)	95% (bootstrap)
$r_0 = 0$	126.50	79.7	94.5
$r_0 = 1$	67.99	56.1	65.1
$r_0 = 2$	41.34	36.2	38.4
$r_0 = 3$	16.24	19.8	23.4

Note: critical values are the 95% quantiles of the asymptotic distribution, simulated with the program DisCo (Nielsen, 1994), and the 95% quantiles derived within a bootstrap procedure

Bootstrap procedures have been suggested to generate small sample critical values and have also been analysed in simulation studies. Van Giersbergen (1996) considers a parametric bootstrap procedure in their analysis. The Monte Carlo studies provide mixed evidence with respect to the usefulness of bootstrap procedures. There seems to be no formal

hypothesis (see also Saikkonen & Lütkepohl, 2000b).

proof of an improved convergence rate in case of the bootstrap procedure. However, the results for the bootstrap procedure carried out in Hubrich (1999) for the sample from 1979(1) to 1994(2) are presented in Table 3.8 for comparison. In addition to the critical values simulated using DisCo, the empirical critical values have been derived from a parametric bootstrap procedure allowing for a restricted step dummy ($Dstep90$), unrestricted impulse dummies ($D903i$ and $D933i$) and a constant as well as seasonal dummies.[64] Based on these critical values, the trace test indicates a cointegration rank of three. Thus, the result is the same as on the basis of the asymptotic critical values simulated using DisCo (see Table 3.8). The result for this shorter sample also suggests that the finding of a cointegration rank of three is robust against a variation in the sample.[65] Also, the recursive eigenvalues presented in Figure 3.5 indicated at least three cointegration relations.

Concluding from all results, a cointegration rank of $r = 3$ is assumed in the following. The model without a linear deterministic trend in the cointegration relation is underlying the following analysis to avoid problems with the interpretation of the linear trend.

It has been argued that a linear trend should be included in the cointegration relation a priori to model e.g. the technological progress in the economy (see Doornik et al., 1998). On the other hand, the inclusion of a trend might lead to a problem of interpretation. An output gap relation has often been suggested as an economically plausible cointegration relation including the linear trend. The relation between the deviation of output from its trend, $y - t$, and, say, the real interest rate has sometimes been considered to represent a cointegration relation (see e.g. Juselius, 1996, 1998). This implies that $y - t$ is nonstationary. The question arises whether this is a plausible assumption. It would mean, that the output might diverge infinitely from its trend, rather than fluctuating around it. This implication appears to be economically implausible.

Furthermore, since the tests for the cointegration rank lead to the same result whether a linear trend is included in the cointegration relation or not, and since no further misspecification due to the exclusion of the linear trend from the system is indicated, the following analysis is based on a system without a linear trend in the cointegration relation.

[64] The bootstrap procedure has been based on 10000 replications.

[65] For further analysis of the robustness of the presented results, see Section 3.4.3.2.

3.4.3 Testing Restrictions on the Cointegration Space

The Johansen procedure facilitates tests of restrictions on the adjustment coefficients α and the cointegration vectors β. In these tests the likelihood function is maximized allowing for restrictions on α and/or β. Consistent with the result of the test for the cointegration rank, the likelihood ratio tests for testing restrictions are carried out under the assumption of three cointegration vectors.

3.4.3.1 Weak Exogeneity and Stationarity of the Variables

In single-equation procedures for estimation or testing it is implicitly assumed that the knowledge of the data generating process of the explanatory variables would not provide any information for the parameters of interest. Richard (1980) and Engle, Hendry & Richard (1983) have introduced and developed different concepts of exogeneity of a variable with respect to a particular parameter.[66]

Here, we are interested in the concept of weak exogeneity. Weak exogeneity of regressors ensures that there is no loss of information about parameters of interest from analysing only the conditional distribution. z_t is weakly exogenous for a set of parameters if inference concerning these parameters can be made conditional on z_t without any loss of information relative to using the joint density of y_t and z_t. One might be interested in estimating e.g. the demand for money within a single-equation approach. However, to receive efficient estimators from single equation estimation of a money demand function by OLS, the precondition of weak exogeneity of the variables in the monetary system (except of money) would have to be fulfilled. Otherwise the cointegration parameters are inherently cross-linked between the equations, i.e. single equation estimation will lead to a loss of information (Banerjee et al., 1993, p.252).

Results from testing weak exogeneity of the variables in the economic system considered here are presented in Table 3.9. Testing weak exogeneity of the variables means testing each equation in the system for the presence of any cointegration relation. More precisely, zero restrictions on the adjustment coefficients α of each cointegration relation are tested under the assumption $r = 3$. The null hypothesis $\alpha_{j,1} = \alpha_{j,2} = \alpha_{j,3} = 0$

[66]These concepts include weak, strong and super exogeneity, also see e.g. Banerjee et al. (1993), Ericsson et al. (1998) or Ericsson & Irons (1994).

for the 3 cointegration relations is tested where j denotes the jth equation of the system ($j = 1, \cdots, n$ with $n = 5$).[67]

Weak exogeneity of the variables of the economic system is rejected for the EMS period except for real income y^r and the short-term interest rate r^s, but the p-value for r^s is near the 5% level.[68] Therefore, of the variables that would enter a money demand equation, weak exogeneity is strongly rejected for the inflation rate. Thus, modelling German money demand using dynamic single equation estimation by OLS would result in inefficient estimators. A systems approach is, therefore, preferred over a single equation approach to account for all three cointegrating relationships. Furthermore, fully efficient estimators are obtained by applying the systems approach. Moreover, the aim of the study is not only the analysis of the German money demand, but also the analysis of the conditions for German monetary policy in general characterized by the long-run relationships between important macro-economic variables. Further, this approach could be extended to model the interdependencies within the system.

Some studies, especially Juselius (1996), have drawn policy conclusions from the weak exogeneity results. However, this might be problematic since the analysis of α coefficients does not take short-run relations into account. If, for example, it is concluded from the weak exogeneity of income that there is no long-run effect of money, this conclusion might, in fact, be wrong since it does not take into account the effects of the long-run monetary relation that might influence the income equation via the change in the inflation rate.

Table 3.9: Weak Exogeneity Tests: Restrictions on α

Variable	m^r	y^r	r^l	r^s	Δp
χ^2-statistic	11.509**	3.747	8.005*	7.539	33.297**
	[0.009]	[0.29]	[0.05]	[0.06]	[0.00]

Note: p-values in brackets, ** and * denote results significant at 1% and 5%, respectively

[67] The switching algorithm applied to carry out these tests will be described in Section 3.4.3.2.

[68] If restrictions on the three cointegration vectors derived in the following section are additionally taken into account, weak exogeneity is neither rejected for r^s nor for r^l.

3.4.3.2 Tests of Long-Run Relationships Suggested by Economic Theory

From the Johansen procedure the cointegration space is estimated consistently. The adjustment coefficients α and the cointegration vector β can be determined once r is known and normalization or identification restrictions are specified. However, the statistical identification and normalization of α and β is arbitrary and any non-singular linear combinations of these matrices provide equivalent representations. Therefore, identifying restrictions have to be derived from economic theory. These economically plausible restrictions can be tested within the Johansen approach conditional on the selected cointegration rank.

Johansen and Juselius (e.g. Johansen & Juselius, 1994) have suggested some tests for that purpose.[69] However, Doornik (1995) argues that it is often more convenient to specify the restrictions directly on the elements of β. Therefore, he proposes a testing method that allows general restrictions on α and β, possibly non-linear.

Various algorithms for estimation under general restrictions are implemented in PcFiml 9.0 (Doornik & Hendry, 1997a, p.230/231), the program which has been used for the analysis in this chapter. In the present analysis a non-linear switching algorithm has been chosen, i.e. the maximization of the likelihood function switching between β and α fixing the other.[70]

Exact identification is possible if the number of restrictions s_i in the ith cointegration relation is equal to $s_i = r-1$ just identifying restrictions as well as one normalization on each vector are imposed. Exact identification does not change the likelihood function, and testing exactly identifying restrictions is therefore not possible (Johansen & Juselius, 1994). Only overidentifying restrictions can be tested, i.e. when more than $r-1$ restrictions are imposed on each equation (Johansen & Juselius, 1994). However, it is possible to test some hypotheses on the parameters without necessarily identifying the system first (Johansen, 1995, p.72). Such a strategy has been applied below testing stationarity of the variables as well as single cointegration vectors. If all r cointegration relations are

---

[69] For an overview of different tests, see Doornik & Hendry (1997a, p.227).

[70] Although it is not known that the switching algorithm converges to the global maximum of the likelihood function, the switching algorithm works in practice. It converges fast if given suitable starting values and is chosen because it is reasonably robust. With respect to the algorithms implemented in PcFiml, the starting values are determined from the unrestricted parameters, assuming rank r. For details on numerical optimization and numerical accuracy, see Doornik & Hendry (1997a, pp 247).

tested simultaneously, identification has to be checked. Identification in cointegrated systems has been discussed in Johansen (1995, p.76). Checking identification is implemented in the software package PcFiml 9.0 employed for the computations in this chapter (Doornik & Hendry, 1997a, p.232). Since quite general restrictions are imposed here, the generic identification check of Doornik (1995) is used.

Conditional likelihood ratio test statistics, for a given cointegration rank, follow asymptotically a standard χ^2 distribution. Some studies have also presented simulation results for small samples. Podivinsky (1992) and Jacobson (1995) find relatively modest size distortions based on very simple 2- or 3-dimensional DGPs with one cointegration vector and few lags. Therefore, they have a small number of parameters to be estimated. Jacobson, Vredin & Warne (1998) consider a four-dimensional DGP with r=2, two exogenous variables and a set of seasonal dummies. They find severe size distortions for a sample size typical for macroeconomic applications. Podivinsky (1998) analyses the effect of misspecification of the number and nature of cointegration vectors on the LR tests for cointegration. Podivinsky (1998) finds that critical values may be inappropriate when applied to sample sizes of 100 or smaller. Gredenhoff & Jacobson (1998) suggest a bootstrap procedure for testing restrictions to avoid size distortions in small samples. The power of this procedure is similar to that of the asymptotic test.

Johansen (1998) derives a Bartlett corrected likelihood ratio test for some linear restrictions to improve the finite sample approximation. In simulations he finds that the correction improves the size of the tests, but that a correction factor under less restrictive assumptions has to be developed.

Despite the small sample problems pointed out in several simulation studies, it seems reasonable to apply the asymptotic tests of linear restrictions in empirical studies as long as an applicable finite sample correction has not been suggested. Therefore, tests of restrictions on cointegration vectors are applied to the five variable system analysed in this chapter.

Stationarity Tests First, stationarity of each variable in the system has been tested under the assumption of $r = 3$. Stationarity of money, income and inflation is postulated in the respective hypotheses H_1 (see Table 3.10), testing single cointegration vectors normalized on the respective variable and restricting all other parameters to zero. Stationarity of each interest rate is tested in the hypotheses H_1 and H_2 for the interest rates. Stationarity is rejected by the LR tests for all variables in the system. These results are consistent with the results of the univariate tests of the order of integration. Note, that, in contrast to the Augmented Dickey Fuller and Perron test, the null hypothesis is stationarity here. As stationarity is rejected, this is an even stronger indication that the variables are actually non-stationary. To test stationarity of y^r and m^r the step dummy for reunification has been included.

Table 3.10: LR Tests for Cointegration Relationships (r=3), Sample Period: 1979(1) - 1997(4)

		m^r	y^r	r^l	r^s	Δp	$Dstep90$	$D9495$		p-value
money										
$H_1 : \beta'=$	(	1	0	0	0	0	-0.47	0	)	0.003**
$H_2 : \beta'=$	(	1	-1	0	0	0	-0.11	0	)	0.02*
income										
$H_1 : \beta'=$	(	0	1	0	0	0	-0.36	0	)	0.0007**
interest rates										
$H_1 : \beta'=$	(	0	0	1	0	0	0	0	)	0.008**
$H_2 : \beta'=$	(	0	0	0	1	0	0	0	)	0.01**
$H_3 : \beta'=$	(	0	0	1	-1	0	0	0	)	0.05*
$H_4 : \beta'=$	(	0	0	1	-1	0	0	0.001	)	0.26
inflation										
$H_1 : \beta'=$	(	0	0	0	0	1	0	0	)	0.01**
$H_2 : \beta'=$	(	0	0	0	0	1	0.002	0	)	0.008**
$H_3 : \beta'=$	(	0	0	1	0	-3.90	0	0	)	0.53
$H_4 : \beta'=$	(	0	0	0	1	-2.69	0	0	)	0.70
$H_5 : \beta'=$	(	0	0	1	0	-4	0	0	)	0.69
$H_6 : \beta'=$	(	0	0	0	1	-4	0	0	)	0.39
$H_7 : \beta'=$	(	0	0	1	0	-4	0.006	0	)	0.87
$H_8 : \beta'=$	(	0	0	0	1	-4	0.002	0	)	0.27

Note: ** and * denote significance at a 1% and 5% level respectively; the p-values correspond to the LR test of the respective restriction; the values with modulus unequal to 1, 0 or 4 are freely estimated

Single Cointegration Vectors Further, Table 3.10 displays restrictions tested on single cointegrating vectors using likelihood ratio tests. These restrictions are motivated by economic theory of the long-run relationships between the variables considered in this analysis (see the discussion in Section 3.3).

According to these theoretical considerations money demand can be viewed to be mainly a function of income and of opportunity costs of holding money as well as an own interest rate of money. Since testing restrictions on a single cointegration vector requires more than $r - 1$ restrictions for the vector to be overidentified, the money demand relation will be tested simultaneously with the other relationships, later.

In the context of testing single cointegration vectors, the velocity of money, which has a considerable impact on the transmission process of monetary policy, can be tested. Stationarity of the inverse velocity $(m^r - y^r)$ including the step dummy for reunification (H_2) is tested and rejected (see Table 3.10). This result is considered to be plausible as velocity in Germany is assumed to have a negative trend (see e.g. Issing & Tödter, 1995).[71] The hypothesis of income homogeneity of money demand will be considered again when simultaneous tests of three cointegration vectors are carried out.

The expectations theory of the term structure suggests a long-run one-to-one relationship between long-term and short-term interest rates as shown in Section 3.3 under the assumption of rational expectations and stationarity of the term premium.

Table 3.10 shows that a long-run (1,-1) relationship between the two interest rates is not rejected by Johansen's likelihood ratio test if a dummy is introduced for a period where a sharp increase in the long-term interest rate is not paralleled by the short-term interest rate (H_4). This result indicates that the spread is stationary. Therefore, the necessary condition for the expectations theory of the term structure to hold is fulfilled.

In the following, the Fisher equation of the form

$$r_{r,t} = r_t - \pi_t + \epsilon_t$$

is tested, where $\pi_t = 4 \times \Delta p_t$ represents the full Fisher effect. The coefficient of the inflation rate has been transformed to account for using a quarterly inflation rate and interest rates measured in percent per annum in the analysis. The coefficient of -4 for the quarterly inflation rate implies a (1,-1) cointegration vector between annual nominal interest rates

[71] Wolters et al. (1998) have argued that this negative trend can be captured by the inflation rate introduced in the money demand relation.

and the annual inflation rate. Arguments have been brought forward in the literature for a Fisher relation between the short-term yield and the inflation rate as well as the long-term interest rate and the inflation rate.

Therefore, the Fisher equation has been tested for r^l and r^s presented in Table 3.10 (H_3 to H_8). Stationarity of a vector including the inflation rate and the long-term (H_3) or the short-term interest rate (H_4) is not rejected. The absolute value of the estimated coefficients of the inflation rate is smaller than 4. This would mean that the interest rates do not fully account for the inflation rate. The coefficients indicate a higher increase in the long-term interest rate in comparison with the short-term interest rate if inflation increases, and therefore plausibly suggest a higher term premium for investments in long-term assets. However, the full Fisher effect is tested and not rejected for both the short-term and the long-term interest rate at a 5% significance level whether the step dummy for reunification is excluded (H_5 and H_6) or included (H_7 and H_8). This result is consistent with the stationarity of the spread because the Fisher effect has to hold for the short-term interest rate as well as for the long-term interest rate if the expectations theory of the term structure holds.

Simultaneous Tests Based on the results of the LR tests of restrictions on single cointegrating vectors, simultaneous tests of economically reasonable long-run relationships have been carried out. The most interesting results are presented in Table 3.11. All hypotheses tested include a long-run monetary relationship, a cointegration vector for the two interest rates and a third cointegrating vector including the inflation rate and the long-term interest rate.

In the first hypothesis H_1^* the money relation is normalized on the monetary aggregate and the interest rate spread is included as one variable in the money demand relation, i.e. the coefficients of the interest rates are restricted to have the same size but opposite sign. The second cointegration vector is normalized on the long-term interest rate and the coefficient of the short-term interest rate is restricted to -1, as suggested by the expectations theory. Other variables except $D9495$[72] are excluded. The third vector of the first hypothesis representing the full Fisher effect is normalized on the long-term interest rate, and the coefficient for the inflation rate is restricted to -4. The step dummy $Dstep90$ has been included to allow for a structural break in the real interest rate due to reunification.

[72]For an explanation of $D9495$, see Section 3.4.1.3.

Table 3.11: LR Tests of Simultaneous Restrictions on $\hat{\beta}'$, r=3, 1979(1) - 1997(4)

		m^r	y^r	r^l	r^s	Δp	$D9495$	$Dstep90$	p-value
H_1^*	$\beta_1'=$	(1	-1.23	1.84	-1.84	7.28	-0.04	-0.02)	
	$\beta_2'=$	(0	0	1	-1	0	0.01	0)	0.45
	$\beta_3'=$	(0	0	1	0	-4	0	0.005)	
H_2^*	$\beta_1'=$	(1	-1	-2.11	2.11	10.77	-0.003	-0.09)	
	$\beta_2'=$	(0	0	1	-1	0	0.01	0)	0.047*
	$\beta_3'=$	(0	0	1	0	-4	0	0.005)	

Note: ** and * denote significance at a 1% and 5% level respectively; the p-values correspond to the LR test of the simultaneous restrictions; the values with modulus unequal to 1, 0 or 4 are freely estimated

These three vectors (H_1^*) are simultaneously tested and are not rejected.[73] It should be noted that H_1^* in Table 3.11 is not identified, since on the first cointegration vector only one restriction is imposed. However, additional restrictions could be imposed. If the coefficient of income is additionally restricted to one to test for income homogeneity of money, the LR test rejects (see H_2^*). Furthermore, it is of interest whether the velocity trend in Germany has changed after reunification, i.e. whether the step dummy $Dstep90$ is significant in the money demand relation.

In Table 3.12 the parameter estimates are presented for the case where the interest rate spread as well as the dummy $D9495$ is excluded from the money demand relation, thereby restricting those variables to zero that enter the second cointegration relation. The resulting system with three cointegration relations is identified and therefore the t statistics[74] for the estimated coefficients are also presented.

It becomes apparent that $Dstep90$ is not significant, i.e. that it can

[73] Consistent with the expectations hypothesis of the term structure, a similar result is found if r^s instead of r^l is included in the Fisher relation.

[74] The t statistics for the coefficients of the identified system are calculated on the basis of the standard errors provided by PcFiml 9.0 (Doornik & Hendry, 1997a, p.283).

Table 3.12: LR Tests of Simultaneous Restrictions on $\hat{\beta}'$, r=3, Sample Period: 1979(1) - 1997(4), Identified

		m^r	y^r	r^l	r^s	Δp	$D9495$	$Dstep90$	p-value
H_2^{id}	$\beta_1'=$	(1	-1.23	0	0	6.69	0	-0.02)	
			(20.5)			(9.16)		(1.0)	
	$\beta_2'=$	(0	0	1	-1	0	0.02	0)	0.56
							(5.0)		
	$\beta_3'=$	(0	0	1	0	-4	0	0.005)	
								(1.0)	

Note: * denotes significance at a 5% level; the p-value corresponds to the LR test of the simultaneous restrictions; the values with modulus unequal to $1, 0$ or 4 are freely estimated; t-statistics are in brackets

be excluded from the money demand relation as well as from the Fisher relation. Therefore, money and income seem to have changed to the same extent due to reunification, meaning that the velocity trend has not changed. Further, there has been no break in the real interest rate due to reunification. Table 3.13 presents the estimates of the cointegration relations of the identified system with additional exclusion restrictions on $Dstep90$.

The economic interpretation of the cointegration relations in Section 3.4.3.3 is based on the non-identifying restrictions imposed in H_3^* in Table 3.13 since the resulting cointegration vectors allow a more plausible interpretation of the money demand equation. The vectors presented in H_3^* in Table 3.13 are compatible with the identified set of cointegration vectors H_3^{id} in Table 3.13 that is not rejected.

Sensitivity Analysis Several small sample simulation studies have found that results of the Johansen procedure - of the rank test as discussed in Chapter 2 and the tests for the cointegration relations as discussed in the introduction of Section 3.4.3.2 - depend on the sample size as well as on the lag order of the VAR underlying the analysis. Therefore, the robustness of the empirical results presented above is discussed in the following.

Estimates and tests within Johansen's maximum likelihood procedure have been carried out for smaller samples, e.g. for samples from 1979(1)

Table 3.13: LR Tests of Simultaneous Restrictions on $\hat{\beta}'$, r=3, Sample Period: 1979(1) - 1997(4)

		m^r	y^r	r^l	r^s	Δp	$D9495$	$Dstep90$	p-value
H_3^{id}	$\beta_1'=$	(1	-1.28	0	0	5.96	0	0)	
			(64.0)			(8.64)			
	$\beta_2'=$	(0	0	1	-1	0	0.01	0)	0.56
							(2.50)		
	$\beta_3'=$	(0	0	1	0	-4	0	0)	
H_3^*	$\beta_1'=$	(1	-1.28	2.86	-2.86	6.39	0.04	0)	
	$\beta_2'=$	(0	0	1	-1	0	0.01	0)	0.47
	$\beta_3'=$	(0	0	1	0	-4	0	0)	

Note: ** and * denote significance at a 1% and 5% level respectively; the p-values correspond to the LR test of the simultaneous restrictions; the values with modulus unequal to 1, 0 or 4 are freely estimated; H_3^{id} represents an identified set of restrictions, H_3^* an unidentified set of restrictions; t-statistics are in brackets

until 1994(2) (Hubrich, 1999) as well as until 1996(4). The result of the Johansen rank test is robust with respect to a variation of the sample size. Also, the three specific cointegration vectors found for the sample period 1979(1) to 1997(4) appear to be very robust in smaller samples with only small variations in the coefficients (see e.g. the results from Hubrich (1999) presented in Table 3.14). Further, residual based ADF tests have been carried out to check stationarity of the cointegration vectors. Nonstationarity is rejected for all three cointegration relationships and, therefore, the multivariate result is confirmed.

Recursively computed tests for cointegration restrictions (Doornik & Hendry, 1997a, p.283) are also carried out and are presented in Figure 3.6. They do not indicate any rejection of the restrictions in a range of smaller samples. Thus, the cointegration relations found in the empirical analysis presented in this chapter display considerable robustness over different samples.

Table 3.14: LR Tests of restrictions on β', r=3, Sample Period: 1979(1) - 1994(2)

		m^r	y^r	r^l	r^s	Δp	$Dstep90$	p-value
H_3^* :	β_1'=	(1	-1.188	3.777	-3.777	7.053	-0.025)	
	β_2'=	(0	0	1	-1	0	0)	0.146
	β_3'=	(0	0	0	1	-4	0.013)	
H_4^* :	β_1'=	(1	-1	3.327	-3.327	10.43	-0.098)	
	β_2'=	(0	0	1	-1	0	0)	0.034*
	β_3'=	(0	0	0	1	-4	0.014)	

Note: * denotes significance at a 5% level; the p-values correspond to the LR test of the simultaneous restrictions; the values with modulus unequal to $1, 0$ or 4 are freely estimated

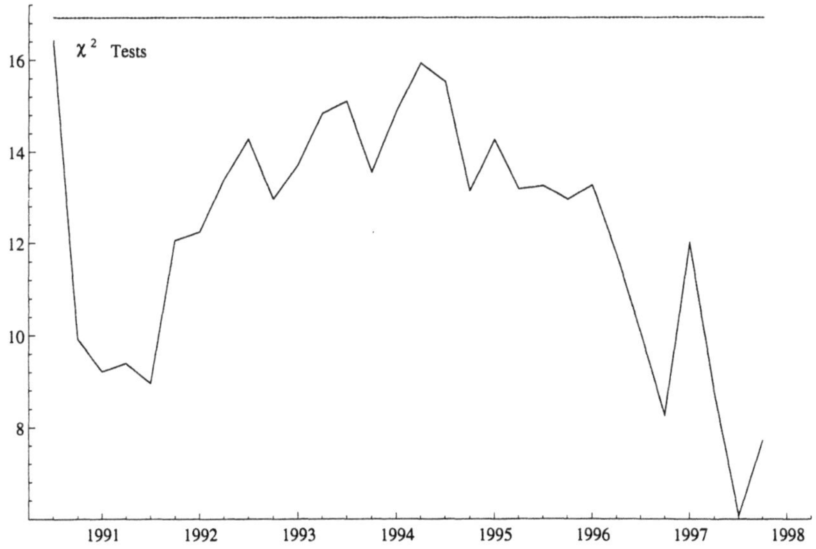

Figure 3.6: Recursive Tests of Simultaneous Restrictions on Cointegration Vectors (H_3^{id}, Table 3.13, $r = 3$)

Table 3.15: LR Tests of Simultaneous Restrictions on $\hat{\beta}'$, r=3, 1979(1) - 1997(4)

		m^r	y^r	r^l	r^s	Δp	$Dstep90$	p-value
H^{od}	$\beta_1'=$	(1	-1.26	0	0	4.19	0)	
			(63.0)			(5.90)		
	$\beta_2'=$	(0	0	1	-1	0	0)	0.16
	$\beta_3'=$	(0	0	1	0	-4	0)	

Note: the p-values correspond to the LR test of the simultaneous restrictions; the values with modulus unequal to 1, 0 or 4 are freely estimated; t-statistics are in brackets

The outcome of the Johansen procedure for the VAR(2) has not been compared with results based on other lag orders as the misspecified VAR(1) should not be taken as the basis for further tests since misspecification can lead to size distortions of the tests. On the other hand, higher order VAR models include too many parameters relative to the number of observations. Furthermore, the sensitivity of the results with respect to the inclusion of dummy variables is tested. In a system without $D9495$ a cointegration rank of $r = 3$ is found as well. Table 3.15 shows that even in such a system with the coefficient of the step dummy restricted to zero three cointegration vectors are not rejected. However, the system including the dummy variable $D9495$ has been preferred because of its better fit.

Since the step dummy is not significant in the model with $D9495$ (Table 3.12) and it can also be restricted to zero in a model without $D9495$ for the same sample period (Table 3.15), the cointegration rank is tested in a system without $Dstep90$ and without $D9495$. The cointegration rank is found to be $r = 3$ as before. In such a system, the three cointegration relationships are not rejected on a 5% significance level, either.

3.4.3.3 The Cointegration Vectors: Economic Interpretation

The interpretation of the cointegration vectors is based on the restrictions imposed in H_3^* in Table 3.13 where the dummy variable *Dstep*90 is excluded from the cointegration vectors since it is found to be insignificant. As mentioned earlier, the first cointegrating vector can be interpreted as a long-run money demand relationship

$$EC_1 : m^r = 1.28y^r - 2.86(r^l - r^s) - 6.39\Delta p - 0.04D9495$$

All coefficients in this cointegration vector show the theoretically expected signs. The income coefficient is 1.28 and therefore exceeds unity. This result justifies the derivation of the annual target for M3 announced by the Bundesbank which is based on the assumption that velocity is falling in Germany. An income coefficient greater than one can be due to wealth effects (monetary wealth does grow faster than the GNP) or can be caused by an increase of the unobservable transaction volume which is stronger than the increase in GNP (see e.g. Issing & Tödter, 1995).[75]

The result is similar to the estimates that Wolters et al. (1998) obtained from a single equation approach. The coefficient derived within the Johansen procedure is smaller than the coefficient of the inflation rate in the single equation estimate of Wolters et al. (1998), but the coefficient of the interest rate spread representing opportunity costs of holding money is nearly the same as that obtained from the single equation approach by these authors, using the same variables.[76]

The second cointegrating vector is the spread between the long-term and the short-term interest rate:

$$EC_2 = r^l - r^s + 0.01D9495$$

This result is consistent with the expectations theory of the term structure and implies that expectations of future short-term rates essentially determine the current long-term interest rates. This is in contrast to the findings of other authors (see Section 3.3) for data with different observation frequency. The different sample periods as well as frequency of the data might explain the differences in results. An ADF test based

[75]The estimated adjustment coefficient of the first cointegration vector is $\alpha = -0.09$. The coefficient is significant and the negative sign implies that money is adjusting in case of a deviation from the long-run equilibrium represented by the first cointegration vector. Therefore, this long-run relationship can be interpreted as a money demand relation.

[76]However, the income elasticity can be restricted to one in Wolters et al. (1998).

on the sample period considered in the present study also rejects non-stationarity of the spread.

The third cointegrating vector can be interpreted to represent the Fisher relation:

$$EC_3 = r^l - \pi \qquad (\pi = 4 \times \Delta p)$$

where π is the annual inflation rate, i.e. $\pi = 4 \times \Delta p$ with Δp representing the quarterly inflation rate. r^l represents the annual yields on bonds in circulation. The full long-run Fisher effect, where the coefficient of the annual inflation rate is unity, states that under rational expectations the inflation rate is the dominant force to determine the nominal interest rate. Notably, Yuhn (1996) found a long-run relationship between the inflation rate and a short-term as well as a long-term interest rate, analysing German data within a systems approach. Note, that the step dummy *Dstep*90 has been found to be insignificant (Table 3.12). Therefore, German reunification has not led to a change in the German real interest rate.

To summarize, three stable long-run relationships between the variables considered suggested by economic theory are confirmed by the empirical analysis, i.e. a money demand relationship, the interest rate differential and a relationship reflecting the long-run Fisher effect.

3.4.4 Conclusion

In the empirical analysis in this chapter, three long-run relationships influencing German monetary policy are identified within the framework of the Johansen procedure. Johansen's rank test indicates a cointegration rank of $r = 3$, i.e. a rank larger than the one found applying the trend-adjusted LR test suggested by Saikkonen & Lütkepohl (2000b). Further analysis is based on $r = 3$ since Johansen's test has higher power in situations with several dummy variables.

Weak exogeneity of the variables of the money demand equation is rejected by the data. Restrictions have been tested on the estimated cointegration relations using likelihood ratio tests. These tests indicate that there are three stable cointegration relationships between the variables of the money demand system: a money demand relationship, the yield spread and a Fisher equation. These relationships are found to be stable over the period of the EMS where the structural break of German reunification can be modelled by dummy variables and a change in the weights of the own interest rate.

The result of this analysis is remarkable as these three long-run relationships suggested by economic theory can be identified simultaneously within the system considered. The stable long-run relationships obtained in this study are crucial for German monetary policy, because the stability of the long-run money demand relationship as well as the long-run Fisher effect and the long-run relationship between short- and long-term interest rates have important implications for the conduct and transmission process of monetary policy.

In addition to its monetary target M3, the Bundesbank also monitors other indicators, e.g. the term structure of interest rates, to obtain information on potential inflationary risks. Therefore, one interesting result of this study is the finding of a stationary interest rate spread. Further, the finding that money demand in Germany is still stable after reunification (if the structural break is modelled) is an important argument that the policy of monetary targeting was an appropriate strategy for the Bundesbank. Possible implications for the monetary policy of the ECB are discussed in Chapter 4.

Chapter 4

Concluding Remarks and Outlook

4.1 Small Sample Performance of Systems Cointegration Tests

For empirical analyses in a cointegration framework it is of great importance to detect the number of cointegration relations in a system of variables, since further analysis, e.g. causality or impulse response analysis, are based on the cointegration rank found. Therefore, the relative small sample properties of alternative cointegration rank tests help to guide the methodological choice in applied research. In Chapter 2 a wide range of systems cointegration tests has been compared with respect to their underlying assumptions as well as their small sample performance.

One objective has been to present the tests in a general unifying framework in order to compare the underlying assumptions of the different test procedures. In applied work, it is very important to know the assumptions under which a test procedure is supposed to work in order to be able to choose the appropriate test. Important aspects in this context are the assumption about the trend parameters of the process and whether the test statistics depend on these parameters. Therefore, one focus of the simulation study was to analyse the sensitivity of the test performance to the trending properties of the data generating process.

Furthermore, the aim of the simulations was the analysis of size and power of a broad range of systems cointegration tests in small samples. Previous simulation studies suggest that in small samples some multivariate tests for the cointegration rank often show size and/or power distortions in certain situations. These results have been investigated further in new simulations.

In contrast to most previous studies, the scope of the small sample comparison in Chapter 2 is very broad as it comprises, besides some well-known test procedures, a number of systems cointegration tests about which limited knowledge of their properties has been available so far. The aim of the simulation study was to explore the strengths and weaknesses of the different systems cointegration tests by carrying out a comparison on the basis of some simple DGPs. The idea was that tests which do not work well for a simple DGP cannot in general be trusted in more complicated situations, even if they have been shown to perform well in specific complicated situations. It has been found that the canonical correlation tests, the Stock & Watson tests as well as the Bierens tests perform very poorly even under ideal conditions. Therefore their use cannot be recommended for applied work. Generally, likelihood based methods have been found to perform better, but they also have deficiencies in some situations.

A small sample simulation for a data-based DGP with structural breaks has been carried out so as to receive some information on how the respective LR tests work if dummy variables have to be taken into account. The results indicate that Johansen's LR test performs better for this particular DGP. This finding is of importance for the empirical analysis in Chapter 3 where dummy variables are included to model structural breaks. However, the DGP employed is very specific and further research has to be carried out to explore the relative small sample performance of these tests in the presence of dummy variables further.

Recommendations for the application of cointegration rank tests have been provided drawn from the results presented that are relevant also for the empirical analysis in Chapter 3.

4.2 Empirical Analysis of a German Monetary System

A German monetary system has been analysed in Chapter 3 to identify long-run relationships that influence the transmission process of the Bundesbank's monetary policy. The simulation results in Chapter 2 indicate that the LR based tests perform best. Therefore, Johansen's original LR test as well as the trend-adjusted LR test suggested by Saikkonen & Lütkepohl (2000b) has been applied. Johansen's LR test indicates $r = 3$, a higher cointegration rank than the trend-adjusted LR test. This is not surprising as Johansen's LR test has been found to display higher power in the data-based simulations, i.e. for a high-dimensional system where structural breaks have to be taken into account (see Section 2.6). Therefore, the cointegration rank has been assumed to be $r = 3$ for further analysis.

Since the Johansen procedure facilitates a broad empirical analysis, this framework has been chosen to test restrictions on the cointegration space in Section 3.4.3. Economic theory suggests three stable cointegration relationships between the variables of the money demand system: a money demand relationship, the yield spread and a Fisher equation. These restrictions have been tested empirically. The stable long-run relationships obtained are of major interest in the context of monetary policy in Germany, because the stability of the long-run money demand relationship as well as the long-run Fisher effect and the long-run relationship between short- and long-term interest rates have implications for the conduct and transmission process of monetary policy. In addition to its monetary target M3, the Bundesbank also monitored other indicators, e.g. the term structure of interest rates, to obtain information on potential inflationary risks.

The cointegration vectors obtained from the systems procedure have been interpreted and the stability of these long-run relationships has been analysed. Tests based on recursive estimation indicate that the results for the three cointegration relations are robust with respect to variations in the sample size. It has been shown that the structural break of German reunification can be modelled and that money demand in Germany continues to be stable after reunification. Therefore, one precondition for the policy of monetary targeting by the Bundesbank was fulfilled. The question of the stability of money demand remains an essential issue for the monetary policy of the ECB.[1] The lessons that can be drawn from empirical results found for Germany are discussed in Section 4.4 below. How to model the structural break that will occur due to the European Monetary Union will be a main challenge for future research regarding the euro area.

4.3 Further Research

Methodology The exploration of the small sample properties of systems cointegration tests presented in this work mainly includes simula-

[1] A considerable number of studies on aggregate European money demand have been published, e.g. Fagan & Henry (1998), Fase & Winder (1998) and Wesche (1997).

tions for 2- and 3-dimensional DGPs of order one or two. The aim has been to compare a broad range of tests on the basis of relatively simple DGPs and select the best-performing tests in terms of relative size and power. Such an approach is plausible since tests that exhibit size distortions and/or low power on the basis of simple DGPs will not perform well for more complicated DGPs of higher dimension, either. However, it would provide further insight to compare the performance of original and mean- as well as trend-adjusted LR tests that have been found to perform best in the simulations presented for more complicated DGPs. One first step in that respect is the simulation comparison on the basis of the data-based 5-dimensional DGP in Section 2.6. Previous simulation studies have analysed the performance of tests in many respects, e.g. their dependence on the dimension as well as the order of the process. However, a simulation study systematically analysing the dependence on the inclusion of seasonal dummies, one or more shift dummies as well as constant and a linear trend term in systems of different orders and dimensions would be of great interest for applied work.

Monetary Policy Analysis The analysis of long-run relationships within an economy is of importance since long-run relationships determine the principle behaviour in the economy. In contrast to the short-run dynamics, about which we have little theoretical knowledge, economic theory provides testable propositions for long-run relationships. Further, long-run relationships are important with respect to long-run effects of policy actions. However, it is often of interest to take short-run dynamics into account in empirical analysis, e.g. to analyse the transmission process of monetary policy. For such a purpose the multivariate analysis presented should be extended and the long-run relationships employed as a basis for modelling a dynamic cointegrated system. Approaches in that direction are impulse response analysis, structured VAR analysis as well as SVAR modelling. However, from a structured VAR analysis alone (resulting in a VECM), it is problematic to get a clear picture of the interdependences in the model. Impulse response analysis, taking into account the long-run relationships, can be more helpful in this respect. One approach in that direction, using the same variables as the empirical analysis presented here, has been considered by Lütkepohl & Wolters (1998).

A different approach of analysing the effect of shocks on a system is structural VAR analysis which has become a very popular instrument of monetary policy analysis and this approach has been discussed extensively in the literature, e.g. by Christiano, Eichenbaum & Evans (1997), Bagliano & Favero (1998), Faust (1998) and Uhlig (1998).

On the basis of the approaches mentioned above questions with respect to the controllability of money by the central bank as well as the causal link between money and inflation within EMU should be analysed further[2] to provide policy recommendations for the ECB. One interesting question in that context concerns methodologies: To what extent are differences in conclusions due to different econometric methods employed in the analyses?

Furthermore, it will be of interest to analyse data for the euro area as a whole and compare the results with national experiences. However, the data made available by the ECB are aggregated data for the period from 1985 until 1996, and are from the consolidated balance sheet of the euro area from 1997 onwards. Therefore, the problem arises how to link pre-1999 data to post-1999 euro area statistics (European Central Bank, 1999b). Moreover, it is not clear what aggregated data for the time period before EMU mean in the light of the different initial conditions in the countries with respect to monetary policy and central bank constitution.

4.4 Outlook: Lessons from German Monetary Policy for the European Central Bank?

A central question with respect to European Monetary Union is whether conclusions can be drawn from the analysis of past monetary policies in the participating European nations for the monetary policy of the ECB. In this respect, especially the question of the relevance of the German experience arises.

Several arguments can be brought forward to consider German past monetary policy experience as important for the ECB's policy. First, as mentioned in the introduction of this thesis, the behaviour of German economic agents will play a major role in the transmission process of the monetary policy of the ECB since Germany is the largest economy in EMU. Second, Germany has played a prominent role in the EMS as the Deutsche Mark was its anchor currency. Third, the ECB has in many respects been modelled according to the blueprint of the Bundesbank. And fourth, due to the success of the Bundesbank's monetary targeting strategy in terms of price stability, the ECB has assigned a prominent role to money in its monetary policy strategy.

[2] A few studies analysing those questions have been discussed in Chapter 3.

The following important conclusions for policy decisions in EMU from past experience have been brought forward as arguments for a policy strategy by the ECB with a central role devoted to monetary aggregates (European Central Bank, 1999a): First, aggregate European money demand has been found stable and to be strongly influenced by the stability of German money demand. Second, broad European monetary aggregates have been leading indicators for price developments in the euro area.

Furthermore, a Taylor rule, characterizing the response in short-term interest rates to deviations of inflation from the target and to deviations of output from potential, based on the parameter estimates for Germany can be used as a benchmark for the evaluation of the ECB's policy (International Monetary Fund, 1998).

However, conclusions for the ECB policy from past experience have to be considered with some caution. Especially, considerable uncertainties exist concerning the behaviour of economic agents in Germany and elsewhere in the EMU with respect to the medium- and long-term change due to the regime shift, for example because of the higher integration of European financial markets. Moreover, high uncertainties concerning changes in expectations of economic agents and future developments in the world economy lead to numerous questionmarks concerning the transfer of past experience to EMU. There are some issues the ECB has to face that national central banks did not have to deal with to the same extent. First, the ECB is responsible for a large number of sovereign countries. Furthermore, these countries are in different stages of the economic cycle which makes appropriate central monetary policy rather difficult. Another complication is represented by differences across countries in the transmission process of monetary policies. Additionally, the ECB has to face the negative effects of asymmetric shocks to a larger extent than the national central banks. Especially, migration within a European country is quite common while migration between European countries is restricted to a small range of professions due to language and cultural barriers. Similarly, the asymmetric shocks will not be compensated by financial transfers to the same extent as within single European nations since the common EU budget is very small compared to financial transfers within the member states.

However, as regards the general policy implementation of the ECB, it is worthwhile to consider the national and, especially, the German experience as a benchmark against which to evaluate the new situation in EMU.

Appendix A

Trend-adjusted LR Tests: Dummy Variables

Saikkonen & Lütkepohl (2000b) suggest to estimate the deterministic terms by a GLS procedure and adjust the time series for these terms in a first step. The second step, then, is to carry out a rank test based on the adjusted data. Allowing for 2 impulse and 2 step dummies (one of those can be considered to be an extended impulse dummy) as well as seasonal dummies, the DGP has the form

$$\begin{aligned} y_t &= \mu_0 + \mu_1 t + \delta_{01} di_{1t} + \delta_{02} di_{2t} + \delta_1 ds_t + \delta_2 ds_t^i \\ &\quad + \delta_{s1} sd_{1,t} + \delta_{s2} sd_{2,t} + \delta_{s3} sd_{3,t} + x_t, \qquad t = 1, 2, \ldots, \end{aligned} \tag{1.1}$$

where

$$di_{1t} = \begin{cases} 1, & t = T_{01} \\ 0, & t \neq T_{01} \end{cases}, \qquad di_{2t} = \begin{cases} 1, & t = T_{02} \\ 0, & t \neq T_{02} \end{cases},$$

$$ds_t = \begin{cases} 1, & t < T_1 \\ 0, & t \geq T_1 \end{cases}, \qquad ds_t^i = \begin{cases} 0, & t < T_{21} \\ 1, & T_{21} \leq t \leq T_{22} \\ 0, & t \geq T_{22} \end{cases},$$

$$sd_{it} = \begin{cases} 1, & i + t \\ 0, & otherwise \end{cases} \qquad \text{for} \quad i = 1, ..., 3 ,$$

where di_{1t} and di_{2t} are impulse dummies, ds_t and ds_t^i are step dummies and sd_{it}, $t = 1, ..., 3$ are seasonal dummies, whereas $\delta_{0j}, j = 1, 2$ and $\delta_j, j = 1, 2$ as well as $\delta_{si}, i = 1, ..., 3$ are the respective parameters.

The model below is explicitely derived for $p = 2$. Let x_t follow a VAR(2):

$$x_t = A_1 x_{t-1} + A_2 x_{t-2} + \varepsilon_t$$

This can be rewritten in an ECM under the null hypothesis:

$$\Delta x_t = \Pi x_{t-1} + \Gamma_1 \Delta x_{t-1} + \varepsilon_t$$

where ε_t is normally identically distributed, i.e. $\varepsilon_t \sim NID(0, \Omega)$. Multiplying (1.1) by the lag polynomial $A(L) = I_n - A_1 L - A_2 L^2$ and writing in EC form results in

$$\begin{aligned} \Delta y_t &= \nu_0 + \nu_1 t + \alpha\beta' y_{t-1} + \Gamma_1 \Delta y_{t-1} \\ &+ \delta_{01} di_{1,t} - A_1 \delta_{01} di_{1,t-1} - A_2 \delta_{01} di_{1,t-2} \\ &+ \delta_{02} di_{2,t} - A_1 \delta_{02} di_{2,t-1} - A_2 \delta_{02} di_{2,t-2} \\ &+ \delta_1 \Delta ds_t - \Gamma_1 \delta_1 \Delta ds_{t-1} - \alpha\beta' \delta_1 ds_{t-1} \\ &+ \delta_2 \Delta ds_t^i - \Gamma_1 \delta_2 \Delta ds_{t-1}^i - \alpha\beta' \delta_2 ds_{t-1}^i \\ &+ \delta_{s1} sd_{1,t} + \delta_{s2} sd_{2,t} + \delta_{s3} sd_{3,t} + \varepsilon_t, \end{aligned} \tag{1.2}$$

where $\nu_0 = -\Pi\mu_0 + (\Psi + \Pi)\mu_1$, $\nu_1 = -\alpha\beta'\mu_1$ and $\Psi = I_n - \Gamma_1 = I_n + A_2$. Please note, that since the constant enters unrestrictedly in this model, a fourth seasonal dummy is not needed and the lagged seasonal dummies drop out.

If the nonlinear restrictions on the coefficients of the dummies are ignored, (1.2) simplifies to (1.3):

$$\begin{aligned} \Delta y_t &= \nu + \alpha(\beta' y_{t-1} - \tau(t-1) - \theta_1 ds_{1,t-1} - \theta_2 ds_{2,t-1}) \\ &+ \Gamma_1 \Delta y_{t-1} + \gamma_{01,0} di_{1,t} + \gamma_{01,1} di_{1,t-1} + \gamma_{01,2} di_{1,t-2} \\ &+ \gamma_{02,0} di_{2,t} + \gamma_{02,1} di_{2,t-1} + \gamma_{02} di_{2,t-2} \\ &+ \gamma_{1,0} \Delta ds_t - \gamma_{1,1} \Delta ds_{t-1} \\ &+ \gamma_{2,0} \Delta ds_t^i - \gamma_{2,1} \Delta ds_{t-1}^i \\ &+ \gamma_{s1} sd_{1,t} + \gamma_{s2} sd_{2,t} + \gamma_{s3} sd_{3,t} + \varepsilon_t, \end{aligned} \tag{1.3}$$

with $\nu = -\alpha\beta'\mu_0 + \Psi\mu_1$, $\tau = \beta'\mu_1$ and $\theta_1 = \beta'\delta_1$ as well as $\theta_2 = \beta'\delta_2$. Note, that $\Delta ds_{1,t-j}$ is an impulse dummy which is one at $t = t_1 + j$, so that

$$\Delta ds_t = \begin{cases} 1, & t = T_1 \\ 0, & otherwise \end{cases},$$

$$\Delta ds_{1,t-1} = \begin{cases} 1, & t = T_1 + 1 \\ 0, & otherwise \end{cases}, \qquad \Delta ds_{1,t-2} = \begin{cases} 1, & t = T_1 + 2 \\ 0, & otherwise \end{cases},$$

Before estimating (1.3), check whether the dummy variables are linearly independent. The coefficients are defined as follows: $\gamma_{si} = \delta_{si}$ for $i = 1, \cdots, 3$ and

$$\gamma_{01,j} = \begin{cases} \delta_{01} \quad , & j = 0 \\ -A_j\delta_{01}, & j = 1, ..., p \end{cases},$$

$$\gamma_{02,j} = \begin{cases} \delta_{02} \quad , & j = 0 \\ -A_j\delta_{02}, & j = 1, ..., p \end{cases},$$

$$\gamma_{1,j} = \begin{cases} \delta_1 \quad , & j = 0 \\ -\Gamma_j\delta_1, & j = 1, ..., p-1 \end{cases},$$

$$\gamma_{2,j} = \begin{cases} \delta_2 \quad , & j = 0 \\ -\Gamma_j\delta_2, & j = 1, ..., p-1 \end{cases},$$

In the German monetary system presented in Chapter 3 the first impulse dummy and the first step dummy allow for the structural break of German reunification. Therefore, $di_{1,t}$ and $\Delta ds_{1,t}$ are the same and $\Delta ds_{1,t}$ and $\Delta ds_{1,t-1}$ can be excluded from this representation.

Appendix B

Data

The data analysed are quarterly, not seasonally adjusted time series for the period 1979(1) to 1997(4). Sources are as follows:

- The nominal M3 time series are obtained from the Monthly Reports of the *Deutsche Bundesbank.* The value of the last month of each quarter represents the quarterly value.

- The long-term interest rate is an average yield on bonds in circulation (*durchschnittliche Umlaufsrendite inländischer Inhaberschuldverschreibungen)* which is constructed as a weighted average of bonds in circulation. The value of the last month of each quarter represents the quarterly value.

- The own rate of M3 is constructed as a weighted average of the interest rate on savings deposits *(Spareinlagen mit gesetzlicher Kündigungsfrist)* and the interest rate on time deposits, represented by time deposits of 1 to 3 months to maturity (including deposits between 1 and 5 million DM). The value of the last month of each quarter represents the quarterly value.

- The GNP data are from the German Institute for Economic Research *(Deutsches Institut für Wirtschaftsforschung, Berlin).*

- Prices are represented by the deflator of GNP (1991=100) derived from data published by the German Institute for Economic Research *(Deutsches Institut für Wirtschaftsforschung, Berlin).*

List of Figures

List of Tables

Bibliography

Ahn, S. K. & Reinsel, G. C. (1988). Nested reduced-rank autoregressive models for multiple time series, *Journal of the American Statistical Association* **83**: 849–856.

Bagliano, F. C. & Favero, C. A. (1998). Measuring monetary policy with VAR models: An evaluation, *European Economic Review* **42**: 1069–1112.

Banerjee, A., Dolado, J., Galbraith, J. W. & Hendry, D. F. (1993). *Co-integration, Error-Correction, and the Econometric Analysis of Non-stationary Data*, Oxford University Press, Oxford.

Barnett, W. (1980). Economic monetary aggregates: An application of index numbers and aggregation theory, *Journal of Econometrics* **14**: 11–48.

Barro, R. J. & Gordon, D. B. (1983). Rules, discretion and reputation in a model of monetary policy, *Journal of Monetary Economics* **12**: 101–121.

Barr, D. G. & Cuthbertson, K. (1991). Neoclassical consumer demand theory and the demand for money, *The Economic Journal* **101**: 855–876.

Baumol, W. J. (1952). The transactions demand for cash: An inventory theoretic approach, *Quarterly Journal of Economics* **66**(4): 545–556.

Bernanke, B. S. & Mihov, I. (1997). What does the Bundesbank target?, *European Economic Review* **41**: 1025–1053.

Bernanke, B. S. & Mishkin, F. S. (1997). Inflation targeting: A new framework for monetary policy, *Journal of Economic Perspectives* **111**(2): 97–116.

Bewley, R. & Yang, M. (1995). Tests for cointegration based on canonical correlation analysis, *Journal of the American Statistical Association* **90**: 990–996.

Beyer, A. (1998a). Modelling money demand in Germany, *Journal of Applied Econometrics* **13**: 57–76.

Beyer, A. (1998b). Monetary transmission in Germany: Evidence from a structural econometric model, *Discussion Paper 98-05*, Institute of Economics, University of Copenhagen.

Biefang-Frisancho Mariscal, I. & Trautwein, H.-M. (1994). A cointegration and error correction model of the demand for money (M3) in Germany, *in* G. Bol, G. Nakhaeizadeh & K.-H. Vollmer (eds), *Finanzmarktanwendungen neuronaler Netze und ökonometrischer Verfahren*, Vol. 93 of *Wirtschaftswissenschaftliche Beiträge*, Physica-Verlag, Heidelberg.

Bierens, H. J. (1997a). Cointegration analysis, *in* C. Heij, H. Schumacher, B. Hanzon & C. Praagman (eds), *System Dynamics in Economic and Financial Models*, John Wiley, New York.

Bierens, H. J. (1997b). Nonparametric cointegration analysis, *Journal of Econometrics* **77**: 379–404.

Boswijk, P. & Franses, P. H. (1992). Dynamic specification and cointegration, *Oxford Bulletin of Economics and Statistics* **54**(3): 369–381.

Cabos, K., Funke, M. & Siegfried, N. A. (1998). Some thoughts on monetary targeting vs. inflation targeting, *Quantitative Macroeconomics Working Paper 8/99*, Universität Hamburg.

Campbell, J. Y. & Shiller, R. J. (1987). Cointegration and the tests of present value models, *Journal of Political Economy* **95**: 1062–1088.

Campbell, J. Y. & Shiller, R. J. (1991). Yield spreads and interest rate movements: A bird's eye view, *Review of Economic Studies* **58**: 495–514.

Canzoneri, M. B. & Dellas, H. (1998). Real interest rates and central bank operating procedures, *Journal of Monetary Economics* **42**: 471–494.

Cheung, Y.-W. & Lai, K. S. (1993). Finite-sample sizes of Johansen's likelihood ratio tests for cointegration, *Oxford Bulletin of Economics and Statistics* **55**: 313–328.

Chow, G. C. (1960). Tests of equality between sets of coefficients in two linear regressions, *Econometrica* **28**: 591–605.

Christiano, L. J., Eichenbaum, M. & Evans, C. L. (1997). Monetary policy shocks: What have we learned and to what end?, *Working Paper, December*, NBER.

Clarida, R. & Gertler, M. (1996). How the Bundesbank conducts monetary policy, *Working Paper 5581*, National Bureau of Economic Research.

Crowder, W. J. & Hoffman, D. L. (1996). The long-run relationship between nominal interest rates and inflation: The Fisher equation revisited, *Journal of Money, Credit, and Banking* **28**(1): 102–118.

Darby, M. R. (1975). The financial and tax effects of monetary policy on interest rates, *Economic Inquiry* **13**: 266–69.

Deutsche Bundesbank (1994). Das Geldmengenziel für das Jahr 1994, *Monatsbericht Januar 1994* pp. 19–23.

Deutsche Bundesbank (1995a). Geldnachfrage und Währungssubstitution in Europa, *Monatsbericht Januar 1995*, pp. 33–49.

Deutsche Bundesbank (1995b). Überprüfung der Geldmengenziele und Neuordnung der Mindestreserven, *Monatsbericht Juli 1995.*

Dickey, D. A., Bell, W. R. & Miller, R. B. (1986). Unit roots in time series models: Tests and implications, *American Statistician* **40**: 12–26.

Dickey, D. A. & Fuller, W. A. (1979). Estimators for autoregressive time series with a unit root, *Journal of the American Statistical Association* **74**: 427–431.

Doornik, J. A., Hendry, D. F. & Nielsen, B. (1998). Inference in cointegrating models: UK M1 revisited, *Journal of Economic Surveys* **12**(5): 533–540.

Doornik, J. A. & Hendry, D. F. (1997a). *PcFiml 9.0, Modelling Dynamic Systems Using PcFiml 9.0 for Windows*, Thomson Publishing.

Doornik, J. A. & Hendry, D. F. (1997b). *PcGive 9.0, Empirical Econometric Modelling Using PcGive 9.0 for Windows*, Thomson Publishing.

Doornik, J. A. (1995). Testing general restrictions on the cointegrating space, mimeo, Nuffield College, Oxford.

Efron, B. & Tibshirani, R. (1993). *An Introduction to the Bootstrap*, Chapman and Hall, New York.

Eitrheim, Ø. (1998). The demand for broad money in Norway, 1989–1993, *Empirical Economics* **23**(3): 339–354.

Engle, R. F. & Granger, C. W. J. (1987). Cointegration and error correction: Representation, estimation and testing, *Econometrica* **55**: 251–276.

Engle, R. F., Hendry, D. F. & Richard, J.-F. (1983). Exogeneity, *Econometrica* **51**: 277–304.

Engle, R. F. (1982). Autoregressive conditional heteroscedasticity, with estimates of the variance of United Kingdoms inflations, *Econometrica* **50**: 987–1007.

Ericsson, N. R., Hendry, D. F. & Mizon, G. E. (1998). Exogeneity, cointegration, and economic policy analysis, *Journal of Business and Economic Statistics* **16**(4): 370–387.

Ericsson, N. R. & Irons, J. S. (eds) (1994). *Testing Exogeneity*, Oxford University Press, New York.

Estrella, A. & Mishkin, F. S. (1997). The predictive power of the term sturcture of interest rates in Europe and the United States: Implications for the European Central Bank, *European Economic Review* **41**(7): 1375–1401.

European Central Bank (1998). Press Conference, Tuesday, 13 October 1998, The President's Introductory Statement, Press Release, Internet.

European Central Bank (1999a). *Monthly Bulletin, January 1999.*

European Central Bank (1999b). *Monthly Bulletin, February 1999.*

Evans, M. & Lewis, K. (1995). Do expected shifts in inflation affect estimates of the long-run Fisher relation?, *Journal of Finance* **50**: 225–253.

Fagan, G. & Henry, J. (1998). Long run money demand in the EU: Evidence for area-wide aggregates, *Empirical Economics* **23**(3): 483–506.

Fama, E. F. (1975). Short-term interest rates as predictors of inflation, *American Economic Review* **65**: 269–282.

Fama, E. F. (1984). The information of the term structure, *Journal of Financial Economics* **13**: 509–528.

Fama, E. F. (1990). Term structure forecasts of interest rates, inflation, and real returns, *Journal of Monetary Economics* **25**(1): 59–76.

Fase, M. M. G. & Winder, C. C. A. (1998). Wealth and the demand for money in the European Union, *Empirical Economics* **23**(3): 507–524.

Faust, J. (1998). The robustness of identified VAR conclusions about money, *Carnegie-Rochester Conference Series on Public Policy* **49**: 207–244.

Fisher, I. (1911). *The Purchasing Power of Money*, Macmillan, New York.

Fisher, I. (1930). *The Theory of Interest*, Macmillan, New York.

Friedman, M. (1956). The quantity theory of money – A restatement, *in* M. Friedman (ed.), *Studies in the Quantity Theory of Money*, University of Chicago Press, Chicago.

Fuller, W. A. (1976). *Introduction to Statistical Time Series*, John Wiley, New York.

Gaab, W. & Liedtke, O. (1992). On the long-run relationship between money, output and interest rates: A cointegration analysis for West Germany, *Recherches Economiques de Louvain* **58**(3–4): 455–471.

Gaab, W. & Mullineux, A. (1996). Financial innovation, monetary aggregates and monetary policy in the UK and Germany, *in* D. Duwendag (ed.), *Finanzmärkte, Finanzinnovationen und Geldpolitik*, Duncker & Humblot, pp. 73–110.

Gaab, W. (1996). On the demand for Divisia and simple-sum M3 in Germany, 1960-93, *in* A. Mullineux (ed.), *Financial Innovation, Banking and Monetary Aggregates*, Edward Elgar, pp. 160–186.

Garcia, R. & Perron, P. (1996). An analysis of the real interest rate under regime shifts, *The Review of Economics and Statistics* **78**(1): 111–125.

Gennari, E. & Juselius, K. (1998). Monetary transmission mechanisms in Italy, mimeo. European University Institute.

Gerlach, S. (1997). The information content of the term structure: Evidence for Germany, *Empirical Economics* **22**: 161–179.

Gonzalo, J. & Lee, T.-H. (1998). Pitfalls in testing for long run relationships, *Journal of Econometrics* **86**: 129–154.

Gonzalo, J. & Pitarakis, J.-Y. (1998). Specification via model selection in vector error correction models, *Economics Letters* **60**(3): 321–328.

Gonzalo, J. & Pitarakis, J.-Y. (1999). Dimensionality effect in cointegration analysis, *in* R. Engle & H. White (eds), *Cointegration, Causality, and Forecasting. A Festschrift in Honour of Clive W.J. Granger*, Oxford University Press, Oxford, pp. 212–229.

Gonzalo, J. (1994). Five alternative methods of estimating long-run equilibrium relationships, *Journal of Econometrics* **60**: 203–233.

Goodhart, C. (1975). Problems of monetary management: The U.K. experience, *in* Courakis (ed.), *Inflation, Depression and Economic Policy in the West*, Totowa, New York.

Granger, C. W. J. & Teräsvirta, T. (1993). *Modelling Nonlinear Economic Relationships*, Oxford University Press, Oxford.

Granger, C. W. J. (1981). Some properties of time series data and their use in econometric model specification, *Journal of Econometrics* **16**: 121–130.

Gredenhoff, M. & Jacobson, T. (1998). Bootstrap testing and approximate finite sample distributions for tests of linear restrictions on cointegrating vectors, presented at the ESEM98 in Berlin. Stockholm School of Economics.

Green, J. H. (1996). Inflation targeting: Theory and policy implications, *Staff Papers 4*, IMF.

Haldane, A. G. (1997). Some issues in inflation targeting, *Working Papaer Series 74*, Bank of England.

Hamilton, J. D. (1994). *Time Series Analysis*, Princeton University Press, Princeton, New Jersey.

Hansen, G. & Kim, J. R. (1995). The stability of German money demand. Tests of the cointegration relation, *Weltwirtschaftliches Archiv* **131**: 286–301.

Hansen, G. (1997). The domestic term structure and international interest linkages: A cointegration analysis, *Weltwirtschaftliches Archiv* **132**: 675–689.

Hansen, H. & Johansen, S. (1993). Recursive estimation in cointegrated VAR-models, *Preprint 1*, Institute of Mathematical Statistics, University of Copenhagen.

Hardouvelis, G. A. (1994). The term structure spread and future changes in long and short rates in the G7 countries, *Journal of Monetary Economics* **33**: 255–283.

Harvey, A. C. (1990). *The Econometric Analysis of Time Series*, 2nd edn, Philip Allan, Hemel Hempstead.

Hassler, U. & Nautz, D. (1998). The link between German short- and long-term interest rates. Some evidence against the term structure oriented monetary policy, *Jahrbücher für Nationalökonomie und Statistik* **217**(2): 214–226.

Hassler, U. (1994). Einheitswurzeltests - Ein Überblick, *Allgemeines Statistisches Archiv* **78**(2): 207–228.

Haug, A. A. (1996). Tests for cointegration: A Monte Carlo comparison, *Journal of Econometrics* **71**: 89–115.

Hendry, D. F. & Doornik, J. A. (1994). Modelling linear dynamic econometric systems, *Scottish Journal of Political Economy* **41**(1): 1–33.

Hendry, D. F. (1984). Monte Carlo experimentation in econometrics, *in* Z. Griliches & M. Intriligator (eds), *Handbook of Econometrics*, Elsevier Science Publishers BV.

Hendry, D. F. (1995). *Dynamic Econometrics*, Oxford University Press, Oxford.

Hoffmann, J. (1998). Probleme der Inflationsmessung in Deutschland, *Diskussionspapier 1*, Deutsche Bundesbank.

Hoffman, D. L. & Rasche, R. H. (1996). *Aggregate Money Demand Functions*, Kluwer Academic Publishers, Boston.

Ho, M. S. & Sørensen, B. E. (1996). Finding cointegration rank in high dimensional systems using the Johansen test: An illustration using data based Monte Carlo simulations, *Review of Economics and Statistics* **78**(4): 726–732.

Hubrich, K., Lütkepohl, H. & Saikkonen, P. (2000). A review of systems cointegration tests, *Econometric Reviews, forthcoming.*

Hubrich, K. (1999). Estimation of a German money demand system - A long-run analysis, *Empirical Economics* **24**(1): 77–99.

International Monetary Fund (1998). *World Economic Outlook, Oktober.*

Issing, O. & Tödter, K.-H. (1995). Geldmenge und Preise im vereinten Deutschland, *in* D. Duwendag (ed.), *Neuere Entwicklungen in der Geldtheorie und Währungspolitik*, Duncker & Humblot, Berlin, pp. 97–123.

Issing, O. (1992). Theoretische und empirische Grundlagen der Geldmengenpolitik der Deutschen Bundesbank, *Wirtschaftsdienst* **10**: 537–548.

Issing, O. (1995). Die Geldmengenstrategie der Deutschen Bundesbank, *in* J. Siebke & H. Thieme (eds), *Geldpolitik. Zwanzig Jahre Geldmengensteuerung in Deutschland*, Nomos Verlagsgesellschaft, Baden-Baden, pp. 9–34.

Issing, O. (1997). Monetary targeting in Germany: The stability of monetary policy and of the monetary system, *Journal of Monetary Economics* **39**: 67–79.

Jacobson, T., Vredin, A. & Warne, A. (1998). Are real wages and unemployment related?, *Economica* **65**: 69–96.

Jacobson, T. (1995). Simulating small sample properties of the maximum likelihood cointegration method: Estimation and testing, *Finnish Economic Papers* **8**: 96–107.

Johansen, S. & Juselius, K. (1990). Maximum likelihood estimation and inference on cointegration – With applications to the demand for money, *Oxford Bulletin of Economics and Statistics* **52**: 169–210.

Johansen, S. & Juselius, K. (1994). Identification of the long-run and the short-run structure. An application to the ISLM model, *Journal of Econometrics* **63**: 7–36.

Johansen, S. & Nielsen, B. (1993). Manual for the simulation program DisCo. Institute of Mathematical Statistics, University of Copenhagen.

Johansen, S. (1988). Statistical analysis of cointegration vectors, *Journal of Economic Dynamics and Control* **12**: 231–54.

Johansen, S. (1991). Estimation and hypothesis testing of cointegration vectors in Gaussian vector autoregressive models, *Econometrica* **59**(6): 1551–81.

Johansen, S. (1992). Determination of cointegration rank in the presence of a linear trend, *Oxford Bulletin of Economics and Statistics* **54**: 383–397.

Johansen, S. (1994). The role of the constant and linear terms in cointegration analysis of nonstationary time series, *Econometric Reviews* **13**: 205–231.

Johansen, S. (1995). *Likelihood-based inference in cointegrated vector autoregressive models*, Oxford University Press, Oxford.

Juselius, K. (1996). The changing role of the German Bundesbank. An empirical analysis of German monetary policy before and after 1983, *Oxford Bulletin of Economics and Statistics* **58**: 791–819.

Juselius, K. (1998). Changing monetary transmission mechanism within the EU, *Empirical Economics* **23**(3): 456–482.

Juselius, K. (1999). A structured VAR under changing monetary policy, *Journal of Business and Economic Statistics, forthcoming.*

Keynes, J. M. (1930). *A Treatise on Money*, Macmillan, London and New York.

Keynes, J. M. (1936). *The General Theory of Employment, Interest, and Money*, Macmillan, London and New York.

King, M. (1996). Direct inflation targets, *in* Deutsche Bundesbank (ed.), *Monetary Policy Strategies in Europe*, Verlag Vahlen, München, pp. 141–166.

Kirchgässner, G. & Savioz, M. (1995). Is the interest rate spread a valid predictor for real and nominal economic development? An empirical investigation for the Federal Republic of Germany, *Discussion Paper 9510*, Department of Economics, University of St. Gallen.

Kirchgässner, G. & Wolters, J. (1990). Sind die Realzinsen stationär? Theoretische Überlegungen und empirische Ergebnisse, *Kredit und Kapital* **23**(4): 468–495.

Kirchgässner, G. & Wolters, J. (1993). Are real interest rates stable? An international comparison, *in* G. Schneeweiß & K. Zimmermann (eds), *Studies of Applied Eonometrics*, Physica-Verlag, Heidelberg.

Kiviet, J. F. & Phillips, G. D. A. (1992). Exact similar tests for unit roots and cointegration, *Oxford Bulletin of Economics and Statistics* **54**(3): 349–367.

Kole, L. S. & Meade, E. E. (1995). German monetary targeting: A retrospective view, *Technical Report 10*, Federal Reserve Bulletin.

König, R. (1996). The Bundesbank's experience of monetary targeting, *in* Deutsche Bundesbank (ed.), *Monetary Strategies in Europe*, Verlag Vahlen, München, pp. 107–140.

Kugler, P. (1996). Long term bond yields, monetary policy and the expectations hypothesis of the term structure of interest rates, *Diskussionsschriften 96-6*, Universität Bern.

Kwiatkowski, D., Phillips, P. C. B., Schmidt, P. & Shin, Y. (1992). Testing the null of stationarity against the alternative of a unit root: How sure are we that the economic time series have a unit root?, *Journal of Econometrics* **54**: 159–178.

Kydland, F. E. & Prescott, E. C. (1977). Rules rather than discretions: The inconsistency of optimal plans, *Journal of Political Economy* **85**: 473–491.

Laidler, D. E. W. (1993). *The Demand for Money: Theories, Evidence, Problems*, 2nd edn, HarperCollins College Publishers, New York.

Leiderman, L. & Svensson, L. E. O. (eds) (1995). *Inflation Targets*, Centre of Economic Policy Research, London.

Lin, C.-F. J. & Teräsvirta, T. (1994). Testing the constancy of regression parameters against continuous structural change, *Journal of Econometrics* **62**: 211–228.

Lütkepohl, H. & Poskitt, D. S. (1998). Consistent estimation of the number of cointegration relations in a vector autoregressive model, *in* R. Galata & H. Küchenhoff (eds), *Econometrics in Theory and Practice. Festschrift for Hans Schneeweiß*, Physica-Verlag, Heidelberg, pp. 87–100.

Lütkepohl, H. & Saikkonen, P. (1999a). A lag augmentation test for the cointegration rank of a VAR process, *Economics Letters* **63**(1): 23–27.

Lütkepohl, H. & Saikkonen, P. (1999b). Order selection in testing for the cointegrating rank of a VAR process, *in* R. Engle & H. White (eds), *Cointegration, Causality, and Forecasting. A Festschrift in Honour of Clive W.J. Granger*, Oxford University Press, Oxford, pp. 168–199.

Lütkepohl, H. & Saikkonen, P. (1999c). Testing for the cointegrating rank of a VAR process with a time trend, *Journal of Econometrics* **95**: 177–198.

Lütkepohl, H. & Wolters, J. (1998). A money demand system for German M3, *Empirical Economics* **23**(3): 371–386.

Lütkepohl, H. (1991). *Introduction to Multiple Time Series Analysis*, Springer Verlag, Berlin.

Lütkepohl, H. (1995). Kointegration und gemeinsame Trends, *in* K. Oppenländer (ed.), *Konjunkturindikatoren: Fakten, Analysen, Verwendung*, Oldenbourg Verlag, pp. 144–176.

MacDonald, R. & Murphy, P. D. (1989). Testing for the long run relationship between nominal interest rates and inflation using cointegration techniques, *Applied Economics* **21**: 439–447.

MacKinnon, J. G. (1991). Critical values for co-integration tests, *in* R. Engle & C. Granger (eds), *Long-Run Economic Relationships*, Oxford University Press, pp. 267–76.

Maddala, G. S. & Kim, I.-M. (1998). *Unit Roots, Cointegration and Structural Change*, Cambridge University Press, Cambridge.

McCallum, B. T. & Goodfriend, M. S. (1987). Demand for money: Theoretical studies, *in* J. Eatwell, M. Millgate & P. Newman (eds), *The New Palgrave: A Dictionary of Economics*, Macmillan, London.

McCallum, B. T. (1989). *Monetary Economics. Theory and Policy*, Macmillan, New York.

Mishkin, F. S. & Posen, A. S. (1997). Inflation targeting: Lessons from four countries, *Economic Policy Review* **3**(3): 9–96.

Mishkin, F. S. (1992). Is the Fisher effect for real? A reexamination of the relationship between inflation and interest rates, *Journal of Monetary Economics* **30**: 195–215.

Müller, C. (1998). Der Einfluß der Wahl der Ordnung eines Vektorautoregressiven Prozesses auf Kointegrationstests, Diplomarbeit (Master's thesis). Humboldt-Universität zu Berlin.

Nautz, D. & Wolters, J. (1996). Die Entwicklung langfristiger Kreditzinssätze: Eine empirische Analyse, *Kredit und Kapital* **29**(4): 481–510.

Nautz, D. (1995). Zur Feinsteuerung des Geldmarktes durch Wertpapierpensionsgeschäfte der Deutschen Bundesbank, *Zeitschrift für Wirschafts- und Sozialpolitik* **115**: 623–644.

Nielsen, B. (1994). DisCo. Institute of Mathematical Statistics, University of Copenhagen.

Osterwald-Lenum, M. (1992). A note with fractiles of the asymptotic distribution of the maximum likelihood cointegration rank test statistics: Four cases, *Oxford Bulletin of Economics and Statistics* **54**: 461–72.

Patinkin, D. (1989). *Money, Interest and Prices*, 2nd, abridged edn, MIT Press, Cambridge, Massachusetts.

Perron, P. & Campbell, J. Y. (1993). A note on Johansen's cointegration procedure when trends are present, *Empirical Economics* **18**: 777–789.

Perron, P. (1988). Trends and random walks in macroeconomic time series: Further evidence from a new approach, *Journal of Economic Dynamics and Control* **12**: 297–232.

Perron, P. (1989). The great crash, the oil price shock, and the unit root hypothesis, *Econometrica* **57**(6): 1361–1401.

Pesaran, M. H. & Smith, R. P. (1998). Structural analysis of cointegrating VARs, *Journal of Economic Surveys* **12**(5): 417–422.

Pfann, G. A., Schotman, P. C. & Tschernig, R. (1995). Nonlinear interest rate dynamics and implications for the term structure, *Journal of Econometrics* **74**: 149–176.

Phillips, P. C. B. & Hansen, B. E. (1990). Statistical inference in instrumental variables regression with I(1) processes, *Review of Economic Studies* **57**: 99–125.

Phillips, P. C. B. (1988). Reflections on econometric methodology, *Economic Record* **64**: 344–359.

Phillips, P. C. P. & Perron, P. (1988). Testing for a unit root in time series, *Biometrika* **75**: 335–346.

Plosser, C. I. & Rouwenhorst, K. G. (1994). International term structure and real economic growth, *Journal of Monetary Economics* **33**(1): 133–155.

Podivinsky, J. M. (1992). Small sample properties of tests of linear restrictions on cointegration vectors and their weights, *Economics Letters* **39**: 13–18.

Podivinsky, J. M. (1998). Testing misspecified cointegrating relationships, *Economics Letters* **60**: 1–9.

Quintos, C. E. (1998a). Analysis of cointegration vectors using the GMM approach, *Journal of Econometrics* **85**: 155–188.

Quintos, C. E. (1998b). Fully modified vector autoregressive inference in partially nonstationary models, *Journal of the American Statistical Association* **93**(442): 783–795.

Rahbek, A. C. (1994). The power of some multivariate cointegration tests, *Preprint 6*, Department of Theoretical Statistics, University of Copenhagen.

Ramaswamy, R. & Sloek, T. (1997). The real effects of monetary policy in the European Union: What are the differences?, *IMF Working Paper WP/97/160*, International Monetary Fund.

Reimers, H. E. (1991). *Analyse kointegrierter Variablen mittels vektorautoregressiver Modelle*, Physica-Verlag, Heidelberg.

Reimers, H. E. (1992). Comparisons of tests for multivariate cointegration, *Statistical Papers* **33**: 335–359.

Reinsel, G. C. & Ahn, S. K. (1992). Vector AR models with unit roots and reduced rank structure: Estimation, likelihood ratio test, and forecasting, *Journal of Time Series Analysis* **13**: 353–375.

Richard, J.-F. (1980). Models with several regimes and changes in exogeneity, *Review of Economic Studies* **47**: 1–20.

Rogoff, K. (1985). The optimal degree of commitment to an intermediate monetary target, *Quarterly Journal of Economics* **100**: 1169–1189.

Rose, A. (1988). Is the real interest rate stable?, *Journal of Finance* **43**: 1094–1112.

Saikkonen, P. & Lütkepohl, H. (1999). Local power of likelihood ratio tests for the cointegrating rank of a VAR process, *Econometric Theory* **15**: 50–78.

Saikkonen, P. & Lütkepohl, H. (2000a). Testing for the cointegrating rank of a VAR process with an intercept, *Econometric Theory, forthcoming.*

Saikkonen, P. & Lütkepohl, H. (2000b). Testing for the cointegrating rank of a VAR process with structural shifts, *Journal of Business & Economics Statistics, forthcoming.*

Saikkonen, P. & Lütkepohl, H. (2000c). Trend adjustment prior to testing for the cointegrating rank of a VAR process, *Journal of Time Series Analysis, forthcoming.*

Saikkonen, P. & Luukkonen, R. (1997). Testing cointegration in infinite order vector autoregressive processes, *Journal of Econometrics* **81**: 93–129.

Samuelson, P. A. (1958). An exact consumption loan model of interest with or without the social contrivance of money, *Journal of Political Economy* **66**(December): 467–482.

Sargent, T. J. & Wallace, N. (1988). The real bills doctrine versus the quantity theory: A reconsideration, *Journal of Political Economy* **90**(December): 1212–1236.

Scharnagl, M. (1996). Geldmengenaggregate unter Berücksichtigung struktureller Veränderungen an den Finanzmärkten, *Diskussionspapier 2/96*, Deutsche Bundesbank.

Scharnagl, M. (1998). The stability of German money demand: Not just a myth, *Empirical Economics* **23**(3): 355–370.

Schich, S. T. (1996). Alternative Spezifikationen der deutschen Zinsstrukturkurve und ihr Informationsgehalt hinsichtlich der Inflation, *Diskussionspapier 8*, Deutsche Bundesbank.

Schmidt, P. & Phillips, P. C. B. (1992). LM tests for a unit root in the presence of deterministic trends, *Oxford Bulletin of Economics and Statistics* **54**: 257–287.

Schwert, G. W. (1989). Tests for unit roots: A Monte Carlo investigation, *Journal of Business and Economic Statistics* **7**: 147–59.

Shiller, R. J. (1990). The term structure of interest rates, *in* B. Friedman & F. Hahn (eds), *Handbook of Monetary Economics*, Elsevier Science Publisher.

Stehle, R., Jaschke, S. & Wernicke, S. (1998). Tax clientele effects in the German bond market, *Discussion Paper 11*, SFB 373, Humboldt-Universität zu Berlin.

Stock, J. H. & Watson, M. W. (1988). Testing for common trends, *Journal of the American Statistical Association* **83**: 1097–1107.

Stock, J. H. & Watson, M. W. (1993). A simple estimator of cointegrating vectors in higher order integrated systems, *Econometrica* **61**: 783–820.

Stock, J. H. (1987). Asymptotic properties of least-squares estimators of cointegrating vectors, *Econometrica* **55**: 1035–1056.

Svensson, L. E. O. (1997). Inflation forecast targeting: Implementing and monitoring inflation targets, *European Economic Review* **41**: 1111–1146.

Svensson, L. E. O. (1998a). Inflation targeting as a monetary policy rule, Manuscript, prepared for the Sveriges Riksbank-IIES Conference on Monetary Policy Rules, Stockholm.

Svensson, L. E. O. (1998b). Monetary policy issues for the ESCB, Manuscript. Institute for International Economic Studies, Stockholm University.

Teräsvirta, T. (1998). Modelling economic relationships with smooth transition regressions, *in* D. Giles & A. Ullah (eds), *Handbook of Applied Economic Statistics*. forthcoming.

Tobin, J. (1956). The interest elasticity of transactions demand for cash, *Review of Economics and Statistics* **38**(3): 241–247.

Tobin, J. (1958). Liquidity preference as behavior towards risk, *Review of Economic Studies* **25**(February): 65–86.

Toda, H. Y. (1994). Finite sample properties of likelihood ratio tests for cointegrating ranks when linear trends are present, *Review of Economics and Statistics* **76**: 66–79.

Toda, H. Y. (1995). Finite sample performance of likelihood ratio tests for cointegrating ranks in vector autoregressions, *Econometric Theory* **11**: 1015–1032.

Tödter, K.-H. (1994). Eine transaktionsorientierte Geldmenge, *Kredit und Kapital* **27**: 319–347.

Tullio, G., de Souza, E. & Giucca, P. (1996). The demand for money functions in Europe and in Germany before and after the fall of the Berlin wall, *in* P. de Grauwe, S. Micossi & G. Tullio (eds), *Inflation and Wage Behaviour in Europe*, Clarendon Press, Oxford, pp. 310–338.

Tzavalis, E. & Wickens, M. R. (1996). Forecasting inflation from the term structure, *Journal of Empirical Finance* **3**: 103–122.

Uhlig, H. (1998). The robustness of identified VAR conclusions about money: A comment, *Carnegie-Rochester Conference Series on Public Policy* **49**: 245–263.

Van Giersbergen, N. P. A. (1994). Comment on nonparametric cointegration analysis, Manuscript. Department of Econometrics, University of Amsterdam, Amsterdam.

Van Giersbergen, N. P. A. (1996). Bootstrapping the trace statistic in VAR models: Monte Carlo results and applications, *Oxford Bulletin of Economics and Statistics* **58**(2): 391–408.

von Hagen, J. & Neumann, M. J. M. (1988). Instability versus dynamics: A study in West German demand for money, *Journal of Macroeconomics* **10**(3): 327–349.

von Hagen, J. & Neumann, M. J. M. (1996). A framework for monetary policy under EMU, *in* Deutsche Bundesbank (ed.), *Monetary Policy Strategies in Europe*, Verlag Franz Vahlen, München, pp. 141–166.

Wallace, M. S. & Warner, J. T. (1993). The Fisher effect and the term structure of interest rates: Tests of cointegration, *The Review of Economics and Statistics–Notes* **75**(2): 320–324.

Wesche, K. (1997). The stability of European money demand: An investigation of M3H, *Open Economies Review* **8**(4): 371–391.

Wolters, J. & Hassler, U. (1998). Die Zinsstruktur am deutschen Interbanken-Geldmarkt: Eine empirische Analyse für das vereinigte Deutschland, *Ifo-Studien* **44**(2): 141–160.

Wolters, J. & Lütkepohl, H. (1997). Die Geldnachfrage für M3: Neue Ergebnisse für das vereinigte Deutschland, *Ifo-Studien* **43**: 35–54.

Wolters, J., Teräsvirta, T. & Lütkepohl, H. (1998). Modelling the demand for M3 in the unified Germany, *The Review of Economics and Statitistics* pp. 399–409.

Wolters, J. (1995a). Kointegration und Zinsentwicklung im EWS. Eine Einführung in die Kointegrationsmethodologie und deren Anwendung, *Allgemeines Statistisches Archiv* **79**: 146–169.

Wolters, J. (1995b). On the term structure of interest rates - Empirical results for Germany, *Statistical Papers* **36**: 193–214.

Wolters, J. (1998). Untersuchung der Renditestruktur am deutschen Kapitalmarkt, 1970–1996, *in* E. Baltensperger (ed.), *Spekulation, Preisbildung und Volatilität auf Finanz- und Devisenmärkten*, Berlin.

Yang, M. & Bewley, R. (1996). On cointegration tests for VAR models with drift, *Economics Letters* **51**: 45–50.

Yap, S. F. & Reinsel, G. C. (1995). Estimation and testing for unit roots in a partially nonstationary vector autoregressive moving average model, *Journal of the American Statistical Association* **90**: 253–267.

Yuhn, K.-H. (1996). Is the Fisher effect robust? Further evidence, *Applied Economics Letters* **3**: 41–44.

Contributions to Economics

Simon Duindam
Military Conscription
1999. ISBN 3-7908-1203-X

Bruno Jeitziner
Political Economy of the Swiss National Bank
1999. ISBN 3-7908-1209-9

Irene Ring et al. (Eds.)
Regional Sustainability
1999. ISBN 3-7908-1233-1

Katharina Müller/Andreas Ryll/
Hans-Jürgen Wagener (Eds.)
Transformation of Social Security: Pensions in Central-Eastern Europe
1999. ISBN 3-7908-1210-2

Stefan Traub
Framing Effects in Taxation
1999. ISBN 3-7908-1240-4

Pablo Coto-Millán
Utility and Production
1999. ISBN 3-7908-1153-X

Frank Riedel
Imperfect Information and Investor Heterogeneity in the Bond Market
2000. ISBN 3-7908-1247-1

Kirsten Ralf
Business Cycles
2000. ISBN 3-7908-1245-5

Michele Bagella/
Leonardo Becchetti (Eds.)
The Competitive Advantage of Industrial Districts
2000. ISBN 3-7908-1254-4

Frank Bohn
Monetary Union and Fiscal Stability
2000. ISBN 3-7908-1266-8

Michael Malakellis
Integrated Macro-Micro-Modelling Under Rational Expectations
2000. ISBN 3-7908-1266-8

Stefan Baumgärtner
Ambivalent Joint Production and the Natural Environment
2000. ISBN 3-7908-1290-0

Henri Capron, Wim Meeusen (Eds.)
The National Innovation System of Belgium
2000. ISBN 3-7908-1308-7

Tobias Miarka
Financial Intermediation and Deregulation
2000. ISBN 3-7908-1307-9

Chisato Yoshida
Illegal Immigration and Economic Welfare
2000. ISBN 3-7908-1315-X

Nikolaus Thumm
Intellectual Property Rights
2001. ISBN 3-7908-1329-X

Johannes Bröcker/Hayo Herrmann (Eds.)
Spatial Change and Interregional Flows in the Integrating Europe
2001. ISBN 3-7908-1352-4

GPSR Compliance

The European Union's (EU) General Product Safety Regulation (GPSR) is a set of rules that requires consumer products to be safe and our obligations to ensure this.

If you have any concerns about our products, you can contact us on ProductSafety@springernature.com

In case Publisher is established outside the EU, the EU authorized representative is:

Springer Nature Customer Service Center GmbH
Europaplatz 3
69115 Heidelberg, Germany

Batch number: 10725973

Printed by Printforce, the Netherlands